# First World War
and Army of Occupation
## War Diary
France, Belgium and Germany

50 DIVISION
Headquarters, Branches and Services
Commander Royal Artillery
1 April 1915 - 31 December 1916

WO95/2813/2

The Naval & Military Press Ltd
www.nmarchive.com
Published in association with The National Archives

Published by

## The Naval & Military Press Ltd

Unit 10 Ridgewood Industrial Park,

Uckfield, East Sussex,

TN22 5QE England

Tel: +44 (0) 1825 749494

www.naval-military-press.com

www.nmarchive.com

*This diary has been reprinted in facsimile from the original. Any imperfections are inevitably reproduced and the quality may fall short of modern type and cartographic standards.*

© **Crown Copyright**
**Images reproduced by permission of The National Archives, London, England, 2015.**

# Contents

| Document type | Place/Title | Date From | Date To |
|---|---|---|---|
| Heading | WO95/2813/2 | | |
| Miscellaneous | 50th Division C.R.A. Apr 1915-Dec 1916 | | |
| War Diary | | 01/04/1915 | 31/05/1915 |
| Heading | 50th Division Hd. Qrs R.A. 50th Division Vol II 1-30.6.15 | | |
| War Diary | | 01/06/1915 | 30/06/1915 |
| Heading | 50th Division Hd. Qrs R.A. 50th Division Vol III 1-31.7.15 | | |
| War Diary | | 01/07/1915 | 31/07/1915 |
| Heading | 50th Division Hd Qrs R.A. 50th Division Vol IV From 1 To 26th. 8.15 | | |
| War Diary | | 01/08/1915 | 31/08/1915 |
| Heading | 50th Division Hd Qrs R.A. 50th Division Vol V Sept 15 | | |
| War Diary | | 01/09/1915 | 30/09/1915 |
| Heading | 50th Division Hd Qrs R.A. 50th Division Vol VI Oct 15 | | |
| War Diary | | 01/10/1915 | 30/11/1915 |
| Heading | H.Q. RA 50th Div Dec 15 Vol VIII | | |
| War Diary | | 01/12/1915 | 31/12/1915 |
| Heading | H.Q. R.A. 50th Div Jan Vol IX | | |
| Miscellaneous | 50th Divisional Artillery | 00/01/1916 | 00/01/1916 |
| War Diary | Reninghelst | 01/01/1916 | 31/01/1916 |
| War Diary | Hooggraaf G25b Sheet 28 | 08/02/1916 | 26/02/1916 |
| War Diary | Ypres Salient | 02/03/1916 | 10/03/1916 |
| Heading | HQ R A 50 Div Feb Vol X | | |
| Heading | HQ R A 50 Div Vol 12 | | |
| Heading | HQ RA 50 Div Vol XI | | |
| War Diary | Hoograaf | 06/04/1916 | 06/04/1916 |
| War Diary | Westoutre Sheet 28 M9c | 07/04/1916 | 30/04/1916 |
| War Diary | Westoutre | 01/05/1916 | 01/05/1916 |
| War Diary | Eecke | 03/05/1916 | 30/05/1916 |
| Heading | War Diary H.Q 50th Divisional Artillery June 1916 Vol 14 | | |
| War Diary | Westoutre | 04/06/1916 | 24/06/1916 |
| Miscellaneous | | | |
| War Diary | Westoutre | 05/06/1916 | 30/06/1916 |
| Operation(al) Order(s) | 50th Divisional Artillery Operation Order No. 17 | 03/07/1916 | 03/07/1916 |
| Operation(al) Order(s) | 50th Divisional Artillery Operation Order No. 18 | 08/07/1916 | 08/07/1916 |
| Operation(al) Order(s) | 50th Divisional Artillery Operation Order No. 19 | 21/07/1916 | 21/07/1916 |
| Miscellaneous | 50th Divisional Artillery Operation Order No. 20 | 26/07/1916 | 26/07/1916 |
| Operation(al) Order(s) | 50th Divisional Artillery Operation Order No. 21 | 27/07/1916 | 27/07/1916 |
| Operation(al) Order(s) | 50th Divisional Artillery Operation Order No. 22 | 28/07/1916 | 28/07/1916 |
| Heading | Headquarters 50th Div. Artillery August 1916 Vol. 16 | | |
| War Diary | Westoutre | 05/08/1916 | 31/08/1916 |
| Miscellaneous | B.M.1506 | 04/08/1916 | 04/08/1916 |
| Miscellaneous | Programme Of Bombardment | | |
| Miscellaneous | 50th Division G.X.2382. | 05/08/1916 | 05/08/1916 |
| Miscellaneous | Brigade Major 50th Div. Artillery | 05/08/1916 | 05/08/1916 |
| Miscellaneous | Programme Of Bombardment | | |

| | | | |
|---|---|---|---|
| Miscellaneous | 50th Division G.X.2382. | 06/08/1916 | 06/08/1916 |
| Miscellaneous | Brigade Major 50th Divisional Artillery | 05/08/1916 | 05/08/1916 |
| Miscellaneous | Staff Officer R.A. V. Corps | 06/08/1916 | 06/08/1916 |
| Miscellaneous | To see & Return Please | 06/08/1916 | 06/08/1916 |
| Miscellaneous | V Corps GX. 6926/2 | 06/08/1916 | 06/08/1916 |
| Operation(al) Order(s) | 50th Divisional Artillery Operation Order No. 24 | 07/08/1916 | 07/08/1916 |
| Miscellaneous | Canadian Corps. 19th Division. | 10/08/1916 | 10/08/1916 |
| Operation(al) Order(s) | 50th Divisional Artillery Operation Order No. 25 | 14/08/1916 | 14/08/1916 |
| Miscellaneous | Relief Table | | |
| Operation(al) Order(s) | 50th Divisional Artillery Operation Order No. 26 | 15/08/1916 | 15/08/1916 |
| Operation(al) Order(s) | 50th Divisional Artillery Operation Order No. 27 | 16/08/1916 | 16/08/1916 |
| Operation(al) Order(s) | 50th Divisional Artillery Operation Order No. 28 | 17/08/1916 | 17/08/1916 |
| Operation(al) Order(s) | 50th Divisional Artillery Operation Order No. 29 | 18/08/1916 | 18/08/1916 |
| Operation(al) Order(s) | 50th Divisional Artillery Operation Order No. 30 | 23/08/1916 | 23/08/1916 |
| Heading | 50th. Division C.R.A. 50th. Divisional Artillery September 1916. | | |
| War Diary | Nr. Albert | 01/09/1916 | 30/09/1916 |
| Map | Map | | |
| Miscellaneous | Headquarters, 50th Division. | 06/09/1916 | 06/09/1916 |
| Miscellaneous | Action Of 50th D.A. | 09/09/1916 | 09/09/1916 |
| Operation(al) Order(s) | 50th Divisional Artillery Operation Order No. 31 | 09/09/1916 | 09/09/1916 |
| Operation(al) Order(s) | 50th Divisional Artillery Operation Order No. 32 | 09/09/1916 | 09/09/1916 |
| Miscellaneous | Addendum To 50th Divisional Artillery Order No. 32 | 11/09/1916 | 11/09/1916 |
| Miscellaneous | 50th Divisional Artillery Operation Order No. 33 | 09/09/1916 | 09/09/1916 |
| Miscellaneous | Centre Group Divisional Artillery | 12/09/1916 | 12/09/1916 |
| Miscellaneous | Addendum No.1 To Centre Group | 11/09/1916 | 11/09/1916 |
| Operation(al) Order(s) | 50th Divisional Artillery Operation Order No. 34 | 12/09/1916 | 12/09/1916 |
| Miscellaneous | A Form Messages And Signals. | | |
| Miscellaneous | Artillery Instructions No.70 | 11/09/1916 | 11/09/1916 |
| Miscellaneous | Headquarters, R.A. | 11/09/1916 | 11/09/1916 |
| Miscellaneous | Addendum No. 1 To Centre Group | 11/09/1916 | 11/09/1916 |
| Miscellaneous | Addendum No.1 To Artillery Instructions No.70 | 12/09/1916 | 12/09/1916 |
| Miscellaneous | A Form Messages And Signals | 12/09/1916 | 12/09/1916 |
| Miscellaneous | Centre Group Divisional Artillery | 11/09/1916 | 11/09/1916 |
| Miscellaneous | Centre Group Divisional Artillery | 12/09/1916 | 12/09/1916 |
| Operation(al) Order(s) | Centre Divisional Artillery Group (Preliminary) Operation Order No. 35 | 12/09/1916 | 12/09/1916 |
| Miscellaneous | O.C. Bde. R.F.A. | 13/09/1916 | 13/09/1916 |
| Miscellaneous | O.C. Bde. R.F.A. | 14/09/1916 | 14/09/1916 |
| Miscellaneous | Warning Order | 19/09/1916 | 19/09/1916 |
| Miscellaneous | Artillery Instructions | 19/09/1916 | 19/09/1916 |
| Miscellaneous | 50th Divisional Artillery | 19/09/1916 | 19/09/1916 |
| Miscellaneous | 50th Divisional Artillery | 23/09/1916 | 23/09/1916 |
| Miscellaneous | 50th Divisional Artillery-S.O.S. Barrages | 25/09/1916 | 25/09/1916 |
| Miscellaneous | O.C. 4 Bde 5 R.F.A. | 26/09/1916 | 26/09/1916 |
| Miscellaneous | 50th Divisional Artillery | 27/09/1916 | 27/09/1916 |
| Miscellaneous | 50th Divisional Artillery | 28/09/1916 | 28/09/1916 |
| Operation(al) Order(s) | 50th Divisional Artillery Operation Order No. 36 | 27/09/1916 | 27/09/1916 |
| Miscellaneous | Programme Of Bombardment | | |
| Operation(al) Order(s) | Right Divisional Artillery Group Operation Order No. 61 | 24/09/1916 | 24/09/1916 |
| Miscellaneous | Time Table Of Fire | | |
| Miscellaneous | Time Table Of Fire-18-Pounders | | |
| Miscellaneous | Addendum No.1 Right Divisional Artillery Group Operation Order No. 61 | 24/09/1916 | 24/09/1916 |
| Miscellaneous | Artillery Instructions | 26/09/1916 | 26/09/1916 |

| | | | |
|---|---|---|---|
| Miscellaneous | Programme Of Bombardment | 26/09/1916 | 26/09/1916 |
| Miscellaneous | 50th Divn G.546 | 24/09/1916 | 24/09/1916 |
| Miscellaneous | A Form Messages And Signals. | 24/09/1916 | 24/09/1916 |
| Miscellaneous | 50th Division. G.546 | 24/09/1916 | 24/09/1916 |
| Operation(al) Order(s) | Fiftieth Division Operation Order Number 55 | 21/09/1916 | 21/09/1916 |
| Miscellaneous | A Form Messages And Signals | 25/09/1916 | 25/09/1916 |
| Miscellaneous | P. S. Targets For To-Night | 25/09/1916 | 25/09/1916 |
| Miscellaneous | O.C. 4 Bde. S R.F.A. | 24/09/1916 | 24/09/1916 |
| Miscellaneous | Artillery Instructions | 23/09/1916 | 23/09/1916 |
| Miscellaneous | Programme Of Bombardment | | |
| Operation(al) Order(s) | 50th Divisional Artillery Operation Order No. 37 | 28/09/1916 | 28/09/1916 |
| Miscellaneous | Artillery Instructions | 28/09/1916 | 28/09/1916 |
| Miscellaneous | A Form. Messages And Signals. | 28/09/1916 | 28/09/1916 |
| Miscellaneous | Programme Of Bombardment | 29/09/1916 | 29/09/1916 |
| Miscellaneous | Artillery Instructions | 01/10/1916 | 01/10/1916 |
| Miscellaneous | Warning Order | 30/09/1916 | 30/09/1916 |
| Miscellaneous | A Form Messages And Signals. | 29/09/1916 | 29/09/1916 |
| Miscellaneous | A Form Messages And Signals. | 30/09/1916 | 30/09/1916 |
| Miscellaneous | A Form Messages And Signals. | 29/09/1916 | 29/09/1916 |
| Miscellaneous | A Form Messages And Signals. | | |
| Miscellaneous | Report On Road From Bazentin-Le-Petit | 30/09/1916 | 30/09/1916 |
| Miscellaneous | 50th Division. G.609/2. | 30/09/1916 | 30/09/1916 |
| Miscellaneous | 50th Division. G.609/1. | 29/09/1916 | 29/09/1916 |
| Miscellaneous | A Form Messages And Signals. | | |
| Miscellaneous | 50th Division. G.609 | 29/09/1916 | 29/09/1916 |
| Miscellaneous | 50th Divisional Artillery | 03/09/1916 | 03/09/1916 |
| Miscellaneous | 50th Divisional Artillery. | 03/09/1916 | 03/09/1916 |
| Miscellaneous | 50th Divisional Artillery. | 04/09/1916 | 04/09/1916 |
| Miscellaneous | 50th Divisional Artillery. | 05/09/1916 | 05/09/1916 |
| Miscellaneous | 50th Divisional Artillery. | 07/09/1916 | 07/09/1916 |
| Miscellaneous | Programme Of Bombardment | 09/09/1916 | 09/09/1916 |
| Miscellaneous | 50th Divisional Artillery. | 09/09/1916 | 09/09/1916 |
| Miscellaneous | Centre Group Divisional Artillery | 10/09/1916 | 10/09/1916 |
| Miscellaneous | Centre Group Divisional Artillery | 11/09/1916 | 11/09/1916 |
| Miscellaneous | Artillery Programme | 15/09/1916 | 15/09/1916 |
| Miscellaneous | A Form Messages And Signals. | 14/09/1916 | 14/09/1916 |
| Miscellaneous | Programme Of Bombardment | 15/09/1916 | 15/09/1916 |
| Miscellaneous | Copy No.9 B.N. 1636/6 | 14/09/1916 | 14/09/1916 |
| Miscellaneous | Artillery Instructions | 13/09/1916 | 13/09/1916 |
| Miscellaneous | Artillery Programme | 15/09/1916 | 15/09/1916 |
| Miscellaneous | Centre Divisional Artillery Group | 14/09/1916 | 14/09/1916 |
| Miscellaneous | Programme Of Bombardment | 15/09/1916 | 15/09/1916 |
| Miscellaneous | Artillery Programme | | |
| Miscellaneous | O.C., Bde. R.F.A. | 14/09/1916 | 14/09/1916 |
| Miscellaneous | Brigade Major 50th D.A. | 13/09/1916 | 13/09/1916 |
| Miscellaneous | Officer Commanding 251 (Northumbrian) Brigade. R.F.A. | 14/09/1916 | 14/09/1916 |
| Miscellaneous | O.C. Bde. R.F.A. | 14/09/1916 | 14/09/1916 |
| Miscellaneous | Communication Between Aeroplanes And Artillery | 14/09/1916 | 14/09/1916 |
| Miscellaneous | C Form (Duplicate). Messages And Signals. | 14/09/1916 | 14/09/1916 |
| Miscellaneous | From Officer Commanding 253rd (Northumbrian) Brigade R.F.A. | 14/09/1916 | 14/09/1916 |
| Miscellaneous | C Form (Duplicate). Messages And Signals. | 14/09/1916 | 14/09/1916 |
| Miscellaneous | Artillery Instructions | 14/09/1916 | 14/09/1916 |
| Miscellaneous | Addendum No.2 To Artillery Instructions No.71 | 15/09/1916 | 15/09/1916 |
| Miscellaneous | Communication Between Aeroplanes And Artillery | 03/09/1916 | 03/09/1916 |

| Type | Description | Date From | Date To |
|---|---|---|---|
| Miscellaneous | C Form (Duplicate) Messages And Signals. | 14/09/1916 | 14/09/1916 |
| Miscellaneous | O.C. Bde. R.F.A. | 14/09/1916 | 14/09/1916 |
| Miscellaneous | Programme Of Bombardment | 15/09/1916 | 15/09/1916 |
| Miscellaneous | Programme Of Bombardment | 17/09/1916 | 17/09/1916 |
| Miscellaneous | Artillery Programme | 16/09/1916 | 16/09/1916 |
| Miscellaneous | Copy Of Telegram. | 17/09/1916 | 17/09/1916 |
| Miscellaneous | O.C. 4 Bde. S. R.F.A. | 17/09/1916 | 17/09/1916 |
| Miscellaneous | Programme Of Bombardment | 17/09/1916 | 17/09/1916 |
| Miscellaneous | Programme Of Bombardment. | 18/09/1916 | 18/09/1916 |
| Miscellaneous | O.C. Bde. R.F.A. | 19/09/1916 | 19/09/1916 |
| Miscellaneous | Programme Of Bombardment. | 20/09/1916 | 20/09/1916 |
| Map | Map | | |
| Miscellaneous | Suggested Plan For Bombing Attack On The Crescent. | 19/09/1916 | 19/09/1916 |
| Miscellaneous | Addenda And Corrigenda To Programme For Bombing Attack On The Crescent. | 19/09/1916 | 19/09/1916 |
| Miscellaneous | O.C. Bde. R.F.A. | 20/09/1916 | 20/09/1916 |
| Miscellaneous | Programme Of Bombardment. | 20/09/1916 | 20/09/1916 |
| Miscellaneous | Programme Of Bombardment. | 21/09/1916 | 21/09/1916 |
| Miscellaneous | Programme Of Bombardment. | 23/09/1916 | 23/09/1916 |
| Miscellaneous | 50th Divn. G.546 | 24/09/1916 | 24/09/1916 |
| Miscellaneous | Artillery Instructions | 23/09/1916 | 23/09/1916 |
| Miscellaneous | Programme Of Bombardment. | 24/09/1916 | 24/09/1916 |
| Miscellaneous | O.C. Bde R.F.A. | 24/09/1916 | 24/09/1916 |
| Miscellaneous | Warning Order | 30/09/1916 | 30/09/1916 |
| Operation(al) Order(s) | Right Divisional Artillery Group Operation Order No. 63 | 30/09/1916 | 30/09/1916 |
| Miscellaneous | Fire Time Table-18-Pounders (To Accompany Right D.A. Group Op. O. No. 63) | | |
| Miscellaneous | Diary Of Information Received | 15/09/1916 | 15/09/1916 |
| Miscellaneous | Daily Diary Of Information | 16/09/1916 | 16/09/1916 |
| Miscellaneous | Daily Diary Of Information | 17/09/1916 | 17/09/1916 |
| Miscellaneous | Daily Diary Of Information | 18/09/1916 | 18/09/1916 |
| Miscellaneous | Daily Diary Of Information | 20/09/1916 | 20/09/1916 |
| Miscellaneous | Daily Diary Of Information | 22/09/1916 | 22/09/1916 |
| Miscellaneous | From Officer Commanding 253rd. (Northumbrian) Bde. R.F.A. | 30/09/1916 | 30/09/1916 |
| Miscellaneous | Daily Diary Of Information | 22/09/1916 | 22/09/1916 |
| Miscellaneous | Daily Diary Of Information | 23/09/1916 | 23/09/1916 |
| Miscellaneous | Daily Diary Of Information | 25/09/1916 | 25/09/1916 |
| Miscellaneous | Daily Diary Of Information | 27/09/1916 | 27/09/1916 |
| Miscellaneous | Daily Diary Of Information | 28/09/1916 | 28/09/1916 |
| Miscellaneous | Daily Diary Of Information | 29/09/1916 | 29/09/1916 |
| Miscellaneous | Daily Diary Of Information | 30/09/1916 | 30/09/1916 |
| Miscellaneous | 50th Divisional Artillery | 29/09/1916 | 29/09/1916 |
| Miscellaneous | 50th Divisional Artillery. | 28/09/1916 | 28/09/1916 |
| Miscellaneous | 50th Divisional Artillery. | 27/09/1916 | 27/09/1916 |
| Miscellaneous | 50th Divisional Artillery. | 26/09/1916 | 26/09/1916 |
| Miscellaneous | 50th Divisional Artillery. | 25/09/1916 | 25/09/1916 |
| Miscellaneous | Daily Intelligence Summary, 9.0 am 24:9:16 to 9.0 am 25:9:16. | 24/09/1916 | 24/09/1916 |
| Miscellaneous | 50th Divisional Artillery | 23/09/1916 | 23/09/1916 |
| Miscellaneous | 50th Divisional Artillery. | 21/09/1916 | 21/09/1916 |
| Miscellaneous | 50th Divisional Artillery. | 22/09/1916 | 22/09/1916 |
| Miscellaneous | 50th Divisional Artillery. | 20/09/1916 | 20/09/1916 |
| Miscellaneous | 50th Divisional Artillery. | 19/09/1916 | 19/09/1916 |
| Miscellaneous | 50th Divisional Artillery. | 18/09/1916 | 18/09/1916 |

| Type | Description | Date From | Date To |
|---|---|---|---|
| Miscellaneous | 50th Divisional Artillery. | 17/09/1916 | 17/09/1916 |
| Miscellaneous | 50th Divisional Artillery. | 13/09/1916 | 13/09/1916 |
| Map | Map | | |
| Heading | Headquarters 50th Div. Artillery October 1916 Vol.18 | | |
| Miscellaneous | Central Registry | | |
| Heading | 50th Divisional Artillery Headquarters. War Diary For Month Of October 1916. Volume XIX | | |
| War Diary | Railway Copse | 01/10/1916 | 01/10/1916 |
| War Diary | Near Millencourt | 03/10/1916 | 29/10/1916 |
| Miscellaneous | 50th Divisional Artillery | 30/09/1916 | 30/09/1916 |
| Miscellaneous | 50th Divisional Artillery | 01/10/1916 | 01/10/1916 |
| Miscellaneous | 50th Divisional Artillery. | 02/10/1916 | 02/10/1916 |
| Operation(al) Order(s) | 50th Divisional Artillery Operation Order No. 38 | 30/09/1916 | 30/09/1916 |
| Miscellaneous | Programme Of Bombardment. | 01/10/1916 | 01/10/1916 |
| Miscellaneous | Programme Of Bombardment For 4.5" Howitzers. | 01/10/1916 | 01/10/1916 |
| Miscellaneous | C Form (Original). Messages And Signals. | 01/10/1916 | 01/10/1916 |
| Miscellaneous | Addendum No.2 To 50th Divisional Artillery Operation Order No. 38 | 01/10/1916 | 01/10/1916 |
| Miscellaneous | Addendum No.3 To 50th Divisional Artillery Operation Order No. 38 | 30/09/1916 | 30/09/1916 |
| Miscellaneous | 50th Divisional Artillery. | 02/10/1916 | 02/10/1916 |
| Operation(al) Order(s) | 50th Divisional Artillery Operation Order No. 39 | 02/10/1916 | 02/10/1916 |
| Miscellaneous | 50th Division G.X.2541/10 | 04/10/1916 | 04/10/1916 |
| Operation(al) Order(s) | 50th Divisional Artillery Operation Order No. 40 | 08/10/1916 | 08/10/1916 |
| Miscellaneous | Attack Of 1st October | 01/10/1916 | 01/10/1916 |
| Miscellaneous | 50th Division. | 08/10/1916 | 08/10/1916 |
| Miscellaneous | Report On Operations On The 1st Inst. As Seen from The Air | 08/10/1916 | 08/10/1916 |
| Operation(al) Order(s) | 50th Divisional Artillery Operation Order No. 41 | 16/10/1916 | 16/10/1916 |
| Miscellaneous | Note. | 01/10/1916 | 01/10/1916 |
| Miscellaneous | Note. | 02/10/1916 | 02/10/1916 |
| Miscellaneous | Daily Diary Of Information | 02/10/1916 | 02/10/1916 |
| Miscellaneous | 253rd (Northumbrian) Brigade R.F.A. | 01/10/1916 | 01/10/1916 |
| Miscellaneous | 251st Brigade R.F.A. | 02/10/1916 | 02/10/1916 |
| Miscellaneous | 253rd (Nth) Bde. R.F.A. | 02/10/1916 | 02/10/1916 |
| Miscellaneous | 252 Brigade R.F.A. | 02/10/1916 | 02/10/1916 |
| Heading | War Diary Volume XX November 1916 50th Divisional Artillery. Vol.19 | | |
| War Diary | Near Millencourt | 01/11/1916 | 04/11/1916 |
| War Diary | X.27.B.98 | 06/11/1916 | 12/11/1916 |
| War Diary | Lozenge Wood | 12/11/1916 | 14/11/1916 |
| War Diary | Bavlincourt | 15/11/1916 | 24/11/1916 |
| Operation(al) Order(s) | 50th Divisional Artillery Operation Order No. 42 | 06/11/1916 | 06/11/1916 |
| Miscellaneous | Programme Of Bombardment. | 09/11/1916 | 09/11/1916 |
| Miscellaneous | Programme Of Bombardment | 10/11/1916 | 10/11/1916 |
| Operation(al) Order(s) | Left Group Divisional Artillery Operation Order No. 43 | 10/11/1916 | 10/11/1916 |
| Miscellaneous | Programme Of Bombardment | 10/11/1916 | 10/11/1916 |
| Miscellaneous | Programme For Bombardment 11.11.16 | 11/11/1916 | 11/11/1916 |
| Miscellaneous | Programme Of Bombardment | 13/11/1916 | 13/11/1916 |
| Operation(al) Order(s) | 50th Divisional Artillery Operation Order No. 44. | 12/11/1916 | 12/11/1916 |
| Operation(al) Order(s) | Left Divisional Artillery Group Operation Order No. 45 | 13/11/1916 | 13/11/1916 |
| Miscellaneous | Programme Of Bombardment | 14/11/1916 | 14/11/1916 |
| Operation(al) Order(s) | Left Divisional Artillery Group Operation Order No. 46 | 13/11/1916 | 13/11/1916 |
| Miscellaneous | Programme Of Bombardment. | 14/11/1916 | 14/11/1916 |
| Operation(al) Order(s) | 50th Divisional Artillery Operation Order No. 47 | 19/11/1916 | 19/11/1916 |
| Miscellaneous | Relief Of Brigades | | |

| | | | |
|---|---|---|---|
| Miscellaneous | Addendum No.1 To 50th Divisional Artillery Operation Order No. 47 | 20/11/1916 | 20/11/1916 |
| Operation(al) Order(s) | 50th Divisional Artillery Operation Order No. 48 | 21/11/1916 | 21/11/1916 |
| War Diary | Bavelincourt | 01/12/1916 | 31/12/1916 |
| Operation(al) Order(s) | 50th Divisional Artillery Operation Order No. 49 | 28/11/1916 | 28/11/1916 |
| Operation(al) Order(s) | 50th Divisional Artillery Operation Order No. 50 | 30/11/1916 | 30/11/1916 |
| Operation(al) Order(s) | 50th Divisional Artillery Operation Order No. 51 | 07/12/1916 | 07/12/1916 |
| Operation(al) Order(s) | 50th Divisional Artillery Operation Order No. 52 | 28/12/1916 | 28/12/1916 |
| Miscellaneous | Relief Of Batteries Of 50th D.A. | | |

WO 95/2813/2

# 50TH DIVISION

C. R. A.

APR 1915-DEC 1916

Army Form C. 2118.

Instructions regarding War Diaries and Intelligence Summaries are contained in F. S. Regs., Part II. and the Staff Manual respectively. Title pages will be prepared in manuscript.

# WAR DIARY
## INTELLIGENCE SUMMARY
*(Erase heading not required.)*

| Hour, Date, Place | Summary of Events and Information | Remarks and references to Appendices |
|---|---|---|
| April 1st | Tactical exercise with Infantry for 2nd & 3rd Brigades. Bdgr and 4. E.L. RTA. orders received by N.S. HQ to move abroad. | |
| 2 | Training proceeding. | |
| 3 | Do | |
| 4 | Do | |
| 5 | Do | |
| 6 | Preparation for proceeding abroad. | |
| 7 | Do | |
| 8 | Do | |
| 10 | Without interest | |
| 12 | Major Thompson proceeded abroad in charge, with 5 Drs, Artillery. | |
| 14 | Horse inspected by Maj. Gen. the R.A and left in care | |
| 15 | Advance stores to covered by Rug ahrs from Pilot the trans under covered orders. | |

Army Form C. 2118.

# WAR DIARY
## ~~INTELLIGENCE~~ SUMMARY
*(Erase heading not required.)*

Instructions regarding War Diaries and Intelligence Summaries are contained in F. S. Regs., Part II. and the Staff Manual respectively. Title pages will be prepared in manuscript.

| Hour, Date, Place | Summary of Events and Information | Remarks and references to Appendices |
|---|---|---|
| 15 cont'd | Zeppelin raid on Newcastle by no damage done in Bellevue area. | |
| 16 | H.Q R.A left W Pheneman left for Southampton and embarked for Havre HAVRE HAZEBROUCK left Havre and reached Hazebrouck on | SOUTHAMPTON |
| 17 | Enemy 4 18. CRA & C LtV NIC and reached Hazebrouck Senes Gay. | |
| 18 | Proceeded to Caestre . CAESTRE | |
| 19 | RngBD RTH began to man war at PREDELLE CAESTRE 2nd or Predelle 2 W or 1st Regt area Coolcap ROUGE CROIX HV at Boeu BORRE Regt lines | |
| 20 | En Cd. at Boeutu . CAESTRE | |
| 21 | Mstuf Bubow | |
| 22 | to | BOESCHEPE |
| 23 | At Arty. Proceeded up to Boescheepe renewed all on gen in Berths and BERTHEN | |

1247  W 3259  500,000  (E) 8/14  J.B.C.&A.  Form/C. 2118/11.

# WAR DIARY
## INTELLIGENCE SUMMARY

*(Erase heading not required.)*

Army Form C. 2118.

Instructions regarding War Diaries and Intelligence Summaries are contained in F. S. Regs., Part II. and the Staff Manual respectively. Title pages will be prepared in manuscript.

| Hour, Date, Place | Summary of Events and Information | Remarks and references to Appendices |
|---|---|---|
| 24 | All Infantry occupy 15t ordered to relieve 17th Brigade in VLAMERTINGHE Area. Moved with 15th Brigade Rear HQ to St Pol Northumberland Int Regt. * | * 1st Regt. informed but cannot POPERINGHE. They Poperinghe having no shelter from heavy. |
| 25 | 5th Artillery moved to Battalion Area. HQ at POPERY, RATTEKOT RATTEKOT, RATTEKOT St LAURENT. | |
| 26 | Moved down to Winnipeg Area. WINNIZEELE | |
| 27 | Moved again to Dunkerque area. | |
| 28 | Training proceeding in billeting areas. | |
| 29 | do | |
| 30 | do | |
| 31 Aug/M | do | |
| 1 | BGRA inspected 1st N.M. Bgd at Winnipeg | VLAMERTINGHE |
| 2 | 5th Artillery attend to essential duties round | |
| 3 | tomorrow. WINNIZEELE | |
| 4 | Making up lists. | |

Army Form C. 2118.

# WAR DIARY
## INTELLIGENCE SUMMARY
*(Erase heading not required.)*

Instructions regarding War Diaries and Intelligence Summaries are contained in F. S. Regs., Part II. and the Staff Manual respectively. Title pages will be prepared in manuscript.

| Hour, Date, Place | Summary of Events and Information | Remarks and references to Appendices |
|---|---|---|
| May 5th | 4th BRIGADE and 'A' Coy Batt. sent up into action east of YPRES. Nothing to report. | |
| 6th | " | |
| 7th | " | |
| 8th | Transport proceeding Reste fairways | |
| 9th | CHURCH PARADE held in VINVIZEELE by Canon CRAWHALL. | |
| 10th | H.Q. moved to St JAN DE BIEZEN, Brigade in area between VATTOU and St JAN DE BIEZEN | |
| 11th | Gigors Knows Smith 9 Road Sillon AE BIEZEN LATTOU arrived and can relieved at some moment. Nothing to report. | |
| 12th | | |
| 13 | Very wet. CRA way up to H.Q.R.A. 28th Div Chateau on Road + LAMERTINGHE - YPRES | |

1247 W 3299 200,000 (E) 8/11 J.B.C.&A. Form C. 2118/11.

Army Form C. 2118.

# WAR DIARY
## *or*
## INTELLIGENCE SUMMARY
*(Erase heading not required.)*

Instructions regarding War Diaries and Intelligence Summaries are contained in F. S. Regs., Part II. and the Staff Manual respectively. Title pages will be prepared in manuscript.

| Hour, Date, Place | Summary of Events and Information | Remarks and references to Appendices |
|---|---|---|
| 14 | 2nd N.Z. Rifle Brig. entrained from YPRES attached to 28th Div. | |
| | Resting the day. | |
| 15. | Thawing & processing. | |
| 16 | Sunday. Weather very fine again. | |
| 17. | Very wet. | |
| 18. | Nothing of moment to report. | |
| 19. | 3rd Batt. 3rd Northumbrian Brig. proceeded I.S. D.B.S. (28 men). | |
| 20 | Nothing to report. | |
| 21 | do | |
| 22 | do | |

# WAR DIARY
## INTELLIGENCE SUMMARY
*(Erase heading not required.)*

Army Form C. 2118.

Instructions regarding War Diaries and Intelligence Summaries are contained in F. S. Regs, Part II. and the Staff Manual respectively. Title pages will be prepared in manuscript.

| Hour, Date, Place | Summary of Events and Information | Remarks and references to Appendices |
|---|---|---|
| 23rd | Nothing to report. | |
| 24. | Heavy bombardment and gas attack in morning. 2nd Northumbrian Brig. lost fighting strength. B.C. 3rd Bath. 3rd Rif. suffered from effects of gas and also silenced gas and battery shoots we withdrew. The bottom of the Riv. Stor. Brig. before went in 2 hrs. ammu. free Ring. 9 4 W. Durham Batt. were expended, and as the Enemies fire on St. H. of Cui and MENIN road was so heavy, it was impossible to replenish therefore it was decided to withdraw the Batt. | |
| 25. | Nothing to report all quiet on the hvy. 1st and 2nd Durham Batt. proceeded to LA MERTINGHE | ? which Bde. 2. or 3rd. ||||  |
| 26 | All quiet. | |

Army Form C. 2118.

# WAR DIARY

## INTELLIGENCE SUMMARY

*(Erase heading not required.)*

Instructions regarding War Diaries and Intelligence Summaries are contained in F. S. Regs., Part II. and the Staff Manual respectively. Title pages will be prepared in manuscript.

| Hour, Date, Place | Summary of Events and Information | Remarks and references to Appendices |
|---|---|---|
| 27. | 2nd Australian Inf. Bde. to unital K Sr VAN TER BIEZEN and 1st Inst. inhran Bnigs would K YLAMERTINGHE, to replace. | |
| 28 | defy sector 1st 2 and 3rd Inf Aust inhrelated Battgs 1st Inst — Inhrian Bnig moved forward into action. | |
| 29 | holding to report. Remainder of 1st Brig went into position | |
| 30 | Nothing to report. | |
| 31 | " " | |

50th Division

HdQrs R.A. 50th Division

Vol II 1 — 30.6.15.

**Army Form C. 2118.**

# WAR DIARY
*or*
## INTELLIGENCE SUMMARY
*(Erase heading not required.)*

Instructions regarding War Diaries and Intelligence Summaries are contained in F. S. Regs., Part II. and the Staff Manual respectively. Title pages will be prepared in manuscript.

| Hour, Date, Place | Summary of Events and Information | Remarks and references to Appendices |
|---|---|---|
| June 1st | All quiet. Div Artill 50th Div moved to T am on POPERINGHE-ABEELE ROAD. Nothing to report. | |
| 2nd | " | |
| 3rd | " | |
| 4th W 50th Div | Artill moved to trans on POPERINGHE - RENINGHELST ROAD. | |
| 5th SW Sty Battey | Pulled out, stepped with from POP. ROAD. In trenches ERINGHE – RENINGHELST. A few shells. | |
| 6th W | Linam Rosie moved up to front again. Rosie returned to for motor van. refused. Dr ROBERTSON E's R.G.A. attached HQ in Kishdrup Rosie & use of respirator. Returned to rpos. 3rd Rosie occupied dug out in S of YPRES - YPar KRUISSTRAAT. | |
| 7th | " | |
| 8th | " | |
| 9th | " | |

Army Form C. 2118.

# WAR DIARY
## or
## INTELLIGENCE SUMMARY

*(Erase heading not required.)*

Instructions regarding War Diaries and Intelligence Summaries are contained in F. S. Regs., Part II. and the Staff Manual respectively. Title pages will be prepared in manuscript.

| Hour, Date, Place | Summary of Events and Information | Remarks and references to Appendices |
|---|---|---|
| June 11. W | Nothing to report. | |
| 12. W | ERA of O.C. 187 Northumd Brig. 23rd Reg RFA came under orders O.C. 187 Northumd Brig. evacuated sick. | |
| 13. Th | All quiet. | |
| 14. F | 2nd E.R battery moved to T 13 D.3.5- under command O.C. 3rd Brig, 2nd & 3rd Northum batteries under command of Major H.S. Ireland. | |
| 15. Sat | BELL D.S.O moved up to N.W of YPRES and was attached to 6th Div howrs. | |
| 15. | H.Q. R.A moved up at 9.40 pm to at M KRUISSTRATT by rusent artillery from hard very heavy fire on right of 15-16 followed by an infantry attack on morning of 16. Several lines of trenches taken by her side of Hooge. Gen Morshead. M.G.-Gen to wound in N. RENIGHELST-POPERINGHE district. | |
| 17. | aqcw | |

# WAR DIARY or INTELLIGENCE SUMMARY

Army Form C. 2118.

| Hour, Date, Place | Summary of Events and Information | Remarks and references to Appendices |
|---|---|---|
| 18. | Instruction trekked. | |
| 19. | " | |
| 20. | 1st Northumbrian Brig moved back to Rillot and 2nd Northumbrian Brig moved into 2nd Co/o area during relief by 2nd Note N'd Brig R.F.A. | |
| 21. | 1st North'umbrian Brig moved into 1st 2nd Co/o area to relieve 2nd Note. Midland Bug R.F.A. | |
| 22. | 3rd North'umbrian Brig R.F.A. moved in batteries into 2nd Co/o area to relieve 1st Nott. N'd Brigade and a portion of Ingots counter bty. | |
| 23. | HQ 2nd N'd Bde and L/L 22nd N'th'd Trench Mortar Batt: moved into new area and completed relief of the North. Midland Brig — 1st Nott. Brig relieved H.H. North. Midland Brig complete. | |

# WAR DIARY
## or
## INTELLIGENCE SUMMARY
*(Erase heading not required.)*

Army Form C. 2118.

| Hour, Date, Place | Summary of Events and Information | Remarks and references to Appendices |
|---|---|---|
| 24. | GO Div Arion, Col went into Div Centre area to relieve 46 Div Arion. Col. HQ 50 D.A. moved to her qua 15 or Chateau to M.2.3.C.7.4. to take over 46 D.A. CRA 50 Div 15th Command a 46" CRA at 12 noon on 24". 10"H.B. and 19 section It.B. Artillery Brigade settled down in new area. Nothing further | |
| 25" | " | |
| 26 | " | |
| 27" | " | |
| 28 | Captain WATSON 2nd in command RH being Hertby by 15th Command D 232" Roy. Army ordered to Cairo RROWLOWSKI. | |
| 29" | " | |
| 30" | Nothing to report. | |

50th Division

121/6160

HdQrs RA. 60th Division
Vol III 1—31.7.15.

**Army Form C. 2118.**

# WAR DIARY
## or
## INTELLIGENCE SUMMARY
*(Erase heading not required.)*

Instructions regarding War Diaries and Intelligence Summaries are contained in F. S. Regs., Part II. and the Staff Manual respectively. Title pages will be prepared in manuscript.

| Hour, Date, Place | Summary of Events and Information | Remarks and references to Appendices |
|---|---|---|
| July 1st | Batteries completed all their registration etc (most) | |
| 2nd | Nothing to report. | |
| 3rd | Weather extremely fine - 1st day of registration in earnest | |
| 4th | } Nothing to report. | |
| 5th | | |
| 6th | Hazy in the early morning; becoming very fine later. | |
| 7th | Dull first half, very wet afternoon. | |
| 8th | Lt.Col. 2/Lt J.M.HILLYARD RHA lost over (wounded) a gun trench trouble to-day. | |
| 9th | Nothing to report. | |
| 10th | CRA carried out a reconnaissance with OC 1st Northumbrian Bry. and OC Batteries and OC 4th Nott - Derby Ropal for 'beg positions'. In afternoon the same proceeded with OC 2nd Northumbrian Bry. | |
| 11. | 2/Lt E. BRONELL joined the (1st) Brigade from Base L.T. MILBURN sick 29 off the Strength. | |

Army Form C. 2118.

# WAR DIARY
## or
## INTELLIGENCE SUMMARY
*(Erase heading not required.)*

Instructions regarding War Diaries and Intelligence Summaries are contained in F. S. Regs., Part II. and the Staff Manual respectively. Title pages will be prepared in manuscript.

| Hour, Date, Place | Summary of Events and Information | Remarks and references to Appendices |
|---|---|---|
| July 12th | Nothing to report. | |
| 13th | Six officers from 2nd Line EAST LANCASHIRE DIVISION and 2nd Line NORTH MIDLAND DIVISION reported at H.Q. 50th D.A. and were posted to Brigades for instruction. | Names of attached officers:— (A) 2nd Line EAST LANCS. Major H.L.R. JACKSON. Captain T.A. HOWSON. 2/Lt E.M. CROSSLAND (B) 2nd Line NORTH MIDLAND. 2/Lt W.E. STEELEY. 2/Lt W.F. WATSON. 2/Lt H.G. DIXIE |
| 14. | Nothing to report. | |
| 15. | Very few shots unable to be brought up. | |
| 16. | 1st Section of 1st + 2nd Northern lines relieved by Sections of Brigades of 23rd Div.; these two Brigades handed their area in (ARMENTIÈRES and 150) over from Section of Brigade of 24th Div. | |
| 17 | Remainder of these two Brigades moved on and all reliefs were completed by 11:15 of 17.18. 1st Section of 4th/5th Batt. 4th Northumbrian Brig. & half 1st Sec. and one Section 4th Batt. went into action itself in their area. Other section of two wagon lines. | 6 pm on 17th. Command passed from CRA 50th DCRA 28th D.A. |

# WAR DIARY
## or
## INTELLIGENCE SUMMARY

*(Erase heading not required.)*

Army Form C. 2118.

| Hour, Date, Place | Summary of Events and Information | Remarks and references to Appendices |
|---|---|---|
| 18. | Remainder of 4th Howitzer Amm with teams, the whole of 1st and Reg. marched with wagon lines of Howitzer area. One of the 1st Durham Rotts. and all the 2nd Durham Battery remained behind till 11th. Old weapons dumps on 16th and 2nd section of 1st Rotts, on all the 3rd/Rotts on 17th. The brigade went into reserve in new area. The remaining section of 1st to Howzs wound with their horsing, the 5th Rott. into action, 4th Howzer hung. | 50th Div. Amm. Col. Marched with new area. |
| 19. | H.Q. 50th D. A. moved with ARMENTIÈRES. H.Q. at RUE SADI CARNOT 83. | |
| 20. | Registering proceeding. T section of 4th Durham Rottr. came into action. | |
| 21. | Every thing very quiet on our front. | |
| 22. | 3rd Gun of 2nd Durham Rotty came into action this after. (one gun of the battery being withdrawn up area.) | 31st Fus. & 9th Howitz. transferred from 24th Bde - 50th. |
| 23. | Nothing to report. | |

Army Form C. 2118.

# WAR DIARY
or
## INTELLIGENCE SUMMARY

*(Erase heading not required.)*

Instructions regarding War Diaries and Intelligence Summaries are contained in F. S. Regs., Part II. and the Staff Manual respectively. Title pages will be prepared in manuscript.

| Hour, Date, Place | Summary of Events and Information | Remarks and references to Appendices |
|---|---|---|
| 24. | Shells dropped in wagon lines of 1st Reif. killing two horses wounding one man. | |
| | 16 Heavy Brigade came under Command of CRA 50th Divn. | |
| 25. | CRA carried on a reconnaissance for bad positions for 14 4H. How. Brig., No 14 Anti-Aircraft gun came under command CRA 50 D.A. | |
| 26. | O.i/C carrying on reconnaissance for subsequent line. | |
| 27. | Everything proceeding satisfactorily. No II Mountain Batty came under command CRA 50th DA. | |
| 28. | Nothing. | |
| 29. | CRA carried on reconnaissance in trenches 67.68. | |
| 30. | G.O.C. Divn. in heavy O.C. 1st & 4th W Riding and major inspected Heavy gun positions. | |
| 31. | A few shots of 17 H.V. Rout was carried out at 6 level crossing. The German have opposite No 40. | |

121/6587

as
986

50th Division

HdQrs R.A. 50th Division

Vol IV

From 1 to 26.8.15

# WAR DIARY
## or
## INTELLIGENCE SUMMARY

*(Erase heading not required.)*

Army Form C. 2118.

Instructions regarding War Diaries and Intelligence Summaries are contained in F. S. Regs., Part II. and the Staff Manual respectively. Title pages will be prepared in manuscript.

| Hour, Date, Place | Summary of Events and Information | Remarks and references to Appendices |
|---|---|---|
| August 1st 1915. | Arrived front, calm on the whole. | |
| 2nd " | Nothing of interest to report, saving ammunition. | |
| 3rd " | 31st French howitzer battery placed at our front SE 6th Corps. | |
| 4th " | Very quiet. Several shells fell in ARMENTIÈRES & Houplines, no material damage. | |
| 5th " | CRA with OC 2nd NORTHUMBRIAN Brigade RFA carried out a reconnaissance for gun positions in WOP at HOUPLINES | |
| 6th " | Nothing to report. | |
| 7th " | Nothing to report. | |
| 8th " | Captain J.I. D'ARCY RA left over the Orchestra Brigade Major during the temporary absence on Major R.C. THOMSON on leave. | |
| 9th " | Enemy being quiet. | |

**WAR DIARY**

or

**INTELLIGENCE SUMMARY**

*(Erase heading not required.)*

Army Form C. 2118.

Instructions regarding War Diaries and Intelligence Summaries are contained in F. S. Regs., Part II. and the Staff Manual respectively. Title pages will be prepared in manuscript.

| Hour, Date, Place | Summary of Events and Information | Remarks and references to Appendices |
|---|---|---|
| Aug 10. | Fourteen officers attached to 2nd Artillery Bde for instruction (as Gunners—boys?). | |
| Aug 11. | Captain the Rev C.M. SMITH attached to 2nd Div. Artillery HQ as "Artillery Chaplain". | |
| 12. | Some shells in 3rd Batt. 2nd position near Ruig's observn. station post. Half disorganised the telephonic system. Repaired to other Batteries. Howd artillery, Bulls of a wider nature. | |
| 13. | | |
| 14. | Nothing doing today. | |
| 15. | 3.05 French Howitzer battery relieved K 50th D.A. wide. (Name? of 2"dlieut A.S. WALKER, Section of 3rd Bdg moved in to take over from 2.W. Bdg (1st Section) | 2dlieut SCUDMORE having been wounded at HOOGE |
| 16. | Relief of 2.W Bdg by the 3rd Bde completed by 8:30AM – by the 3rd Bde 2/15H D. | |

# WAR DIARY
## or
## INTELLIGENCE SUMMARY

*(Erase heading not required.)*

Army Form C. 2118.

Instructions regarding War Diaries and Intelligence Summaries are contained in F. S. Regs., Part II. and the Staff Manual respectively. Title pages will be prepared in manuscript.

| Hour, Date, Place | Summary of Events and Information | Remarks and references to Appendices |
|---|---|---|
| Aug. 17 | Very wet indeed. German artillery more active. |  |
| 18 | Some few towers in HOUPLINES set on fire by enemy's steel fire. Weather very quiet. 3rd Reip fired many shells in retaliation. |  |
| 19 | 3rd Reip completed routine in registration on its new positions. |  |
| 20 | Two beautiful quiet days. No activity on the enemies part. |  |
| 21 |  |  |
| 22 | Previous aeroplanes very busy in photo/reconn. |  |
| 23 | Nothing happened of any interest. |  |
| 24 | Everything very quiet. Best |  |
| 25 | 3rd Section Batt. annoyed by the Frelinghien Ridge Battery began to take up a new position. |  |
| 26 | This relief was finished in the evening of this day. O particularly quiet day. |  |

Army Form C. 2118.

# WAR DIARY
## or
## INTELLIGENCE SUMMARY

(Erase heading not required.)

Instructions regarding War Diaries and Intelligence Summaries are contained in F. S. Regs., Part II. and the Staff Manual respectively. Title pages will be prepared in manuscript.

| Hour, Date, Place | Summary of Events and Information | Remarks and references to Appendices |
|---|---|---|
| Aug 27th | Continual amount of artillery activity. | |
| Aug 28 | Lieut KF WALKER rejoined by Admiralty. | |
| 29 | Very windy. All quiet. | |
| 30 | Renewed artillery showed a little more activity. Several shells few in the Town. Some civilians killed. | |
| 31. | Enemy shelled the old portion of 3rd Bn. Green near HOUPLINES in afternoon. No damage & very quiet work in general. Very few in week of any kind. | |

121/6918

50th Division

H.Q.R.A. 50th Division.

Vol V

Sept. 15

Army Form C. 2118.

# WAR DIARY
## or
## INTELLIGENCE SUMMARY

*(Erase heading not required.)*

Instructions regarding War Diaries and Intelligence Summaries are contained in F. S. Regs., Part II. and the Staff Manual respectively. Title pages will be prepared in manuscript.

| Hour, Date, Place | Summary of Events and Information | Remarks and references to Appendices |
|---|---|---|
| Sept 1st | Nothing of interest to report. | |
| 2nd | Enemy's artillery extremely quiet. | |
| 3rd | A few shells fell in ARMENTIERES in the evening. | |
| 4th | Very heavy rain in the early part of the day. H.Q 50th B.A. moved to Batln HQ at CHAPELLE D'ARMENTIERES to be conveniently and protect HQs generally. The enemy shelled this area for a short while. A little damage was done to the houses on this road. | |
| 5th } 6th } | Two peculiarly quiet days Nothing to report. | |
| 7th | Little war activity. Enemy fired a few shells w/o the town. Hardly any damage. | |
| 8th | Very fine day and warm. All quiet on our front. | |

Army Form C. 2118.

# WAR DIARY
## or
## INTELLIGENCE SUMMARY

*(Erase heading not required.)*

Instructions regarding War Diaries and Intelligence
Summaries are contained in F. S. Regs., Part II.
and the Staff Manual respectively. Title pages
will be prepared in manuscript.

| Hour, Date, Place | Summary of Events and Information | Remarks and references to Appendices |
|---|---|---|
| Sept 1st | Nothing of interest to report. | |
| 2nd | Enemy's artillery extremely quiet. | |
| 3rd | A few shells fell in ARMENTIÈRES in the evening. | |
| 4th | Very heavy rain in the early part of the day. HQ 50th DIV moved to Battle HQ at CHAPELLE D'ARMENTIÈRES to test communications and for practice generally. The enemy shelled this area for a short while. A little damage was done to the houses on the road. | |
| 5th | Two peculiarly quiet days | |
| 6th | Nothing to report. | |
| 7th | Little wind activity. Enemy fired a few shells into the town. Haven't any damage. | |
| 8th | Very fine day and warm. | |
| 9th | Nothing of interest. All quiet on our front. | |

**Army Form C. 2118.**

# WAR DIARY
## or
## INTELLIGENCE SUMMARY

*(Erase heading not required.)*

Instructions regarding War Diaries and Intelligence Summaries are contained in F. S. Regs., Part II. and the Staff Manual respectively. Title pages will be prepared in manuscript.

| Hour, Date, Place | Summary of Events and Information | Remarks and references to Appendices |
|---|---|---|
| Sept 10th | CRA visited wagon lines & to see the new 'Stabourgs'. | |
| Sept 11th | Nothing to report. | |
| 12th | Very fine weather again. | |
| 13th | Enemy aeroplane brought down in early morning near STEENWERCK station. ALBATROS C battery. | |
| 14th | CRA drove to meet three fresh officers to inspect positions of 1st, 2nd, 3rd, 4th NORTHUMBRIAN brigades W. HOUPLINES. | |
| 15th | A very quiet day. | |
| 16th | Nothing to report. | |
| 17th | Team from slipped temporarily and he got 1st Northumbrian Bde fired on German trenches in afternoon. Enemy shelled. No reply from enemy. | |

1247  W 3200  200,000  (E)  8/14  J.B.C.&A.  Forms/C. 2118/11.

# WAR DIARY
## or
## INTELLIGENCE SUMMARY

*(Erase heading not required.)*

Army Form C. 2118.

Instructions regarding War Diaries and Intelligence Summaries are contained in F. S. Regs., Part II. and the Staff Manual respectively. Title pages will be prepared in manuscript.

| Hour, Date, Place | Summary of Events and Information | Remarks and references to Appendices |
|---|---|---|
| Sept 10th | CRA visited wagon lines & to see the new "horselines". | |
| Sept 11th | Arthur to report. | |
| 12th | heavy gun weather again. | |
| 13th | Enemy aeroplane brought down in our lines w/ C heavy STEENWERK station. ALBATROS pattern. | |
| 14th | CRA went to meet the 3 officers to inspect positions for 1st 3rd & 4th NORTHUMBRIAN Brigade in HOUPLINES. | |
| 15th | (very quiet day) | |
| 16th | Arthur to report. | |
| 17th | heavy trench trebot. temporarily 1st Northumbrian Bde fired on few our trenches w/ Gladhaters. Effective shrapnel. No reply from enemy. | |

# WAR DIARY
## or
## INTELLIGENCE SUMMARY

Army Form C. 2118.

*(Erase heading not required.)*

Instructions regarding War Diaries and Intelligence Summaries are contained in F.S. Regs, Part II. and the Staff Manual respectively. Title pages will be prepared in manuscript.

| Hour, Date, Place | Summary of Events and Information | Remarks and references to Appendices |
|---|---|---|
| Sept 18th | Ashturp Dnieper. Very fine weather. | |
| 19h | Very quiet. Nothing of interest. | |
| 20h | Capt J. L. D'ARCY adjutant 4th Yorks Regt: Brig ordered to report to GUARDS DIVISION. Own artillery more active in afternoon than for some considerable time. No serious reply from enemy. | |
| 21h | Heavy bombardment towards the south. | |
| 22d | Arthur Dnieper. | |
| 23 | Extremely wet day. | |
| 24th | Operation orders for 25th Corps out. Brigades getting ready. "Bruere or Chez Nelice." | X. From 5 - 5.5 AM all brigades fired as rapidly as possible from 5.5 - 6 A.M. ahead of the advance front of this Army. Known advance. After that just when Collared with some infantry. |
| 25th | R.A Head Qrs moved to Brigl HQ or ECOLE PROFESSIONELLE at 4.20 am. Artillery fire carried out as follows. X very little reply. Enemy put down a weak rear guard barrage on front during day. Some infantry Brig: Billets on Wood Huts 22 horses Staff officer 9 Brd Malkinshaw. | |

# WAR DIARY or INTELLIGENCE SUMMARY

Army Form C. 2118.

| Hour, Date, Place | Summary of Events and Information | Remarks and references to Appendices |
|---|---|---|
| Sept 18th | Arthur Draper. Very fine weather. | |
| 19th | Very quiet. Nothing of interest. | |
| 20th | Capt. J.I. D'ARCY appointed 4th Notts. Brig. ordered to report to COARGS' DIVISION. Our artillery was active in afternoon bombardment for some considerable time. No serious reply from enemy. | |
| 21st | Heavy bombardment towards the south. | |
| 22nd | Arthur Draper. | |
| 23rd | Relieved. Wet day. | |
| 24th | Operation order of 25th Corps arr. Brigades telling ready. Exarme at short notice. | X. From 5–5.5 PM all brigades fired a rapido as possible from 5.5 – 6 PM fired off the ammunition of their new war allowance. After their had fires called on their infantry |
| 25th | R.A. Headqrs. moved to buildings in ECOLE PROFESSIONELLE at 4.30 am. Artillery fire carried on as follows:- Very little reply from enemy one shell falling in west front Some to sweep up. 6 Bgd. Northumbria Regt. billet in town from 22 hours. | |

Sd/d/e. 6 Bgd Northumbria Regt

Army Form C. 2118.

# WAR DIARY
## or
## INTELLIGENCE SUMMARY

*(Erase heading not required.)*

Instructions regarding War Diaries and Intelligence Summaries are contained in F.S. Regs., Part II. and the Staff Manual respectively. Title pages will be prepared in manuscript.

| Hour, Date, Place | Summary of Events and Information | Remarks and references to Appendices |
|---|---|---|
| Sep. 26th | All quiet on our front. Frequent reports of us French army successes. | |
| 27 | Nothing to report. | |
| 28. | R.A. H.Q. moved back before 12th Bn. 62nd Brig R.F.A. came under command of CRA 50th Div. | |
| 29 | 25th Bde lost over from 12th Bn. 3 brigades of H.A. turned over under command of CRA 50th Div viz 110th, 112th & 113th Bengals R.F.A. | |
| 30 | CRA inspected positions of 112th Brig round LE BIZET & PLOEGSTERT. All very quiet on our front. | |

# WAR DIARY or INTELLIGENCE SUMMARY

Army Form C. 2118.

*(Erase heading not required.)*

Instructions regarding War Diaries and Intelligence Summaries are contained in F. S. Regs., Part II. and the Staff Manual respectively. Title pages will be prepared in manuscript.

| Hour, Date, Place | Summary of Events and Information | Remarks and references to Appendices |
|---|---|---|
| Sep. 26th | All quiet on our front. Frequent reports of 1st and French Army successes. | |
| 27 | Nothing to report. | |
| 28 | R.A. HQ moved back a few miles our HQ. 62nd Brig R.T.A. came under command of CRA SOS Div | |
| 29 | 25th Div took over from 12th Div 3 brigades. No further came under command of CRA 50th Div 110th, 112th, 113th Brigades R.F.A. | |
| 30 | CRA inspected positions of 112th Brig round HE BIZET & PLOEGSTEERT. All very quiet on our front. | |

D/7341

50th Division

H.Q. R.A. 50th Division

Vol VI

Oct 15

# WAR DIARY
or
## INTELLIGENCE SUMMARY
*(Erase heading not required.)*

Army Form C. 2118.

| Hour, Date, Place | Summary of Events and Information | Remarks and references to Appendices |
|---|---|---|
| Oct 1st | Very wet day. Nothing to report. | |
| Oct 2nd | Everything relieved quiet. | |
| Oct 3rd | Lt T ROBINSON 2nd NORTHUMBRIAN Brigade became temporary MDC during the absence on leave of 2/Lt J.L. PRIESTMAN. | |
| 4th | Nothing to report. | |
| 5th | 112th Brigade RFA returned to the 25th Divnl Artillery. Also 113th Brigade, with the exception of 'A' battery. | |
| 6th | Nothing to report. | |
| 7th | The 110th Brigade RFA returned to 25th Divnl Arty, being relieved by 95th Brigade RFA 21st Divnl Arty. 96th Brigade began to relieve the 15th Northumbrian Bde. R.F.A. 2118/11. N.R. battery was relieved by 'C'/115 of 96th Brigade ("D"). battery. | |

**Army Form C. 2118**

# WAR DIARY
## or
## INTELLIGENCE SUMMARY

*(Erase heading not required.)*

Instructions regarding War Diaries and Intelligence Summaries are contained in F. S. Regs., Part II. and the Staff Manual respectively. Title pages will be prepared in manuscript.

| Hour, Date, Place | Summary of Events and Information | Remarks and references to Appendices |
|---|---|---|
| 8th | Asthma shrapnel + Pear batteries began their registration. | |
| 9th | 1st Pontruchies Ridge moved from area near HONDEGHEM to this relief began on Oct 7th was completed. Remaining section of NR battery was relieved. | |
| 10th | A battery 113th Brigade turned to 25th Division on its section. Being relieved by an 8" R.H. 'A' battery 97th Brigade. | |
| 11th | Batteries again registering. by ROBINSON returned to this brigade. | |
| 12th | Wire cutting experiment by begun by 95th & 96th F.A. brigade of six minutes Brigade retaliated on enemy, where they replied. | |
| 13th | Wire cutting continued. These batteries were restrained on the work and the enemy is being unmolested result was led a satisfactory as was expected. | |
| 14th | Reply from enemy expected by us, of a few shells were sent over by them on our heads. | |

# WAR DIARY
## or
## INTELLIGENCE SUMMARY

*(Erase heading not required.)*

Army Form C. 2118.

| Hour, Date, Place | Summary of Events and Information | Remarks and references to Appendices |
|---|---|---|
| 15th | Nothing to report | |
| 16th | Nothing to report. | |
| 17th | G.O.C Division inspected the positions of the batteries of the 96th F.A. Brigade | |
| 18 | G.O.C. inspected positions of batteries of 95th F.A. Brigade. | |
| 19th | 'A' 95th Brigade fired at enemy guns near L'AVENTURE with aeroplane observation. | |
| 20th | G.O.C RA went round hostile covered by 95th Bde batteries on hostile 80. | |
| 21st | The Section of the following batteries were relieved by batteries of 21st Div as follows. 'A' DURHAM Section – 'A' 94th Bde. 2nd DURHAM, relieved by 'B' 94th Bde. R.R. battery by 'D' 96th Bde. 'C' 94th Bde. 'D' 94th Bde being relieved | |

**Army Form C. 2118.**

# WAR DIARY
## or
## INTELLIGENCE SUMMARY
*(Erase heading not required.)*

Instructions regarding War Diaries and Intelligence Summaries are contained in F. S. Regs., Part II. and the Staff Manual respectively. Title pages will be prepared in manuscript.

| Hour, Date, Place | Summary of Events and Information | Remarks and references to Appendices |
|---|---|---|
| 21st. | 4th DURHAM relieved by "B" 97th Brigade. 5th DURHAM by "C" 97th. A.C.s of B/4th front were in Brigade now relieved by R.A.C's of 94th & 97th F.A. Brigades as per turn. | |
| 22nd. | New batteries carrying on their regular row. | |
| 23rd. | Foregoing reliefs were completed. | |
| 24th. | H.Q 50th D.A. handed to CREFSTAF. Handed by H.Q. 21st D.A. all went to 50th D.A. w/E as CpY. 50th D.A.C. went to new area. | |
| 25th. | 50th D.A.C. moved into new area. | |
| 26th. | Brigades settling into new area & proceeding with training. | |

# WAR DIARY
## or
## INTELLIGENCE SUMMARY

*(Erase heading not required.)*

Army Form C. 2118

| Hour, Date, Place | Summary of Events and Information | Remarks and references to Appendices |
|---|---|---|
| 27 | 3rd NORTHUMBRIAN Bde moved back to area N of STEENWERCK. Inspection of a Battery of 50th Bde by H.M. KING GEORGE V on road 1st Canad BAILLEUL - NIEPPE Road. | |
| 28 | } Nothing to report. | |
| 29 | | |
| 30 | CRA proceeded to 50th Divl MTMS to see Low cutting experiments. | |
| 31 | CRA proceeded on leave. Lt. Col. A.D. STOCK 151 assumed temporary Command of 50th D.A. | |

# WAR DIARY
## or
## INTELLIGENCE SUMMARY

*(Erase heading not required.)*

Army Form C. 2118.

| Hour, Date, Place | Summary of Events and Information | Remarks and references to Appendices |
|---|---|---|
| Aug 1st | Very wet weather. Horse standings very bad. | |
| 2nd | Supply of trench coverings very slow. | |
| 3rd | Nothing to report. | |
| 4th | All horse lines in shocking condition. 3rd NORTH- | |
| 5th | ERN General Hospital moved near ROOTE- BOOM. | |
| 6th | Nothing to report. | |
| 7th | CRA returned from leave of absence (ENGLAND) | |
| 8th | CRA started inspection of subsection batteries | |
| | in marching order in area in turn. | |
| 9th | DA began to move to new area East of | |
| | CASTRE - HAZEBROUCK railway | |
| 10th | above moves completed. | |
| 11th | Inspection of 4th Army Group 51 Howr. Bty walking | |
| | DMC or exercising horses. Four horses Cpl. 61st Bty | |
| | of 101 × Bde Col R.F.A. being 51 the horse had the | |

# WAR DIARY
## or
## INTELLIGENCE SUMMARY

*(Erase heading not required.)*

Army Form C. 2118.

529

| Hour, Date, Place | Summary of Events and Information | Remarks and references to Appendices |
|---|---|---|
| 1st | Camp owing to bad conditions | |
| 2nd | Nothing doing | |
| 3rd | do | |
| 4th | G.O.C. 50th Division and IRA inspected Battalion | |
| 5th | 9 DAC | |
| 6th | | |
| 6th | 1st half wet weather | |
| 7th | Nothing to report. Birds in classes & teams | |
| | still delayed. | |
| 8th | Major Thomson Brigade Major proceeded on leave | |
| | 9 absence. Captain E. G. MYGUS assumed duties | |
| | of B.M. Captain C. N. BRIMS 105th on sick | |
| | 9 Staff Captain. | |
| 10th | Paraded for Divisional CommdrsShoot & on return | |
| | Commd. in hall. | |

# WAR DIARY
## or
## INTELLIGENCE SUMMARY
*(Erase heading not required.)*

Army Form C. 2118.

| Hour, Date, Place | Summary of Events and Information | Remarks and references to Appendices |
|---|---|---|
| 20th | Brigade completing fresh shelters and huts for Artillery teams. | |
| 21st | | |
| 22nd | Brigade having one horses per Battalion to DRC in preparation for the change to 18hr equipment. | |
| 23rd | A Brigade's total of 9 18hr guns and entire equipment received and 15th equipment to be returned to Base from HOOGEBROUCK Station. | |
| 24th | Remainder of 18hr equipment received. | |
| 25th | Pony carts been drawn 18hr Ammunition harness. HQ & CHESTRE | |

# WAR DIARY
## or
## INTELLIGENCE SUMMARY
*(Erase heading not required.)*

Army Form C. 2118.

| Hour, Date, Place | Summary of Events and Information | Remarks and references to Appendices |
|---|---|---|
| 25 | Saw Div and relieved same post. | |
| 26 | Cold and wet. | |
| 27 | Tour covers test and refused. | |
| 28 | Relieved but one soft in thorn bed anchoria. | |
| 29 | Try wet and cold | |
| 30 | Try fine day. Got Second ARMY especial its artillery of 50% Division the D.R. wanted for the ARMY COMMANDER at a house in STEENWERK - MOOLENACKER road. The interview proved satisfactory. About 41 hrs. The ARMY COMMANDER afterwards visited 23rd & 31st Trench Mortars at BORRE. | |

H.Q. RM 50/-
Dec '15.
VIII
vol 2

121/7929

# WAR DIARY
or
## INTELLIGENCE SUMMARY

*(Erase heading not required.)*

Army Form C. 2118.

Instructions regarding War Diaries and Intelligence Summaries are contained in F. S. Regs., Part II. and the Staff Manual respectively. Title pages will be prepared in manuscript.

| Hour, Date, Place | Summary of Events and Information | Remarks and references to Appendices |
|---|---|---|
| Dec 1st | Nothing of interest. | |
| 2nd | Wet weather. Interview with Inst. of Principals. | |
| 3/4 | Very wet. Nothing to report. | |
| 4/5 | | |
| 5th | 3rd Brigade moved from ROOTS-BOOM to HONDIS GHEM | |
| 6th | 11 Brigade less BACs moved & trained area near WATTEN. H.Q. SO. D.A at BOLLEZEELE. | |
| 7th | Very wet. Brigade not allowed to enter their training fields. | |
| 8th | Rain | |
| 9th | Very wet again. P.O.C. SO. Sowwin inspected SO. D.A. Very muddy and difficult to manœuvre. | |
| 10 | Training still much interfered with by bad weather. | |

Army Form C. 2118.

# WAR DIARY
## or
## INTELLIGENCE SUMMARY

*(Erase heading not required.)*

Instructions regarding War Diaries and Intelligence Summaries are contained in F. S. Regs., Part II. and the Staff Manual respectively. Title pages will be prepared in manuscript.

| Hour, Date, Place | Summary of Events and Information | Remarks and references to Appendices |
|---|---|---|
| 11. | Horse really fine day. Sur' its arrival at D.A. | |
| 12. | Wet after. Its casualty in a difficult state. Brill field and horse lines. Quit stables | |
| 13. | GOC n C 2nd Army inspected the D.A. very fine day and his satisfaction is definite. | |
| 14. | GOC 50th D.A. went over to RENINGHELST area. | |
| 15. | GOE RA 2nd Corps came down and went over training area. | |
| 16. | Brigades settling into new Athlone training area. | |
| 17. | Brigade marched back to an Estro race area 'road OAESTRE, leaving them guns behind in BOLLEZEELE later on by Q.D.A on relief. Hq. 50V D.A again at CAESTRE. | |

Army Form C. 2118.

# WAR DIARY
## or
## INTELLIGENCE SUMMARY

(Erase heading not required.)

Instructions regarding War Diaries and Intelligence Summaries are contained in F.S. Regs., Part II. and the Staff Manual respectively. Title pages will be prepared in manuscript.

| Hour, Date, Place | Summary of Events and Information | Remarks and references to Appendices |
|---|---|---|
| 18th | 5th Corps Commander till G.O.C. RA 5th Corps met CRA in BORRE, he did not inspect wits | |
| 19th | BACs moved up to REMIGHELST area to take over from BACs of 9th Division, for attack on 1st Corps Front. | |
| 20 | Brigade preparing horses to his area | |
| 21st | Hay not Forward moved up to wagon lines to his area 2.10th, over position of q D.A. | |
| 22 | HQ 60th DA moved down the near HOOG - RAAF and CRA remained command I went three by wi-t, HQ and waggon lines in comfortable state of word. | |
| 23 | R.Gen v. A. Robinson arrived Flake over 5 of J.A. | |

1247 W 3239 200,000 (E) 8/14 J.B.C. & A. Forms/C. 2118/11.

# WAR DIARY
## or
## INTELLIGENCE SUMMARY
*(Erase heading not required.)*

Army Form C. 2118.

| Hour, Date, Place | Summary of Events and Information | Remarks and references to Appendices |
|---|---|---|
| Dec. 24 / Dec 25 | Arthur tonight. Brig. Genl. C.G. HENSITAN handed over the Command of 50th D.A. to Brig. Genl. W.A. ROBINSON C.B. | |
| 26th | Queenie artillery were active in Zwalezendan. | |
| 27th | Nothing to report. | |
| 28th | The 50th DA had a Gun trial shoot with No 2 H F R Group. Result deemed satisfactory. Heavy shelling from | |
| 29th | the evening in district of KRUISSTRAAT. Nothing of interest to report. | |
| 30th | Uneventful. No event of activity on both sides. | |
| 31st | At 11 pm our artillery, with the aeroplanes of No 2 Sqdn HAR shelled the Germans for a short period. Result unknown. | |

H.Q. R.A. 50th Div
Jan
XIX

Army Form C. 2118.

# WAR DIARY
## or
## INTELLIGENCE SUMMARY

*(Erase heading not required.)*

Instructions regarding War Diaries and Intelligence Summaries are contained in F. S. Regs., Part II. and the Staff Manual respectively. Title pages will be prepared in manuscript.

| Hour, Date, Place | Summary of Events and Information | Remarks and references to Appendices |
|---|---|---|
| | 50th DIVISIONAL ARTILLERY<br><br>JANUARY 1916 | |

Army Form C. 2118.

# WAR DIARY
## or
## INTELLIGENCE SUMMARY
*(Erase heading not required.)*

| Hour, Date, Place | Summary of Events and Information | Remarks and references to Appendices |
|---|---|---|
| RENINGHELST Jan 1st | Our artillery shelled the enemy at "Le Gheer" (?) Central European time 2 Greenwich time. | |
| Jan 2nd | | |
| Jan 3rd | Nothing important. | |
| Jan 4th | A certain amount of activity on the part of enemy's artillery. | |
| Jan 5th | CRA visited some of the batteries near BLANDE POORT FARM and on the LILLE ROAD. Nothing important, but very few shells & weather which had not favoured its work etc. | |
| Jan 6th | The scheme for firing on HILL 60 and onward by Hector too thick carried out & weather intervened in anaesthesia. | |
| 7th | A quiet day. | |
| 8th | A quiet Sunday. Nothing important. | |

Army Form C. 2118.

# WAR DIARY
## or
## INTELLIGENCE SUMMARY
(Erase heading not required.)

Instructions regarding War Diaries and Intelligence Summaries are contained in F. S. Regs., Part II. and the Staff Manual respectively. Title pages will be prepared in manuscript.

| Hour, Date, Place | Summary of Events and Information | Remarks and references to Appendices |
|---|---|---|

RENINGHELST

9th  The shelled (which was practically in the ruins of) last place was successfully evacuated on the [illegible] [illegible] in exchanges(?) [illegible] from 9th to 10th 2 [illegible] took [illegible] the distance [illegible] between the 11th Brigade on [illegible] the [illegible] & the 12th [illegible]

10th  [illegible] - [illegible]

11th  [illegible]

12th  [illegible] 3rd & 4th Brigades supplied with aeroplane observation

13th  Nothing to report

14th  Ditto

15th  Ditto

16th  Fast movement of artillery activity 3rd & 4th Brigades continued supplying with aeroplane observation

Army Form C. 2118.

# WAR DIARY
## or
## INTELLIGENCE SUMMARY
*(Erase heading not required.)*

Instructions regarding War Diaries and Intelligence Summaries are contained in F. S. Regs., Part II. and the Staff Manual respectively. Title pages will be prepared in manuscript.

| Hour, Date, Place | | Summary of Events and Information | Remarks and references to Appendices |
|---|---|---|---|
| RENINGHELST. | 17 | A continued shoot against Hill 60 took place between 9.30 am & 11.30 am. The results were only faintly successful, retaliation was rather more little than on the 9th inst. | |
| | 18 | Between 11.30 am & 12.10 pm the enemy had an organized shoot against our front & again from 12.30 pm to 2 pm. The damage caused was practically NIL | |
| | 19 | Our Batteries were kept very busy retaliating to heavy hostile fire which lasted about two hours. Nothing to report. | |
| | 20 | Ditto | |
| | 21 | Ditto | |
| | 22 | | |

Army Form C. 2118.

# WAR DIARY
## or
## INTELLIGENCE SUMMARY

*(Erase heading not required.)*

Instructions regarding War Diaries and Intelligence Summaries are contained in F. S. Regs., Part II. and the Staff Manual respectively. Title pages will be prepared in manuscript.

| Hour, Date, Place | Summary of Events and Information | Remarks and references to Appendices |
|---|---|---|
| RENINGHELST Jan 23 | Nothing to report. | |
| 24 | Nothing to report. | |
| 25 | Nothing to report | |
| 26 | Nothing to report | |
| 27 | Nothing to report | |
| 28 | Nothing to report | |
| 29 | Nothing to report | |
| 30 | CRA visited 4th Dhm Bty and 1st Northumberland Bty | |
| 31 | Nothing to report. | |

Army Form C. 2118.

## INTELLIGENCE SUMMARY 50th Div ARTILLERY

*(Erase heading not required.)*

Instructions regarding War Diaries and Intelligence Summaries are contained in F.S. Regs., Part II, and the Staff Manual respectively. Title pages will be prepared in manuscript.

| Hour, Date, Place | Summary of Events and Information | Remarks and references to Appendices |
|---|---|---|
| HOOGGRAAF G25b SHEET 28. | | |
| FEB. 1916 | | |
| 8 | Great Artillery activity over the whole salient was started by the enemy and various excursions made from their trenches in different parts of the line. | |
| 14 | Artillery activity on part of enemy continued & vigorously replied to by us. Two sallies by the enemy opposite the A and B trenches were immediately checked. At about 5 p.m. the enemy captured some trenches of the division on our right during a relief. | |
| 15 | 6. 18 pr guns of the div. artillery (these being all available) assisted the 17th div. in a counterattack to regain the lost trenches. The bombardment lasted from 8.45 – 9.15 p.m. Weather very bad & only slight success achieved. | |

Army Form C. 2118.

# WAR DIARY
## or
## INTELLIGENCE SUMMARY

(Erase heading not required.)

50th Div ARTILLERY H.Q.

| Hour, Date, Place | Summary of Events and Information | Remarks and references to Appendices |
|---|---|---|
| HOOGRAAF G25b SHEET 28 FEB 1916 16–26 | Very inclement weather & unusual quiet on Divisional front. | |
| 5pm 26th | Division on the night gave S.O.S. call & divisional artillery fired the prearranged barrages; no enemy attack was made however. | |
| 21st | D Bty 61st Bde R.F.A. (How) (4.5) joined the 50th D.A. from the Guards Division – Battery Commander Capt R M KNOLLES. | |

# WAR DIARY
## or
## INTELLIGENCE SUMMARY

Army Form C. 2118.

H.Q. 50th Div ARTILLERY

| Hour, Date, Place | Summary of Events and Information | Remarks and references to Appendices |
|---|---|---|
| YPRES SALIENT | | |
| MARCH | | |
| 2nd 4.32am | Division on our right recaptured the BLUFF trenches. Sec. 18-pr guns of 50th D.A. were lent to assist the right group, kept up a barrage on the flank of the operations. | |
| 12 noon | Left group of Division was relieved by 24th Div. | |

HQ RA 50 Div
Feb
Vol X

50

HQ RA 50 Div

Vol 12

50

HQ RA 50 Div
Vol XI

**CONFIDENTIAL**                                                      Army Form C. 2118.

# WAR DIARY
## or
## INTELLIGENCE SUMMARY.   H.Q. 50th DIV. ARTILLERY.
*(Erase heading not required.)*

Instructions regarding War Diaries and Intelligence Summaries are contained in F.S. Regs., Part II. and the Staff Manual respectively. Title pages will be prepared in manuscript.

| Place | Date | Hour | Summary of Events and Information | Remarks and references to Appendices |
|---|---|---|---|---|
| HOOGRAAF | APRIL | | | |
| ~~WESTOUTRE~~ | 6 | 10AM | C.R.A. 1st CANADIAN DIV. took over from C.R.A. 50th Div. C.R.A. moved to WESTOUTRE divisional artillery to rest area in neighbourhood of EECKE. | |
| WESTOUTRE Sheet 28 M19C | night 7/8th | | Leading section of div. artillery relieved 2nd CANADIAN DIV. ARTILLERY. | |
| | 8/9th | | Relief of 2nd CAN. DIV. Artillery completed & C.R.A. 50th Div. took over the command. | |
| | 18 | | Personnel of the three new 18pr batteries arrived. | |
| | 19 | | Major F. BROUSSON R.A. Brigade Major 50th D.A. - Major R.G. THOMSON R.A. to Command 153rd Bde R.F.A. | |
| | 30 | 12.45 A.M. | Enemy released gas between SPANBROEKMOLEN and the DOUVE followed by an assault. The enemy did not penetrate any trenches on the division's front. | |
| | 26/27 | midnight | 3rd Division took over from 50th Div with the exception of the Artillery. | |
| | 30 | 10:30 night | S.O.S. gas by Brigade ~~#~~ Only a little gas was released + no assault followed. | |

J. Brousson Major R.A.
B.M. 50th Div Arty.

**CONFIDENTIAL**

Instructions regarding War Diaries and Intelligence Summaries are contained in F.S. Regs., Part II. and the Staff Manual respectively. Title pages will be prepared in manuscript.

Army Form C. 2118.

# WAR DIARY
## or
## INTELLIGENCE SUMMARY.
(Erase heading not required.)

MAY 1916.

H.Q. 50th Div Arty.

VIC 13

| Place | Date | Hour | Summary of Events and Information | Remarks and references to Appendices |
|---|---|---|---|---|
| WESTOUTRE | MAY 1916 1 | 12 noon | 3rd Div Arty. took over from 50th Div Arty. Relief of batteries by sections on nights 30 April/1 May and 1 May/2 May. 50th Div Arty. in rest area round EECKE | |
| EECKE | 3 | 12 noon | Division in G.H.Q. reserve & ready to entrain at 9 hours notice. Divisional Artillery overhauling equipment, training and being inoculated. C.R.A. went on leave Lieut Col F.B. Moss BLUNDELL acting C.R.A. Brigades came under new establishments :— 1st Northumbrian Bde + 4th Durham (How) Bty became 250th Bde R.F.A. 2nd " + 5 " " " 251st " " 3rd " + D/61 Bty " 252nd " " 3 Newly formed 18 pr btys with 4th Northumbrian (How) Bde H.Q. became 253rd Bde | |
| | 16 | | 253rd Bde RFA moved to WISSANT for training. | |
| | 16 14 | | C.R.A. returned from leave | |
| | 21 | | C.R.A. invalided to England Lieut Col A.V. STOCKLEY recalled from WISSANT to act as C.R.A. | |

G. Unwin Major R.A. B.M. 50th D.A.

CONFIDENTIAL                 MAY 1916    Army Form C. 2118.

WAR DIARY
or
INTELLIGENCE SUMMARY.

H.Q. 50th DIV. ARTILLERY.

(Erase heading not required.)

Instructions regarding War Diaries and Intelligence Summaries are contained in F. S. Regs., Part II. and the Staff Manual respectively. Title pages will be prepared in manuscript.

| Place | Date | Hour | Summary of Events and Information | Remarks and references to Appendices |
|---|---|---|---|---|
| EECKE | 30 | | 50th D.A. relieved 3rd D.A. in the line the command passing at 12 noon May 30th. Batteries relieved by sections on the nights 29/30th and 30/31st May. Div Arty H.Q at WESTOUTRE. | |

J. Anoreur
Major R.A. B.M. 50th D.A.

WAR DIARY    SECRET    Vol 14

H.Q. 50th DIVISIONAL ARTILLERY.

JUNE 1916.  VOL. XV

**CONFIDENTIAL**

Army Form C. 2118.

# WAR DIARY
or
## INTELLIGENCE SUMMARY.
(Erase heading not required.)

JUNE 1916
H.Q. 50th DIV ARTILLERY
VOL 15

| Place | Date | Hour | Summary of Events and Information | Remarks and references to Appendices |
|---|---|---|---|---|
| WESTOUTRE | JUNE 4 | 12·30AM | 50th Div Artillery assisted 24th Div on right in a minor enterprise. Assistance took the form of 15 mins bombardment of enemy front line and 5 mins barrage on their supports. 36 18 prs and 12 4·5" Hows took part. | |
| | 17 | 12·40 A.M. | B/251 fired gas barrages having intercepted an infantry call. Gas was sent over right batt= of right sector + all batteries of 251 Bde fired on this front – All batteries ceased firing at 1·45 AM | |
| | 20 | | Lt Col. A.V. STOCKLEY R.A. appointed Brigadier-General Commanding 50th Div Artillery vice Brig Gen W.A. ROBINSON C.B. R.A. invalided. | |
| | 24th | | Organised bombardment by Divisional Artillery started – programme attached. | XV.1 |

J. Ommmm
Majr R.A.
B.M. 50th Div Arty

XV

| BDE. | "A" DAY. June 24th | "B" DAY. June 26th | "C" DAY. June 27 | "D" DAY. June 28 | "E" DAY. June 30 | AMMUNITION ALLOTTED. |
|---|---|---|---|---|---|---|
| 250. | Wire cut. Keep open at night. Bombard O.13.a. 5½.1¼. at night | At time which will be given. proceed as in paragraph 2 Instructions. | Para. 3 instructions. Wire cut, etc. Bombard O.19.b.1½.6½. | Wire cut, etc., bombard O.19.a.5.1½. | Wire cut etc.; the wire cutting on this day to last longer and look more important. | 9,000 18-pdr. 1,250 4.5". |
| 252. | Wire cut. Keep open at night. Bombard O.13.a. 7.3. at night. | -do- | Para. 3. instructions. Wire cut, etc. Bombard O.20.a.1½.6. | Wire cut, etc., Bombard O.20.b.1½.2¾. | -do- | 8,500 18,pdr. 1,250 4.5". |
| 251 | WORKS | UNDER | 24th | DIVISION. | | |

**CONFIDENTIAL.**

**VOLUME. 16.**

**WAR DIARY**
or
**INTELLIGENCE SUMMARY.**
(*Erase heading not required.*)

**HEADQUARTERS. 50TH DIVISIONAL ARTILLERY.**
Army Form C. 2118.

Instructions regarding War Diaries and Intelligence Summaries are contained in F. S. Regs., Part II. and the Staff Manual respectively. Title pages will be prepared in manuscript.

July 1916

| Place | Date | Hour | Summary of Events and Information | Remarks and references to Appendices |
|---|---|---|---|---|
| WESTOUTRE. | Night 5/6. 6/7 | | Relief of 251st F.A.B.Group, as in operation Order No. 17. attached. | 16/1. |
| | Night 8/9. | | Alteration in tactical command of certain batteries. Operation Order No. 18. attached. | 16/2. |
| | 15th | | X/50. Trench Mortar Battery detached on special duty. | |
| | 22/23. | | B/251 Battery came under O.C. 108. F. A. B. Group. Operation Order No. 19. attached. | 16/3. |
| | 23rd | | X/50. Trench Mortar Battery returned. | |
| | 26th. | | A/172 Battery came under O.C., 153. F. A. B. Group. | |
| | | | A/36. Medium Trench Mortar Battery under tactical command of O.C. 173. F.A.B.Group. } Operation Order No. 20. attached. | 16/4. |
| | | | Y/36. Medium Trench Mortar Battery under tactical command of O.C. 172. F.A.B.Group. | |
| | 27/28. | | Relief of D/173 by D/251. | |
| | | | C/251 went into action. } Operation Order No. 21. | 16/5. |
| | 28/29. | | One Section of B/154 came out of action | |
| | 29/30. | | Relief of 252 F.A.B.Group and attached Trench Mortar Battery by 2nd Canadian Division and relief of 172 F. A. B. Group and Trench Mortars by 252. F. A. B. Group. Operation Order No. 22. attached. | 16/6. |

WAR DIARY 16/1

SECRET.

Copy No. 1

## 50th DIVISIONAL ARTILLERY OPERATION ORDER No. 17.

3. 7. 16.

1. H.Q., 251st (Northbn) Bde. R.F.A. and the following Batteries will be relieved by 24th Division on nights 5th/6th and 6th/7th July :-

   A. 250.
   B. 251.
   C. 251.
   D. 251.
   A. 253.

2. A/251 Battery will remain in action and under orders of 24th Division.

3. All existing communications will be left.

4. All details ~~as to hours~~ of relief will be arranged by 24th Division.

5. As Sections move out they will march to their wagon-lines.

6. All ammunition dumped at gun positions will be handed over.
   Batteries will move out with all vehicles full.
   2nd Section, "A" Echelon, 50th D.A.C. will be relieved by 24th Division on the evening of 4th July. Responsibility for supply of ammunition will pass when this relief is completed.
   Any further details as to ammunition will be issued later.

7. Completion of stages of relief and the handing over of command will be reported to this Office by wire.

8. Acknowledge.

F. Thompson
Major R.A.,
B.M. 50th D.A.

Issued at 8.0p.m.

Copy No. 1 - C.R.A.
" " 2 - H.Q. 50th Division.
" " 3 - C.R.A. 24th Division.
" " 4 - 250th (Nbn) Bde. R.F.A.
" " 5 - 251st " " "
" " 6 - 252nd " " "
" " 7 - 253rd " " "
" " 8 - 50th D.A.C.
" " 9 - Divnl. T.M. Officer.
Copies 10 and 11 Spare.

WAR DIARY 16/2

SECRET.

Copy No. 10

## 50th DIVISIONAL ARTILLERY OPERATION ORDER NO. 18.

8.7.16.

1. On night 8th/9th July, 150th Infantry Brigade will extend its front Southwards, and will take over trenches from 24th Division as far as the KEMMEL - WYTSCHAETE Road inclusive.

2. When the above relief is completed the following batteries will come under the tactical command of Col. Bell's Group, (new Right Group, 50th D.A.). :-

    A/250.
    A/251.
    B/251.

3. Command will pass on completion of relief of front line trenches.

4. The trench mortar of Z.50 Battery, which is at present tactically attached to Col. Moss-Blundell's Group will rejoin Col. Bell's Group, when the Infantry relief is completed.
    Trench Mortars of X.50 Battery will remain tactically attached to 24th Division.

5. O.C. new Right Group, 50th D.A., will have a call on a Howitzer Battery 24th D.A., (D/107) and should arrange communication.

6. Col. Bell will report when he has taken over command as above.

7. Acknowledge.

Issued at 4.0pm.

Major R.A.,
B.M. 50th D.A.

Copy No. 1 - C.R.A.
" 2 - 50th Division.
" 3 - 24th D.A.
" 4 - 250th (Wbn) Bde. R.F.A.
" 5 - 251st " " "
" 6 - 252nd " " "
" 7 - 253rd " " "
" 8 - Divnl. T.M. Officer.
" 9 & 10 - Spare.

SECRET.

Copy No 7

## 50th DIVISIONAL ARTILLERY OPERATION ORDER No. 19.

21. 7. 18.

1. Reference 50th Division Operation Order No. 42.

   On completion of relief therein mentioned, 'B' Battery, 251st (Northbn) Bde. R.F.A. will come tactically under the orders of the O.C., 108th F.A.B. Group, to cover the increase in front of the 151st Infantry Brigade.

2. Acknowledge.

Issued at 3.30pm.

Major R.A.,
B.M. 50th D.A.

Copy Nos. 1 & 2 - C.R.A.
" No. 3 - 50th Division.
" " 4 - 250th F.A.B. Group.
" " 5 - 108th " "
" " 6 - 151st Inf. Bde.
" " 7 - Spare.

WAR DIARY 16/4

Reference Map 1/20,000           SECRET.
Sheet 28 S.W., & Trench Map.       Copy No. 13

## 50th DIVISIONAL ARTILLERY OPERATION ORDER No. 20.

26th July, 1916.

1. The moves of H.Q., 151 and 150 Infantry Brigades and H.Q. 173 F.A.B. Group are postponed until further orders.

2. With reference to Para. 2, Sub-para (c)., A/172 will also come under the tactical orders of 153 F.A.B. Group.

3. A/36 Medium Trench Mortar Battery is under the tactical command of O.C. 173 F.A.B. Group.

   Y/36 Medium Trench Mortar Battery is under the tactical command of O.C. 172 F.A.B. Group.

4. Acknowledge.

F. Brunson
Major R.A.,
B.M. 50th D.A.

Issued at 3.30p.m.

Copy No. 1 - 250 F.A.B. Group.
       2 - 173 " "
       3 - 172 " "
       4 - 153 " "
       5 - 149th Infantry Bde.
       6 - 151 " "
       7 - 50th Divnl. T.M. Officer.
       8 - H.Q., 50th Division.
       9 - C.R.A., 36th (Ulster) Division.
     10 - R. A., V. Copps.
     11 - C.R.A.
     12 and 13 spare.

WAR DIARY 16/5

SECRET.

Copy No. 6

## 50th DIVISIONAL ARTILLERY OPERATION ORDER No. 21.

27. 7. 16.

1.  One section of D/173 Brigade R.F.A. will be relieved in action on night of 27th/28th by one section of D/251. (The enfilade gun will not be relieved on this night)

2.  On night of 28th/29th, remaining 2 guns of D/173 will be relieved by D/251.

3.  C/251 will go into action on night 27th/28th and come under the orders of O.C., 173 F.A.B. Group.

4.  Two guns of B/154 will come out of action on night 28th/29th.

5.  The disposal of the relieved sections will be notified later.

6.  Reliefs not to commence before 10.0pm each night.

7.  Completion of each relief to be reported to this Office.

8.  Acknowledge.

F. Brown
Major R.A.,
B.H. 50th D.A.

Issued at 2.30pm.

Copy No. 1. - 251 F.A.B. Group.
     2. - 173  "   "
     3. - 154  "   "
     4. - C.R.A. 36th Division.
     5. - 50th Division.
     6 and 7. Spare.

Reference Map 1/20,000  
Sheet 28 S.W. & Trench Map.

SECRET

Copy No. 13

## 50th DIVISIONAL ARTILLERY OPERATION ORDER No. 22.

28.7.16.

1.  252 F.A.B. Group will be relieved by 2nd Canadian Division, by Sections, on nights 29th/30th, and 30th/31st.  Sections will proceed to Wagon-lines on relief.
    A/253 will come out of action by sections on nights 29th/30th and 30th/31st, and proceed to wagon-lines. It will go into action under the tactical command of O.C. 252 F.A.B. Group on night 31st/1st, in such position as O.C. 252 F.A.B. Group selects.

2.  B/253 will relieve B/173 by sections, nights 30th/31st & 31st/1st.
    C/253  "      "    C/173  "     "      "      "    "   "   "

3.  252 F.A.B. Group relieves 172 F.A.B. Group by sections on nights 30th/31st and 31st/1st.

4.  H.Q. 251 F.A.Bde. will relieve H.Q. 173 F.A.Bde at 12 noon on 30th, and will assume command of 173 F.A.B. Group.

5.  Y50 Trench Mortar Battery will be relieved by 2nd Canadian Division on night 29th/30th.  Personnel only will be relieved.
    On night 30th/31st, Y.50 Trench Mortar Battery will go into action under 172 F.A.B. Group.
    All details will be arranged by Divisional Trench Mortar Officers.

6.  All reliefs will take place after dark.

7.  Commands will pass on completion of reliefs.

8.  Completion of each relief to be reported to this office.

9.  Details as regards ammunition will be issued separately.

10. Acknowledge.

F. Brown  
Major R.A.,  
B.M. 50th D.A.

Issued at 8.0 p.m.

Copy No. 1 - 250 F.A.B. Group.  
     2 - 251    "     "  
     3 - 252    "     "  
     4 - 253    "     "  
     5 - 172    "     "  
     6 - 173    "     "  
     7 - 154    "     "  
     8 - 50th Divnl. T.M. Officer.  
     9 - C.R.A. 2nd Canadian Divn.  
    10 - C.R.A. 38th Division.  
    11 - H.Q. 50th Division.  
    12 - R.A., V. Corps.  
    13 - War Diary.  
    14 and 15 - Spare.

Vol. 16.

Headquarters
50th Div. Artillery

August 1916.

W. 15517—M. 141.  250,000.  1/16.  L.S.&Co.  Forms/W 3091/2.      Army Form W. 3091.

# Cover for Documents.

Nature of Enclosures.

~~Intelligence~~

Notes, or Letters written.

Army Form C. 2118.

VOLUME XVII

# WAR DIARY
or
## INTELLIGENCE SUMMARY.

AUGUST 1916.

HEADQUARTERS. 50th DIVISIONAL ARTILLERY.

*(Erase heading not required.)*

Instructions regarding War Diaries and Intelligence Summaries are contained in F. S. Regs., Part II. and the Staff Manual respectively. Title pages will be prepared in manuscript.

Vol. 16

| Place | Date | Hour | Summary of Events and Information | Remarks and references to Appendices |
|---|---|---|---|---|
| WESTOUTRE. | 5 | 4.p.m. | Two hour bombardment by Divisional Artillery on trenches in neighbourhood of SPANBROEKMOLEN (28. N.30.c.) in conjunction with trench Mortars and Corps Heavy Artillery :- 6" and 9.2" Hows and 60 pdrs. The 240 mm. Trench Mortar fired for the first time, with considerable success. | 17/1. |
| | Nights 8/9 | | Relief of 50th Divisional Artillery by 19th Divisional Artillery: Operation Order attached | |
| | 9/10. | | Divisional Artillery in EECKE area. | |
| | 11th } 12th } | | Divisional Artillery entrained for 9th Corps area from GODESWAERVELDE, BAILLEUL MAIN and BAILLEUL WEST arriving at DOULLENS MAIN, DOULLENS, South and FIENVILLERS - CANDAS whence they marched to BOISBERQUES area. | |
| | 13th. | | G.H.Q. reserve in Reserve Army. | |
| | 14th. | | G.H.Q. reserve in Reserve Army. | |
| | 14/15 Midnight | | 50th Division transferred to Fourth Army, III Corps. | |
| | 15th | | Divisional Artillery moved to VIGNACOURT: Operation Order No. 25 attached. | 17/2. |
| | 16th | | Divisional Artillery moved to new area: Operation Order No. 26. attached. | 17/3. |
| | 18/19 | | 50th Divisional Artillery relieved 34th Divisional Artillery covering 15th Division front | 17/4. |
| | 19/20 | | Operation Order No. 27 attached (marked 17/4) 250 and 253. Brigades remained in rest area. | 17/5. |
| | | | Operation Order No. 28 (marked 17/5) attached, also part of D.A.C. Operation Order No. 29 (marked 17/6) attached. | 17/6 |

T.134. Wt. W708—776. 50000. 4/15. Sir J. C. & S.

Army Form C. 2118.

# WAR DIARY

## ~~INTELLIGENCE~~ SUMMARY.

*(Erase heading not required.)*

Instructions regarding War Diaries and Intelligence Summaries are contained in F. S. Regs., Part II. and the Staff Manual respectively. Title pages will be prepared in manuscript.

| Place | Date | Hour | Summary of Events and Information | Remarks and references to Appendices |
|---|---|---|---|---|
| | 24/25) 25/26) 19/31 | | 250 Brigade R.F.A. relieved 70th Brigade R.F.A. by sections and came under the command of 15th Divisional Artillery, covering 1st Division Infantry: Operation Order No.30 attached.<br><br>Carried out daily bombardments. | 17/7 |

J. Anderson
Major, R.A.
B.M. 50th Divisional Artillery.

SECRET.

B.M. 1508.

O.C.,

---

A bombardment of enemy's trenches in N.30 and N.36 will take place on the afternoon of August 5th, according to table attached.

Times are shown as from Zero time, which will be notified later.

Watches will be synchronised.

4. 8. 16.

Major R.A.,
B.M. 50th D.A.

## PROGRAMME OF BOMBARDMENT.

| Unit bombarding. | Time. | Objective. | Rate of fire. | No. of Rounds. | Remarks. |
|---|---|---|---|---|---|
| Right Group. D/252 C/252 A/253 | 0. – 1.50 | Front line N.30.c.5.3. – N.36.a.9.2. and C.T.'s leading thereto. | 1 Round per gun per 3 minutes for first hour, 0.–1.00. 2 rounds per gun per minute, 1.00 – 1.50 | 300 A. 300 AX. 900 A. 1100 AX. | |
| B/251 C/251 | 1.50 – 2.00 | Barrage SUNKEN ROAD N.30.c.5½.3. – N.36.b.2.8½. and C.T.'s N.36.b.2.8½ N.36.b.5.6. – N.36.b.0.4½ – N.36.a.7.3. | 2 Rounds per gun per minute. | 400 A. | |
| Centre Group. D/251 (how) | 0. – 2.00 | N.30.c.5.3. – N.36.a.5½.8. | – | 200 BX | |
| D/252 | 0. – 2.00 | N.36.a.5½.8. – N.36.a.9.2. | – | 100 BX | |
| Right Group. A/251 B/253 | 0. – 2.00 | SPANBROEKMOLEN SALIENT. | One round per gun per minute. | 600 A. 360 AX. | To prevent observation on Heavy T.M. |

## PROGRAMME OF BOMBARDMENT.

| Unit Bombarding. | Time. | Objective. | Rate of Fire | No. of Rounds. | Remarks. |
|---|---|---|---|---|---|
| 3" How. | 0. - 1.50 | S.T. N.30.c.3½.2. - N.36.a.9.5. | - | 80 | |
| 60-pdrs. | -do- | C.T. N.36.b.4½.7. - O.31.a.½.8. <br> -do-  -do-  - O.31.a.0.5. | - | 50 | This has been arranged with H.A., V. Corps. |
| 6" How. | 1.50 - 2.00 | S.T. N.30.c.6½.2. - N.33.a.9.5. | - | 20 | |
| 9.2" How. | -do- | S.T. N.30.c.9½.½. - N.36.b.1.7. | - | 20 | |
| 60-pdrs. | -do- | Huts in L'ENFER WOOD. | - | 50 | |
| One 240 mm.T.M. | 0.02 - 2.00 | Trench N.30.c.7.1½ - N.36.a.9½.4½. | | 25 | |
| Four 2" T.M.'s | 0.02 - 2.00 | Front line N.36.a.3.5. - N.36.a.9½.1½. | 20 Rounds per hour. | 160 | |
| One 2" T.M. | 0.02 - 2.00 | Front line N.30.c.2.3. - N.36.a.5.9. | -do- | 40 | |

SECRET.

50th Division.
G.X.2382.

149th Inf. Bde.
150th    "    "
151st    "    "
G.O.C. R.A.
O.C. Signals.

---

The German trenches between N.36.a.9.1. and N.30.c.5.3. will be fired at by Artillery of all natures, including the Heavy T.M., from 4.0 p.m. to 6.0 p.m. today, the 5th instant.

It is advisable to clear the following trenches :- as much as possible during the shoot :-

D.3, D.4, D.5, BULL RING.

2.      The inspection of drafts by the G.O.C. which was arranged for today, will not now take place.

3.      Signal time will be sent by wire to all Infantry Brigades and G.O.C. R.A. at 2.0 p.m. today, 5th instant.

4.      The detail of the Artillery work has been sent to all concerned by the G.O.C. R.A.

H. Harstack.
Lt.Col.,
General Staff,
50th Division.

5th August 1916.

Copies to :-

G.O.C. V Corps H.A.
36th Division.
2nd Canadian Division.
V Corps.

Brigade Major,
    50th Div. Artillery,

C.C
Copy to 2 Army
& Divisions for information

      The 9.45 H.T.M. and four Medium Mortars bombarded targets as indicated in your B.M. 1506.

      The Heavy T.M. was placed in a temporary position on a wooden platform.

      Owing to nature of ground special attention was paid to foundation, i.e., plenty of bricks were used, making it solid and firm.

      After "cease fire" bed was tested and found to be perfectly level.

      Twenty five (25) rounds were expended in one hour.
- (a) One round blind.
- (b)   "   "   air burst.
- (c)   "   "   short (between trenches).

(a) and (b) - I cannot account for these two errors.

(c) - No doubt due to faulty burning of charge, as I noticed after the bomb left the mortar burning cordite fall in front of muzzle.

The mortar answered very well to all corrections.

Considering the rapid rate of fire the mortar was not unduly heated and could have continued firing.

Judging from the amount of material thrown about, considerable damage was done to enemy works.

Huge gaps were observed in support line trenches.

I might mention that today was the first time the detachment had fired the heavy mortar.

It would be an advantage to have special O.P's with a wide field of view for this mortar.

The four 2" mortars expended 197 rounds during the bombardment. Considerable damage was done to the enemy front line trenches, timber, iron, and dugout frames were observed flying through the air.

Today's shoot was in every way successful. The destructive effect of the 9.45 is beyond doubt.

Absolute concealment is necessary or continuous firing from one position would bring heavy retaliation.

                (sd) W.C.HAND, Capt.,

5/8/16.                     50th Div. T.M.Officer.

                B.M.1506/1.

Staff Officer R.A.,
    V Corps.

      Herewith copy of report by 50th Div. T.M.Officer on the firing of the 240 mm. Trench Mortar during the bombardment on 5/8/16, for your information.

                (sd) . . Stockley, Brig. Gen,

6/8/16.                     C.R.A., 50th Div.

## PROGRAMME OF BOMBARDMENT.

| Unit bombarding. | | Time. | Objective. | Rate of fire. | No of Rounds. | Remarks. |
|---|---|---|---|---|---|---|
| Right Group. | B/252 C/252 A/253 | 0. – 1.50 | Front line N.30.c 5.3 – N.36.a 9.2. and C.T's leading thereto. | 1 Round per gun per 2 minutes for first hour. 0. – 1.00. | 500 A. 300 AX. | |
| | B/251 C/251 | 1.50 – 2.00 | Barrage SUNKEN Road N.30.c 5½.5 – N.36.b 2.8½ and C.T's N.36.b 2.8½ – N.36.b 5.6 – N.36.b 0.4½ – N.36.a 7.3. | 2 rounds per gun per minute. 1.00 – 1.50 | 900 A. 1100 AX. | |
| | | | | 2 rounds per gun per minute. | 400 A. | |
| Centre Group. | D/251 (how) | 0. – 2.00 | N.30.c 5.3 – N.36.a 5½.8. | – | 200 BX. | |
| | D/252 | 0. – 2.00 | N.36.a 5½.8 – N.36.a 9.2. | – | 100 BX. | |
| Right Group. | A/251 B/253 | 0. – 2.00 | SPANBROEKMOLEN Salient. | One round per gun per minute. | 600 A. 380 AX. | To prevent observation on Heavy T.M. |

## PROGRAMME OF BOMBARDMENT.

| Unit Bombarding. | Time. | Objective. | Rate of Fire. | No. of Rounds. | Remarks. |
|---|---|---|---|---|---|
| 6" How. | 0. - 1.50 | S.T. N.30.c.6½.2. - N.36.a.9.5. | — | 80 | |
| 60-prs. | —do— | C.T. N.36.b.4½.7. - 0.31.a.½.8.<br>—do— - 0.31.a.0.5. | — | 50 | This has been arranged with H.A., V Corps. |
| 6" How. | 1.50 - 2.00 | S.T. N.30.c.6½.2. - N.36.a.9.5. | — | 20 | |
| 9.2" How. | —do— | S.T. N.30.c.9½.½. - N.36.b.1.7. | — | 20 | |
| 60-prs. | —do— | Huts in L'ENFER WOOD. | — | 50 | |
| One 240 mm T.M. | 0.02 - 2.00 | Trench N.30.c.7.1½ - N.36.a.9½.4½ | | 25 | |
| Four 2" T.Ms. | 0.02 - 2.00 | Front line N.36.a.6.5 - N.36.a.9½.1½ | 20 Rounds per hour | 160 | |
| One 2" T.M. | 0.02 + 2.00 | Front line N.30.c.5.3 - N.36.a.5.9. | —do— | 40 | |

50th Division.
G.X.2382.

V CORPS.

Herewith a copy of a report by the Divisional T.M.Officer on the shooting of the 9.45" Heavy Trench Mortar, which took place yesterday afternoon.

The result appeared to be very satisfactory.

6th August 1916.

Major-General.
Commanding 50th Division.

Brigade Major,
 50th Divisional Artillery.
 ───────────────

The 9.45 H.T.M. and four Medium Mortars bombarded targets as indicated in your B.M.1506.

The Heavy T.M. was placed in a temporary position on a wooden platform.

Owing to nature of ground special attention was paid to foundation, i.e., plenty of bricks were used, making it solid and firm.

After "cease fire" bed was tested and found to be perfectly level.

Twenty five (25) rounds were expended in one hour.

(a) One round blind.
(b) " " air burst.
(c) " " short (between trenches).

(a) and (b) - I cannot account for these two errors.

(c) No doubt due to faulty burning of charge, as I noticed after the bomb left the mortar burning cordite fall in front of muzzle.

The mortar answered very well to all corrections.

Considering the rapid rate of fire the mortar was not unduly heated and could have continued firing.

Judging from the amount of material thrown about, considerable damage was done to enemy works.

Huge gaps were observed in support line trenches.

I might mention that to-day was the first time the detachment had fired the heavy mortar.

It would be an advantage to have special O.P's with a wide field of view for this mortar.

The four 2" mortars expended 197 rounds during the bombardment. Considerable damage was done to the enemy front line trenches, timber, iron, and dug-out frames were observed flying through the air.

To-day's shoot was in every way successful.

The destructive effect of the 9.45 is beyond doubt.

Absolute concealment is necessary or continuous firing from one position would bring heavy retaliation.

5th August 1916.
          (Sgd) W.C.HAND. Capt.
           50th Div. T.M.Officer.

To-day's shoot was in every way successful.

The destructive effect of the 9.45 is beyond doubt.

Absolute concealment is necessary or continuous firing from one position would bring heavy retaliation.

5th August 1916.
(sgd) W.C.HAND, Capt.
50th Div. T.M.Officer.

Brigade Major,
  50th Divisional Artillery.

  ———————

The 9.45 H.T.M. and four Medium Mortars bombarded targets as indicated in your B.M. 1506.

The Heavy T.M. was placed in a temporary position on a wooden platform.

Owing to nature of ground special attention was paid to foundation, i.e., plenty of bricks were used, making it solid and firm.

After 'cease fire' bed was tested and found to be perfectly level.

Twenty five (25) rounds were expended in one hour.

(a) One round blind.

(b) " " air burst.

(c) " " short (between trenches).

(a) and (b) - I cannot account for these two errors.

(c) No doubt due to faulty burning of charge, as I noticed after the bomb left the mortar burning cordite fall in front of muzzle.

The mortar answered very well to all corrections.

Considering the rapid rate of fire the mortar was not unduly heated and could have continued firing.

Judging from the amount of material thrown about, considerable damage was done to enemy works.

Huge gaps were observed in support line trenches.

I might mention that to-day was the first time the detachment had fired the heavy mortar.

It would be an advantage to have special O.P.'s with a wide field of view for this mortar.

The four 2" mortars expended 197 rounds during the bombardment. Considerable damage was done to the enemy front line trenches, timber, iron, and dug-out frames were observed flying through the air.

B.M. 1506/1.

Staff Officer R.A.,

V. Corps.

Herewith copy of report by 50th Divisional Trench Mortar Officer on the firing of the 240 mm. Trench Mortar during the bombardment on 5.8.16., for your information.

6.8.16.

Brig. Gen.,
C.R.A. 50th Division.

G.

To see, & return please.

A. Stokes B.L.

6.8.16.

14/1

V Corps,
GX.6926/2.

GX. 6928/2

6/8/16.

GX6950 att'd

Second Army,

A bombardment of the German trenches on the 50th Division front was carried out on the 5th inst, in accordance with attached programme.

The results have already been reported.

The Heavy Trench Mortar fired exceedingly well. Detailed report regarding this mortar is attached.

(sd) G.F.BOYD, B.G.,

for Lt. General,
Comdg. V Corps.

Copies to 36th & 41st Divs.

WAR DIARY 17/1

Ref. Sheets 27 S.E. and 28 S.W.,　　　　　　　　SECRET.
　　　　1/20,000.　　　　　　　　　　　　　　　Copy No. 12

## 50th DIVISIONAL ARTILLERY OPERATION ORDER No. 24.

7.8.16.

1. 50th D.A. will be relieved in action by 19th D.A. by sections and as soon after dark as possible on nights 8/9 and 9/10 August, as per table attached, and will proceed to V. Corps Rest area No. 4. Guns will not be exchanged.

    A/252 and A/253 will march from their wagon lines and proceed to Rest area on afternoon of 8th Aug.

    50th D.A.C. will be relieved by half sections on the morning of 9th Aug. Relief to be completed by 12 noon.

2. Brigades and D.A.C. will march to the Rest area via WESTOUTRE - MT. KOKEREELE - BOESCHEPE - Road Junction R.1.d.2.4. - GODEWAERSVELDE.

3. The relief of the Trench Mortars (personnel only) will take place on the 9th Aug.

4. Units will move out on relief with all echelons full to establishment with ammunition, including "B" Echelon Divisional Ammunition Column. Surplus ammunition will be handed over to relieving Units; amounts handed over to be reported to this office as soon as relief is completed.

5. Details of reliefs will be arranged by Os. C. Brigades, D.A.C.'s, and Divisional Trench Mortar Officers.

6. Battery Commanders will march with their second sections.

    Command of Groups will pass at noon on the 9th.

    Responsibility for supply of ammunition will pass at noon on 9th, when O.C., D.A.C. will move to new area.

    Command of Divisional Artillery will pass at noon on the 9th, after which hour H.Q., R.A., 50th Division will be at EECKE.

7. Log books, Defence schemes, Orders, Maps, Photographs and all useful information will be handed over. (See this Office No. S.C. 619 dated 4.8.16).

8. O.C. 253 Bde. will hand over on the morning of the 8th the special work of which he is in charge to O.C., 89th Brigade R.F.A.

9. Completion of each stage of relief and the handing over of command will be reported to this office by wire.

10. Acknowledge.

　　　　　　　　　　　　　　　　　　　　　F. Brown
　　　　　　　　　　　　　　　　　　　　　Major R.A.,
Issued at 10.0a.m.　　　　　　　　　　　　　B.M. 50th D.A.

　　Copy No. 1 - 250 (Nbn) Bde. R.F.A.　Copy No. 8 - H.Q. 50th Divn.
　　　　　　2 - 251　　"　　"　　"　　　　　　9 - A.D.M.S. 50th Dn.
　　　　　　3 - 252　　"　　"　　"　　　　　 10 - 50th Div. Train.
　　　　　　4 - 253　　"　　"　　"　　　　　 11 - R.A., V. Corps.
　　　　　　5 - 50th D.A.C.　　　　　　　　　 12 - War Diary.
　　　　　　6 - 50th Div. TM. Officer.　13, 14 and 15　Spare.
　　　　　　7 - C.R.A., 19th Divn.

SECRET.

V Corps.
GX.6999.
10/8/16.

Canadian Corps.
19th Division.

Smoke discharge, accompanied by two minutes shrapnel, on enemy's trenches will be carried out by the 41st Division. on night 11th/12th at 10.p.m.

(sd) G.F.Boyd
B.G.G.S.
V Corps.

36th Division informed.

124/47  17

Reference Maps, Sheet 11, LENS and
17 AMIENS, 1/100,000.

**WAR DIARY** 17/2

SECRET.
Copy No. 13

## 50th DIVISIONAL ARTILLERY OPERATION ORDER No. 25.

14. 8. 1916.

1. The 50th Division is to be transferred at midnight 14/15 Aug. from G.H.Q. Reserve in Reserve Army to Fourth Army, Third Corps, and will march on 15th Aug. from the BERNAVILLE area to Area C., about VIGNACOURT.

2. The 50th Divisional Artillery will march to billots as under on morning of 15th Aug.:-

   250 R.F.A. Bde. )                    251 R.F.A. Bde. )
   252 R.F.A. Bde. ) BOURDON.                            ) BETHENCOURT
   50th D.A.C.     )                    253 R.F.A. Bde. ) ST. OUEN.

3. Routes will be as follows :-

   250 Bde.    HARDINVAL - FIENVILLERS - MONTRELET - CANAPLES -
               Rly. Crossing 3/4 mile N.W. of V of VIGNACOURT - VIGNACOURT -
               South of FORET DE VIGNACOURT - X Rds. 1/4 mile South of
               U of B. DU GARD.

   251 Bde :-  Rd. Junct. at 1st E of BOISBERGUES - MT. RENAULT FM -
               Rd. Junct. just North of B of BERNAVILLE - ST. HILAIRE -
               Rd. Junct. 1 mile North of M of LE CLAPET MIN -
               ST. LEGER LES DOMART - Left bank of R. NIEVRE.

   252 Bde :-  X. Rds. 1/4 mile South of 1st E of HEUZECOURT -
               BEAUMETZ - RIBEAUCOURT - FRANKQUEVILLE - X. Rds. 1/2 mile
               S.E. of U of DOMART EN PONTHIEU - HALTE (North of ST. OUEN)-
               Right Bank of R. NIEVRE - FLIXECOURT.

   253 Bde :-  MT. RENAULT FM. - Rd. Junct. just North of B of
               BERNAVILLE - ST. HILAIRE - Rd. Junct. 1 mile North of
               M of LE CLAPET MIN - ST. LEGER LES DOMART - Left bank of
               R. NIEVRE.

   D.A.C. :-   Rd. Junct. just North of 1st E of BERNAVILLE -
               BERNEUIL - PERNOIS - Rd. Junct. 1 mile West of V of
               VIGNACOURT - North of FORET DE VIGNACOURT - N of BOURDON.

4. 253 Bde. will march at 4.0a.m. 251 Bde. will march immediately in rear of 253 Bde. and will not cross the BERNAVILLE - LE MEILLARD Road until 253 Bde. is clear.

5. Heads of Columns will not move South of the line DOMART EN PONTHIEU - BERNEUIL - MONTRELET before 7.45a.m.

6. All Columns must be South of a line through ST. OUEN - LAVICOGNE by 10.0a.m.

7. 50th D.A. Heavy and Medium T.M. Batteries will move at 3.0a.m. direct to MONTIGNY area by mechanical transport.

8. 50th D.A. Headquarters will close at BERNAVILLE at 7.0a.m. on 15th Aug. and open at VIGNACOURT at 11.0a.m. on 15th Aug.

9. Brigade billeting parties will meet Staff Captain at R.A. H.Q's. VIGNACOURT at 2.30p.m., 15th August.

10. Acknowledge.

Issued at 7.30 p.m.

Major R.A.,
B.M. 50th D.A.

Copies to -
```
         1 - 250 F.A.Bde.
         2 - 251 F.A.Bde.
         3 - 252 F.A.Bde.
         4 - 253 F.A.Bde.
         5 - 50th D.A.C.
         6 - 50th D.T.M.O.
         7 - H.Q., 50th Divn.
         8 - 50th Div. Train.
         9 - R.A., III Corps.
        10 - IX. Corps.
        11 - X. Corps.
        12 - III Corps.
        13 - War Diary.
        14, 15, 16, Spare.
```

RELIEF TABLE.

| 50th Division. | Gun position or Bde. H.Q. | Relieved by 19th Division | Time of Relief. | Normal zone giving trenches in our lines covered by each (inclusive). | Wagon lines. | Remarks. |
|---|---|---|---|---|---|---|
| Left Group | | | | | | |
| 250 Bde RFA | N.13.c.2.9. | | | | M.12.c.3.5. | |
| A/250 | M.28.b.6.1. | A/88. | On nights 8/9 & 9/10 Aug. | Brigade zone. | M.16.c.2.8½. | |
| B/250 | N.15.b.9.6. | B/88 | | H.1.A. - J.2. | M.12.b.0.3. | |
| C/250 | N.14.a.8.9. | C/88. | | K.2.A. - L.5. | M.12.c.6.3½. | |
| D/250 | N.10.a.2½.3½. | D/88. | | Brigade zone. | M.11.d.3.7. | |
| C/253 | N.14.c.9.0½. | C/89. | | J.3. - K.2. | M.14.a.5.9. | |
| | N.10.a.3.8. | | | | | |
| Centre Group | | | | | | |
| 251 Bde.RFA. | N.20.d.2.5. | | | | M.12.c.6½.7. | |
| A/251 | N.16.a.7.3. | A/87 | | G.3. - G.4.A. | M.17.a.7.6. | |
| B/251 | N.15.d.2.2. | B/87 | | F.2. | M.17.b.2.4. | |
| C/251 | T.28.a.2½.9½. | C/87. | -do- | Brigade zone | M.16.c.3.8. | |
| D/251 | N.26.c.8.7. | D/87 (3 how) | | Brigade zone. | M.11.d.3.6. | |
| " (F'wd gun at | T.5.c.3.8. | | | | | |
| B/253. | N.27.a.8½.¼. | D/87 (2 how) | | F.4. - G.1. | M.15.c.4.6. | |
| | | B/89. | | | | |
| Right Group | | | | | | |
| 252 Bde.RFA. | M.25.d.9.5. | | | | M.10.b.8.6. | |
| B/252 | N.26.d.7.0. | B/86. | -do- | D.5. - E.2. | -do- | |
| C/252 | N.33.a.8.0. | C/86. | | D.3. - D.4. | -do- | |
| D/252 | N.27.a.1.3. | D/86. | | Brigade zone. | -do- | |
| 50th D.A.C. | M.22.b.7.7. | | | | M.11.c.4.0. | |
| 1st Section. | | 19th D.A.C. | On morning of 9th Aug. | | M.17.a.5.5. | |
| 2nd -do- | | | | | M.11.c.2.7. | |
| 3rd -do- | | | -do- | | M.8.c.6.1. | |
| 4th -do- | | | | | | |
| Trench Mortars. | M.18.d.8.5. | | Noon, 8th August. | | M.10.b.8.6. | |
| A/252 | (Not in action) | A/86 | | | M.12.a.5.0. | |
| A/253 | | A/89 | On morning of 9th Aug. | | | |
| 253 F.A.Bde. | M.15.b.8.9. | | | | R.13.a.8.8. | |

WAR DIARY 17/3

Ref. Maps Sheet 11, LENS, and
17 AMIENS, 1/100,000.

SECRET.

Copy No. 12

## 50th DIVISIONAL ARTILLERY OPERATION ORDER NO. 36.

15. 8. 16.

1. The 50th D.A. will march as below to area FRECHENCOURT - BAVELINCOURT - BEAUCOURT on 16th Aug. :-

| UNIT. | Time of leaving Billets. | ROUTE. | BILLETS. |
|---|---|---|---|
| LEFT COLUMN :- | | | |
| 253 Bde. | 3.15am. | ST. OUEN - CANAPLES - HAVERNAS - NAOURS - TALMAS - PIERREGOT - MIRVAUX. | BAVELINCOURT. |
| 251 Bde. | 3.45am. | | BEAUCOURT SUR L'HALLUE. |
| RIGHT COLUMN :- | | | |
| 250 Bde. | 1.15am. | BOURDON - VIGNACOURT - VILLERS BOCAGE - MOLLIENS AU BOIS. | FRECHENCOURT. |
| 252 Bde. | 1.45am. | | BEHENCOURT. |
| D.A.C. | 2.15am. | | FRECHENCOURT. |

Tails of both Columns to be East of the main road AMIENS - DOULLENS by 8.30a.m.

2. Intervals of half a mile will be kept between Brigades of Artillery or D.A.C.

3. 50th D.A. H.Q.'s will close at VIGNACOURT at 9.30a.m. and open at BAVELINCOURT at 11.0a.m. on 16th August.

4. Acknowledge.

F. Brown
Major R.A.,
B.M. 50th D.A.

Issued at 8.30p.m.

Copies to -
1 - 250 F.A.Bde.
2 - 251 " "
3 - 252 " "
4 - 253 " "
5 - 50th D.A.C.
6 - Div. T.M.O.
7 - H.Q. 50th Divn.
8 - 50th Div. Train
9 - R.A., 111 Corps.
10 - 111 Corps.
11 - 34th D.A.
12 - War Diary.
13, 14, & 15 Spare.

Ref. 1/100,000 Sheet 17 AMIENS.                    SECRET.

WAR DIARY 17/4

Copy No. 13

## 50th DIVISIONAL ARTILLERY OPERATION ORDER NO. 27.

16. 8. 16.

1. 50th D.A. will relieve 34th D.A. (Left Group, D.A., 111 Corps), covering 15th Division front, by sections, on the nights 18/19 and 19/20 Aug. Relief to be completed by 6.0a.m. on 20th Aug. Guns will not be exchanged.

2. On completion of above relief, the Left Group D.A., 111 Corps will consist of 47th D.A. and 50th D.A. Brig. Gen. E.W.Spedding, C.M.G., R.A., will command the Group.

3. 50th D.A. will march via BAIZIEUX - HENENCOURT - MILLENCOURT. Reliefs will be as follows :-

250 Bde. (Lt. Col H.S.Bell, D.S.O.) relieves 160 Bde. (Lt. Col. C. N. Warburton.)
251 Bde. (  "  F.B.Moss-Blundell)      "      175 Bde. (Lt. Col. W. Furnivall).
252 Bde. (  "  F.L.Pickersgill)        "      176 Bde. (Lt. Col. E.B. Cotter).
253 Bde. (  "  H. E. Hanson, D.S.O.)   "      152 Bde. (Lt. Col. Kincaid-Smith, C.M.G., D.S.O.).

5. 50th D.A.C. will relieve 34th D.A.C. by half echelons on the 18th and 19th August.

6. V50 Heavy.T.M. Battery will take over one Heavy T.M. from V34 Heavy T.M. Battery on 19th August.

7. All telephone wires, maps, etc., will be taken over by 50th D.A. from 34th D.A.

8. All ammunition left by 34th D.A. will be taken over by 50th D.A. Amount taken over to be reported to this office by wire as soon as relief is completed.

9. Lt. Cols. Commanding Brigades 50th D.A., their Orderly Officers, and two telephonists each will proceed by motor bus to 34th D.A. area on morning of 17th inst., and will remain in 34th D.A. area.

10. Battery Commanders, one Officer, and three telephonists per Battery will proceed by motor bus to 34th D.A. on morning of 18th. Battery Commanders and telephonists will remain in 34th D.A. area. The other officer in each case will return to 34th D.A. wagon lines to bring in the first sections.

11. Command of Batteries, Brigades and Divisional Artillery will pass at 6.0pm on 19th. Command of D.A.C. will pass at 12 noon on 19th, after which hour O.C. 50th D.A.C. will be responsible for supply of ammunition.

12. Other details of reliefs will be arranged by O.C. Brigades, D.A.C.'s and Divisional T.M. Officers.

13. Completion of each stage of relief and handing over of command will be reported to this office by wire.

14 *acknowledge*

Issued at 11.0p.m.

Major R.A.,
B.M. 50th D.A.

Copy No. 1 - 250 Bde. R.F.A.          Copy No. 8 - H.Q., 50th Divn.
         2 - 251 Bde.   "                      9 - C.R.A. 34th Divn.
         3 - 252 Bde.   "                     10 - 111 Corps.
         4 - 253 Bde.   "                     11 - R.A. 111 Corps.
         5 - 50th D.A.C.                      12 - Brig. Gen. E.W.Spedding.
         6 - 50th D.T.M.O.                    13 - War Diary.
         7 - O.C. 50th Div. Train.            14, 15, 16 Spare

WAR DIARY  17/5

SECRET.

Copy No. 13

## 50th DIVISIONAL ARTILLERY OPERATION ORDER NO. 28.

17.8.16.

1. That portion of 50th Divisional Artillery Operation Order No. 27 dated 16.8.16. which refers to the 250 and 253 Brigades R.F.A. is cancelled.

2. Acknowledge.

F. Brown
Major R.A.,
B.M. 50th D.A.

Issued at 7.0p.m.

Copies to -
```
        1 - 250 Bde. R.F.A.
        2 - 251   "      "
        3 - 252   "      "
        4 - 253   "      "
        5 - 50th D.A.C.
        6 - 50th D.T.M.C.
        7 - 50th Div. Train.
        8 - H.Q. 50th Divn.
        9 - C.R.A. 34th Divn.
       10 - 111 Corps.
       11 - R.A., 111 Corps.
       12 - Brig. Gen. E.W.Spedding, C.M.G., R.A.
       13 - War Diary.
       14, 15, 16 Spare.
```

WAR DIARY   17/6

Ref: Map, Sheet 62D, 1/40,000.

SECRET.

Copy No. 12

50th DIVISIONAL ARTILLERY OPERATION ORDER NO. 29.

18. 8. 16.

1.      With reference to Para. 5 of 50th D.A. Operation Order No. 27 dated 13.8.16, the half of 1st Section, "A" Echelon, and the half of "B" Echelon, 50th D.A.C., will not march on the 19th Aug., from MONTIGNY area.

The half of 1st Section, "A" Echelon, and the half of "B" Echelon which proceeded to 34th D.A. area on the 18th will march at 8.0a.m., back to MONTIGNY area, on the 20th inst.

2.      Acknowledge.

F. Brown
Major R.A.
B.M. 50th D.A.

Issued at 8.0p.m.

Copies to -
```
 1 - 250 Bde R.F.A.
 2 - 251   "    "
 3 - 252   "    "
 4 - 253   "    "
 5 - 50th D.A.C.
 6 - 50th D.T.M.O.
 7 - 50th Div. Train.
 8 - H.Q. 50th Divn.
 9 - C.R.A. 34th Div.
10 - B.R. 111 Corps.
11 - Brig. Gen. E.R. Spedding, C.M.G., R.A.
12 - War Diary.
13, 14, 15 Spare.
```

WAR DIARY 17/7

SECRET.

Copy No. 10

## 50th DIVISIONAL ARTILLERY OPERATION ORDER NO. 30.

1. 250 (Northbn) Bde. R.F.A., 50 D.A., will relieve the 70 Bde. R.F.A. 15 D.A., by sections, on nights 24/25 and 25/26 Aug. 1916. Relief to be completed by 6.0 a.m. on Aug. 27. Guns will not be exchanged.

2. On completion of relief, 250 Bde. R.F.A. will come under the orders of C.R.A., 1st Division for all purposes.

3. 250 Bde. R.F.A. will march via BAIZIEUX - HENENCOURT - HILLENCOURT.

4. Ammunition dumped at gun positions will be taken over by 250 Bde. R.F.A. Amount taken over to be reported to this office on completion of relief.

5. All telephone wire, maps, etc., required by 250 Bde. R.F.A. will be handed over by 70 Bde. R.F.A.

6. 1st D.A.C. will be responsible for supply of ammunition to 250 Bde. R.F.A.

7. One Subaltern per battery of 70 Bde. R.F.A. will be left behind for such time as O.C. relieving battery may require his services.

8. Other details of reliefs will be arranged by O.C. Bdes.

9. The 70 Bde. R.F.A. will take over the billets of 250 Bde. at FRECHENCOURT.

10. Completion of each stage of relief will be reported to this office by wire.

11. Acknowledge.

F. Brown
Major R.A.,
B.M. 50th D.A.

Issued at 7.0 p.m.
Aug. 23rd, 1916.

Copies to -
1 - 250 Bde. R.F.A.
2 - 251 " "
3 - 252 " "
4 - 253 " "
5 - 50 D.A.C.
6 - H.Q. 50 Div.
7 - C.R.A. 1st Div.
8 - R.A. lllrd Corps.
9 - 50 Divnl. Train.
10 - War Diary.
11. 12. 13 Spare.

50th. DIVISION

C. R. A.

50th. DIVISIONAL ARTILLERY

SEPTEMBER 1916.

Page 1.

Army Form C. 2118.

vol. XVIII

# WAR DIARY H.Q. 50th Divisional Artillery.

## INTELLIGENCE SUMMARY.

September, 1916.

*(Erase heading not required.)*

Instructions regarding War Diaries and Intelligence Summaries are contained in F. S. Regs., Part II. and the Staff Manual respectively. Title pages will be prepared in manuscript.

Vol XX 17.

| Place | Date | Hour | Summary of Events and Information | Remarks and references to Appendices |
|---|---|---|---|---|
| Nr. ALBERT | Sept. 1 to 9th | | Bombardments as in attached programmes | |
| | | 6 | 18 Pdr. Batteries of 251 and 252 Bdes. R.F.A. called on to assist in repelling counter attack against 1st Div. in HIGH WOOD. Action taken being as in attached appendix. | 18/1. |
| | 10th to 12th | | Redistribution of Brigades and zones as per attached Operation Orders Nos.31, 32, and 33. | 18/2, 18/3 18/4. |
| | 12th | 6.0am on- wards | Preliminary bombardment as per appendix | 18/5. |
| | 14th | 6.0pm | H.Q. Div. Arty. moved to advanced H.Q. | |
| | 15th | 6.20 a.m. | The 50th Div. attacked in conjunction with the 15th Div. on its left and 47th Div. on its right. The artillery barrages lifted in 3 stages corresponding to the three stages of the infantry objective. Programme attached | |
| | 16th | 9.25 a.m. | 50th Division attack PRUE TRENCH after 15 minutes bombardment by Div.Arty. A and B Btys. 253 Bde. R.F.A. D/250 and C/251 moved forward and registered their barrage lines. | |
| | Night 16/17 | | Enemy's artillery fairly quiet. | |

Army Form C. 2118.

# WAR DIARY
## INTELLIGENCE SUMMARY.
Vol. XVIII.

(Erase heading not required.)

| Place | Date | Hour | Summary of Events and Information | Remarks and references to Appendices |
|---|---|---|---|---|
| Nr. ALBERT | Sept. 17th | | B,C and D btys. 276 Bde.R.F.A.moved forward also A,B and D btys. 251 Bde. R.F.A. and A/250. All moves done by sections | |
| | 18th | | Div.Arty. ordered by Corps R.A. to do counter battery work on their zone. | |
| | 19th | | Minor bombing attacks by enemy repulsed. | |
| | 20th | | Report received that enemy lights were mistaken for S.O.S.calls from our own infantry during night 19/20. | |
| | 21st | 11.57 P.M. | Enemy vacated STARFISH trench which 50 Div.Infantry occupied. | |
| | 22nd | 9.55am 11.30 A.M. 5.30 P.M. | Btys. ordered to cease firing as infantry patrols are out in front. Infantry established in PRUE TRENCH with patrols out on MARTINPUICH - EAUCOURT L'ABBAYE road. Enemy aircraft active over Bty. positions. Many enemy digging parties were seen throughout the day well in rear. Heavy Artillery informed. A/252, C/250 and D/250 ordered to move forward by sections. | |
| | 23rd | | | |
| | 24th | | Quiet day. | |
| | 25th | 12.35 P.M. | Attack by Fourth Army. 50 D.A. carried out 3 mins. intense bombardment. All objectives by 1st Div. on the right easily gained. Various small parties of enemy sniped by 18 pdrs. during the afternoon. | |

Page 3.

Army Form C. 2118.

Vol. XVIII.

# WAR DIARY
## INTELLIGENCE SUMMARY.
*(Erase heading not required.)*

Instructions regarding War Diaries and Intelligence Summaries are contained in F. S. Regs., Part II. and the Staff Manual respectively. Title pages will be prepared in manuscript.

| Place | Date | Hour | Summary of Events and Information | Remarks and references to Appendices |
|---|---|---|---|---|
| Nr.ALBERT | Sept. 26th | 12.35 P.M. | Attack by Reserve Army. 50 D.A. put up three minutes intense barrage before zero. Enemy artillery quiet on Corps front and little movement observed. | |
| | 27th | 10.20 A.M. | Leading sections of A/253 and B/250 reported to be in their new positions and registering. | |
| | | 3p.m. | 150 Bde. bombing parties gained ground and ask for barrage to be lifted to FLERS LINE at 3.0 p.m. to enable them to advance further. Operation Order No. 36 attached | 18/6. |
| | 28th | | Relief of 276 Bde. R.F.A. 55 Div. by 39 Bde. R.F.A. 1st Div. commenced. Operation Order No. 37 attached. | 18/7. |
| | 29th | 1.40 P.M. | Relief of personnel of B/250 by C/253 reported complete. Relief of 276 Bde. R.F.A. by 39 Bde. R.F.A. completed. | |
| | 30th | | A and C Btys. 250 Bde. R.F.A. came out of action and personnel went to their wagon lines. 39 Bde. R.F.A. took over 250 Bde. guns that they required to complete them. Warning order for operations on Oct. 1st attached. | 18/8. |

T/134. Wt. W708-776. 500000. 4/15. Sir J. C. & S.

**CRA**  Issued with A.O 54

Identification Trace for use with Artillery Maps.

29  35  5  =

26  32  2  8

M  S

NOTE:—(1) These traces are intended to facilitate the communication of information as to the position of targets, which have been located on a squared map.
(2) The squares on this trace are 1,000 yards in length on the 1:20,000 scale, and 2,000 yards in length on the 1:40,000 scale.
(3) The squares on the trace are fitted to the squares of the map containing the targets, which are then drawn on the trace. Sufficient letters and numbers must also be added to enable the recipient to place the trace in the correct position on his own map. Other detail may also be traced, but this is not essential. The name and scale of the map to which the trace refers must be always given. The trace can be used for either the 1:20,000 or 1:40,000 scale.

G.S.G.S. 4023

Tracing taken from Sheet _____
of the 1: 10000 map of _____
Signature _____ Date _____

SECRET.

B.M. 1620.

Headquarters,
    50th Division.
    ----------

Reference your G.X. 2603.

1.    The gun positions to be occupied, Brigade Headquarters, and O.P.'s are shewn in attached tracing.

2.    This gives 36 18-pdrs. and 12 4.5" Howitzers to cover the Division, the guns, N.C.O.'s and men of the three other 18-pdr. batteries being held in reserve to fill casualties to equipment and personnel.  Under the present rates of firing at least six 18-pdrs. will generally be in the hands of I.O.M. At the present moment we have 10, as all guns requiring new springs have to be taken out of action and sent to I.O.M.

3.    All O.P.'s are in want of improvement and strengthening. I would suggest R.E. making as a commencement one really strong O.P. and dug-out for each Brigade - others might be improved later if time allowed.

    The O.P.'s shewn in Square S.9. are positions of observation in a trench.  The Division at present in occupation found permanent use of them impossible as communications could not be kept up.  When necessary to use one for any special purpose a wire would be run out and reeled in when done with.  The O.P.'s in use give a very good view.

4.    There are no positions further forward which would be tenable until our line goes a good deal further forward than it is at present, but the ranges from present positions are quite effective, and would still be so after a considerable advance.

5.    I propose relieving the 3 18-pdr. batteries and Headquarters of 250 Brigade by the 253 Brigade, leaving D/250 Battery in action.

6.9.16.                                    Brig. Gen
                                C.R.A. 50th Division.

## Action of 50th D.A.                                9.9.16.

5.0p.m.     All Batteries 252 Bde. ordered to search and sweep area
M.25.d. and 32.a.    Rate :- 18-pdrs. 3 rds. per gun per min.
                            Hows.,    2  "   "   "   "   "

5.30pm.    251 Bde. ordered by 18th D.A., through 50th D.A., to reduce rate on barrage to half present rate.

5.40pm.    252 Bde. ordered to reduce rate to :-

18pdrs. 2 rds. per gun per minute.
Hows. 1 rd.  "   "   "   "   "

and to continue to search and sweep, dropping 500 yards.

6.20pm.    One Bty. 252 Bde. ordered to search back from line S.1.b.7.8. - 31.d.2.3. to S.W. of MARTINPUICH; three rounds per gun per minute.

6.55pm.    251 Bde. ordered by 18th D.A. through 50th D.A. and also through Liaison Officer to stop firing.

7.0pm.     252 Bde. ordered to revert to ordinary bombardment programme.

WAR DIARY

18/2

SECRET.

Copy No. 15

## 50th DIVISIONAL ARTILLERY OPERATION ORDER NO. 31.

9. 9. 16.

1. Prior to forthcoming operations the 50th D.A., less 1 Brigade (Centre D.A. Group, commanded by Brig. Gen A. U. Stockley) will be responsible for the following zone :-

   From line through M.34.c.6.0. and M.29.c.0.0. to line through M.32.d.7.0. and M.32.d.7.7.

   The re-distribution to effect this will be complete by 12 noon on 12th.

2. C.R.A.'s of 15th and 50th Divl. Artilleries will take over command of Groups as follows at 12 noon, 10th instant :-

   Centre Group.    Brig. Gen. A. U. Stockley.

   15th Div. Arty., less 1 Brigade. (70, 72 & 73 Bdes. R.F.A.).
   Portion of 47th Div. Arty (237 and 238 bdes. R.F.A.) covering new zone of Centre Group.

   Left Group.    Brig. Gen. E. B. Macnaghten, D.S.O.

   50th Div. Arty., less 2 Brigades. (251 and 252 Bdes. R.F.A.).
   Portion of 47th Div. Arty. covering new front of Left Group.

3. A change of personnel of 50th and 15th Divl. Artilleries will take place gradually during afternoon of 10th and during 11th instant, to be completed by 12 noon, 11th; arrangements to be made between Lt.-Cols. comdg: concerned; guns will remain in position and not moved.
   By evening of 11th inst., Groups will be as follows :-

   Centre Group.
          50th Div. Arty, less 2 Brigades.
          Portion of 47th Div. Arty. covering new zone of
   Centre Group.

   Left Group.
          15th Div. Arty., less 1 Brigade.
          Portion of 47th Div. Arty. covering new zone
   of Left Group.

4. At 12 noon on 12th inst., the following transfer will take place :-

   (a) 47th Div. Arty. to Right Group from Centre and Left Groups.

   (b) Brigade of 50th Div. Arty., (250 Bde. R.F.A.) attached Right Group, to Centre Group.

5. Signalling Officer R.A. will arrange for communications to be complete by 12 noon on 10th instant, at which hour H.Q., 50th D.A., (Centre Group) will be at the Camp in D.6.b.

6. Ammunition at gun positions to be handed over to relieving Units. Amounts handed over at old positions and taken over at new positions to be reported to this office by wire as soon as relief is completed.
   Responsibility for supply of ammunition will change with the change of personnel mentioned in Para. 3 at 12 noon on the 11th, and in the case of 250 Bde. R.F.A., with the change of command at 12 noon on 12th.

## SHEET 2.

7. Liaison Officers of 50th D.A. will hand over and take over from Liaison Officers of 15th D.A. at 12 noon on the 11th.

8. Trench Mortars in the line will be taken over. Arrangements will be made by D.T.M.O.'s concerned.

9. All maps, photos, etc., will be handed over on relief to formations taking over.

10. Completion of each relief to be reported by wire to this office.

11. Acknowledge.

Issued at 11.30a.m.

Major R.A.,
B.M. 50th D.A.

Copies to :-
```
        1 - 250 Bde. R.F.A.
        2 - 251 Bde. R.F.A.
        3 - 252 Bde. R.F.A.
        4 - 253 Bde. R.F.A.
        5 - 50th D.A.C.
        6 - 50th D.T.M.O.
        7 - H.Q. 50th Div.
        8 - R.A., lllrd Corps.
        9 - H.A., lllrd Corps.
       10 - C.R.A. 47th Div.
       11 - C.R.A.,15th Div.
       12 - C.R.A., 1st Div.
       13 - 50th Div. Train A.S.C.
       14 - A.D.M.S. 50th Div.
       15 - War Diary.
       16, 17, 18, 19 Spare.
```

WAR DIARY 18/3

SECRET.
Copy No. 15

## 50th DIVISIONAL ARTILLERY OPERATION ORDER NO. 32.

9. 9. 16.

1. 253rd Brigade R.F.A. will relieve 250th Bde. R.F.A., less D/250, personnel only, on the afternoon of 12th inst.
   Relief will be completed by 4.0p.m., at which hour D/250 will come under the tactical command of O.C., 253rd Bde. R.F.A.

2. 250 Bde. R.F.A., less D/250, will proceed straight to MONTIGNY Rest area on the afternoon of 12th, and occupy billots vacated by 253rd Bde. R.F.A.
   Details will be arranged by Lt-Cols. Comdg: Bdes. R.F.A.

3. Brigades will march via BAIZIEUX - HENENCOURT - HILLENCOURT.

4. Telephone wires, necessary maps, etc., will be handed over.

5. Completion of relief will be reported to this office by wire.

6. Acknowledge.

Major R.A.,
B.M. 50th D.A.

Issued at 5.30p.m.

Copies to :-
1 - 250 Bde. R.F.A.
2 - 251 Bde. R.F.A.
3 - 252 Bde. R.F.A.
4 - 253 Bde. R.F.A.
5 - 50th D.A.C.
6 - 50th D.T.MO.
7 - H.Q., 50th Divn.
8 - R.A., IIIrd Corps.
9 - H.A., IIIrd Corps.
10 - C.R.A. 47th Div.
11 - C.R.A. 15th Div.
12 - C.R.A. 1st Div.
13 - 50th Div. Train A.S.C.
14 - A.D.M.S., 50th Div.
15 - War Diary.
16, (17,) 18, 19 Spare.

Adjt 253/Bde.

Ref. Map, Sheetx 62D, 1/40,000          Copy No 17     SECRET.

## ADDENDUM TO 50th DIVISIONAL ARTILLERY ORDER NO. 32.

11.9.16.

1. Reference Para. 2. 250 Brigade R.F.A., less D/250 will proceed to Wagon Lines at E.8.d.5.5; instead of to MONTIGNY Rest Area.

2. Acknowledge.

Issued at 11.30p.m.

F. Brown
Major R.A.,
B.M. 50th D.A.

Copies to :-
    1 - 250 Bde. R.F.A.
    2 - 251 Bde. R.F.A.
    3 - 252 Bde. R.F.A.
    4 - 253 Bde. R.F.A.
    5 - 50th D.A.C.
    6 - 50th D.T.M.O.
    7 and 8 - H.Q. 50th Div.
    9 - R.A., IIIrd Corps.
    10 - IIIrd Corps H.A.
    11 - C.R.A. 47th Div.
    12 - C.R.A. 15th Div.
    13 - C.R.A. 1st Div.
    14 - A.D.M.S., 50th Div.
    15 and 16 - 50th Div. Train A.S.C.
    17 - War Diary.
    18, 19 20 Spare.

WAR DIARY 18/4

Ref: Map Sheet 62D, 1/40,000.  SECRET.

Copy No. 11

## 50th DIVISIONAL ARTILLERY OPERATION ORDER NO. 33.

9. 9. 18.

1. 50th.D.A.C., less

 Headquarters,

 1st Section,

 28 G.S. Wagons (complete with teams)

 4 N.C.O.'s and 75 gunners,

 will march at 9.0a.m., 10th September to CAMP at D.3.c.3.8.

2. Details of D.A.C. now at FRECHENCOURT will also march to same Camp on 10th September.

3. Completion of moves to be reported to this Office.

4. Acknowledge.

F. Brown

Major R.A.,
B.M. 50th D.A.

Issued at 9.0p.m.

Copies to :-
1 - 250 Bde. R.F.A.
2 - 251 Bde. R.F.A.
3 - 252 Bde. R.F.A.
4 - 253 Bde. R.F.A.
5 - 50th D.A.C.
6 - 50th D.T.M.O.
7 - H.Q. 50th Div.
8 - 50th Div. Train A.S.C.
9 - A.D.M.S., 50th Div.
10 - R.A., IIIrd Corps.
11 - War Diary.
12, 13, 14 Spare.

WAR DIARY 18/5

BM1636

Ref: 1/10,000 Trench Map.

SECRET.

Copy No. 13

## CENTRE GROUP DIVISIONAL ARTILLERY, IIIrd CORPS.

Programme from 6.0a.m. 12/9/16 till further orders.

1. Preliminary bombardment will start at 6.0a.m. to-morrow, 12th inst., and last till further orders.

2. By day, 4.5" howitzers will bombard from 6.0a.m. to 6.30p.m.

3. 18-pdrs. will take up fire at 6.30p.m. and prevent any repair or work being done on trenches which have been bombarded by day.

4. Howitzers will fire P.S. gas shell by night.

5. 18-pdrs. will not fire by day.

6. From 10.0a.m. to 12 mid-day an aeroplane will be up to observe but will only be able to send mostly short or mostly over. To assist aeroplane observation 4.5" Hows. will fire in salvoes as far as possible.

7. Zones of trench to be bombarded are shown roughly on attached tracing.

8. No guns are to be fired fast; every effort must be made by resting guns alternately to keep all guns in action.

9. Fire during day to be continuous.

10. Acknowledge by wire.

F. Bronson
Major R.A.,
B.M. 50th D.A.

11. 9. 16.

Copies to :-

    1 - 250 Bde. R.F.A.
    2 - 251 Bde. R.F.A.
    3 - 252 Bde. R.F.A.
    4 - 253 Bde. R.F.A.
    5 - Right Group D.A.
    6 - Left Group D.A.
    7, 8, 9, 10, H.Q. 50th Div.
    11 - R.A. IIIrd Corps.
    12 - IIIrd Corps H.A.
    13 - War Diary.
    14, 15, 16, 17 Spare.

CENTRE GROUP DIVISIONAL ARTILLERY, IIIrd CORPS.     SHEET 1.

Programme from 6.0a.m. 12/9/16 till further orders.

| Serial No. | Time. | Unit. | Objective. | Remarks. |
|---|---|---|---|---|
| 1. | 6.0a.m. to 10.0a.m. | D/250 | Trench S.2.b.0.8. to S.3.a.0.8. | For first half hour 1 round per how. per minute; afterwards slow steady observed fire. } 560 EX. |
| 2. | 10.0a.m. to 12 noon & onwards to 3.30pm. | -do- | Trench M.33.c.0.8. to M.33.c.99.80. | As aeroplane observation is available; when not available return to (1) |
| 3. | 12 midnight. | -do- | Company H.Q. at M.32.d.2540. | 160 P.S. First ten rounds fast, remainder at 1 round per minute. |
| 4. | 5.30pm to 6.0am | 353 Bde RFA 18-pdrs. | Trenches bombarded by howitzers in day time, also nest of trenches in M.32.d. | 1200 A and AX. |

SHEET 2.

| Serial No. | Time. | Unit. | Objective. | Remarks. |
|---|---|---|---|---|
| 5. | 6.0a.m. to 10.0am. | D/251 | Trench S.3.a.0.8. to S.3.a.9980. | For first half-hour, 1 round per how. per minute; afterwards slow steady observed fire. } 560 BX. |
| 6. | 10.0am to 12 noon and onwards to 6.30pm | -do- | Trench H.32.c.9980 to H.33.c.5.5. to H.33.a.9980. | As aeroplane observation is available; when not available return to (5) |
| 7. | 12-midnight. | -do- | Battalion H.Q. at H.33.a.2.6. | 160 P.S. First ten minutes fast, remainder at 1 round per gun per 1½ minutes. |
| 8. | 6.30pm to 6.0am. | 251 Bde. RFA. 18-pdrs. | Trenches bombarded by howitzers in day-time. | 1200 A and AX. |

SHEET 3.

| Serial No. | Time. | Unit. | Objective. | Remarks. |
|---|---|---|---|---|
| 9. | 6.0a.m. to 10.0a.m. | D/252. | Trench S.3.a.9980 to S.3.b.9.8. | For first half-hour 1 round per how per minute; afterwards slow steady observed fire. } 580 BX. |
| 10. | 10.0a.m. to 12 noon & onwards to 5.30pm. | -do- | Trench M.33.d.9980 to M.34.b.3.0. | As aeroplane observation is available; when not available return to (9). |
| 11. | 11.0p.m. to 12 midnight | -do- | Nest of trenches M.33.b.6.5. | 160 P.S. First ten rounds fast, remainder at 1 round per minute. |
| 12. | 6.30p.m. to 6.0a.m. | 252 Bde. RFA 18-pdrs. | Trenches bombarded by Hows. in day-time, also nest of trenches M.33.b.6.5. | 1200 A and AX. |

SECRET.

Copy No. 13

ADDENDUM NO. 1 to CENTRE GROUP D.A. No. B.M. 1636 dated 11/9/16.

----

1. Para. 3.    Aeroplane will also observe from 2.0pm to 4.0pm.

2. In order to identify howitzer batteries of 50th D.A. that are firing, aeroplane will send following ~~calls~~ :-

   Objective of D/250 Bde. R.F.A.,    Call "D"
   "   "  " 251  "    "            Call "E"
   "   "  " 252  "    "            Call "F"

   4.5" How. batteries will fire 12 salvoes per hour at different times.

   Times will be as follows :-

   | 250 Bde. | 251 Bde. | 252 Bde. |
   |----------|----------|----------|
   | 10.0     | 10.5     | 10.2     |
   | 10.7     | 10.10    | 10.9     |
   | 10.11    | 10.15    | 10.12    |
   | 10.17    | 10.20    | 10.18    |
   | 10.22    | 10.24    | 10.21    |
   | 10.26    | 10.29    | 10.27    |
   | 10.31    | 10.34    | 10.32    |
   | 10.36    | 10.37    | 10.35    |
   | 10.39    | 10.42    | 10.40    |
   | 10.44    | 10.47    | 10.45    |
   | 10.49    | 10.53    | 10.51    |
   | 10.55    | 10.58    | 10.56    |

   and repeat at 11.0a.m., 2.0p.m., and 3.0p.m.

Distribution :-

   As for B.M. 1636.

Major R.A.,
B.M. 50th D.A.
11.9.16.

SECRET.

Copy No. 16.

## 50th DIVISIONAL ARTILLERY OPERATION ORDER NO. 34.

13. 9. 1916.

1.   O.C. 250 Bde. R.F.A. will arrange for three 4-gun batteries of 18-pdrs. to be prepared to go into action on the night 13/14.
Eight guns will be provided by 1st D.A. who will deliver them to-day at 250 Bde. Wagon-lines, E.6.d.5.5.

2.   O.C. 251, 252, and 253 Bdes. R.F.A. will each select a position and arrange for one of these batteries to go into action on afternoon of 13th, or on night 13/14, when they will come under their tactical command until further orders.
These three batteries will register first thing on the morning of 14th.
H.Q. 250 Bde. R.F.A. will remain in their present wagon-lines.
All details will be arranged by Lt.-Cols. Comdg:

3.   Report will be made to this office when batteries are in action.

4.   Acknowledge.

Issued at 3.30p.m.

F. Brown

Major R.A.,
B.M. 50th D.A.

Copy No. 1 - 250 Bde. RFA.
       2 - 251 Bde. RFA.
       3 - 252 Bde. RFA.
       4 - 253 Bde. RFA.
       5 - 50th D.A.C.
       6 and 7 - 50th Div.
       8 - R.A. IIIrd Corps.
       9 - IIIrd Corps H.A.
      10 - Left Group D.A.
      11 - Right Group D.A.
      12 - C.R.A. 1st Div.
      13 - A.D.M.S., 50th Div.
      14 - War Diary.
      15, 16, 17 Spare.

NOTE :-
The position selected for Battery of 250 Bde. should be as far forward as possible, but it must be able to fire from the commencement of operations.

"A" Form.  Army Form C. 2121.
## MESSAGES AND SIGNALS.

| Prefix | Code | In. | Words | Charge | This message is on a/c of: | Recd. at ___ m. |
| --- | --- | --- | --- | --- | --- | --- |
| Office of Origin and Service Instructions. | | | Sent | | ...................Service. | Date |
| | | | At ___ m. | | | From |
| | | | To | | | By |
| | | | By | | (Signature of "Franking Officer.") | |

TO { FH / 10 / FU

| Sender's Number | Day of Month | In reply to Number | | AAA |
| --- | --- | --- | --- | --- |
| BM966 | Sept 12 | | | |

| 4.5" | how | salvos | this | afternoon |
| will | commence | at | 2.40 | pm |
| and | cease | at | 3.20 pm | and |
| not | as | previously | ordered | aaa |

From F. J.
Place
Time 1.15 pm

Signature of Addressor: J Brownmt Major RA

"A" Form.  Army Form C. 2121.
## MESSAGES AND SIGNALS.

| Prefix | Code | m. | Words | Charge | This message is on a/c of: | Recd. at ... m. |
| --- | --- | --- | --- | --- | --- | --- |
| Office of Origin and Service Instructions. | | | Sent At ... m. To By | | ................. Service. (Signature of "Franking Officer.") | Date From By |

| TO | F A |
| --- | --- |
| | 10 |
| | F U |

| Sender's Number. | Day of Month | In reply to Number | | A A A |
| --- | --- | --- | --- | --- |
| * BM967 | Sept 12 | | | |
| 4.5" | How | salvos | will | commence |
| at | 3.40 | p.m. | and | cease |
| at | 4.20 | p.m. | and | not |
| as | previously | ordered | see | BM966 |

From F J
Place
Time 2.10 p.m.

The above may be forwarded as now corrected.   (Z)  [signature]
                                                          Major R.A.
Censor.  Signature of Addressor or person authorised to telegraph in his name.

SECRET
✳✳✳✳✳✳✳✳✳

Copy No. 4

ARTILLERY INSTRUCTIONS NO. 70
BY
THE G.O.C., R.A., IIIrd CORPS.

H.Q., R.A., III Corps.
11th September, 1916

Commencing 6 a.m. to 6.30 p.m.

Divisional Artillery.

Bombardment of Hostile system of trenches. *opposite*

1. All 4.5" Hows. will bombard hostile defences their own front.

Rate of fire 6.0 a.m. to 6.30 a.m. daily will be 1 round per gun per minute.

Total number of rounds to be fired between 6 am and 6.30 pm.

140 rounds per gun.

By night. 40 rounds per gun gas shell.

Arrangements to be made for the fire during the day to be continuous.

2. 18-pdrs. should fire as little as possible by day, but must seize opportunities of inflicting losses on the enemy and preventing hostile movement.

By night they must be very active.

3. Day will be 6 a.m. to 6.30 p.m.

Night will be 6.30 p.m. to 6 a.m.

4. Acknowledge. BM9bl

Issued at 6 p.m.

Copy No. 1 1st Division
2 15th Division
3 50th Division
4 Left Div. Arty. Group
5 Centre Div. Arty. Group
6 Right Div. Arty. Group
7 Heavy Artillery
8 34th Squadron, R.F.C.
9 No.6 Kite Balloon Sect.
10 No.14 Kite Balloon Sect.
11 Arty. XVth Corps
12 Arty. Canadian Corps
13 Arty. Fourth Army.
14 IIIrd Corps "G.S"
15-18 Filed

Major.
Staff Officer to G.O.C., R A.,
III Corps.

S E C R E T  &  U R G E N T.　　　　　　　　Headquarters, R.A.,

　　　　　　　　　　　　　　　　　　　　　　　IIIrd Corps.
1st Div. Arty.
15th Div. Arty.
47th Div. Arty.　　　　　　　　　　　　No.R.A/01/54/2
50th Div. Arty.
55th Div. Arty.
IIIrd Corps "G.S"
IIIrd Corps "A & Q"
A.D.A.S. IIIrd Corps.
Arty. XVth Corps.
Arty. Canadian Corps.
-----------------------

1. Reference R.A/01/54 and R.A/01/54/1 when the re-distribution has been completed on 12th instant, the Divisional Artillery covering the Corps front will now be:-

Right Group.　　　　(Commander, Brig:Genl: E.W. Spedding, C.M.G)

　　　47th Divnl. Artillery (less 1 Brigade)

　　　1 Brigade, 1st Divnl. Artillery.

Centre Group.　　　(Commander, Brig: Genl: A.U. Stockley)

　　　50th Divisional Artillery (less 1 Brigade)

Left Group.　　　　(Commander, Brig: Genl: E.B. Macnaghten, D.S.O)

　　　15th Divnl. Artillery (less 1 Brigade)

　　　1 Brigade, 1st Divnl. Artillery

2. Zones allotted to Groups.

Zones as laid down in R.A/01/54 are cancelled and the following substituted:-

Right Group.

　　　From line through S.10. central and S.5 central
　　　　to line through S.3. central and M.34.a.0.0

Centre Group.

　　　From line through S.3.d.2.9 and M.34. central
　　　　to line through S.2.a.6.1 and M.27.c.2.0.

Left Group.

　　　From line through S.2 central and M.27.d.0.0

　　　To line through R.36.c.0.0 and M.25.d.0.0.

3. For defence purposes the two flank Groups will assist the Centre Group with their overlap; owing to Centre Group having 1 Brigade less in the line.

4. On nights 12th/13th and 13th/14th the two Brigades of the 1st Division will each be relieved by a Brigade of 55th Divl. Artillery.

The Centre Group will also be reinforced by one Brigade of 55th Divl. Artillery on the same nights.

- 2 -

The reliefs and reinforcement will be carried out by Sections.

(The two- 6-gun batteries of Left 1st Divnl. Arty. Brigade will be replaced by three 4-gun 18-pdr batteries)

5. C.R.A. 55th Divisional Artillery will please send up Brigade and Battery Commanders to report at 10 a.m. 12th inst. as follows:-

   To 47th Divl. Arty. Hqrs.  at E.8.b.9.0
   To 50th Divl. Arty. Hqrs.  at D.6.b. central
   To 15th Divl. Arty. Hqrs.  at W.26.c.3.3

6. Guides.

Divisional Artillery Group Commanders will arrange for guides to meet Sections and conduct them to the gun positions.

Centre Group Commander will select positions for the batteries of reinforcing Brigade.

7. Further Reinforcements.

Group Commanders will each reconnoitre positions for one Brigade which will probably be forthcoming from the 23rd Divl. Arty. all preliminary arrangements to be complete by 14th inst.

8. Group Commanders will arrange that no serviceable guns are taken out of the line and that all batteries in action are complete with serviceable guns.

They will in addition be prepared to make up batteries from serviceable guns in rest and put them into the line on night 13th/14th.

9. The 1st Div. Arty. will on relief rejoin their Division and take over the billets and bivouacs of the 3 Brigades of 55th Div. Arty. in BAVLINCOURT and BEHENCOURT.

10. The 55th D.A.C. will relieve the 1st D.A.C. at E.6.c.3.2 on 14th inst; on relief 1st D.A.C. will go into billets and bivouacs at ST. GRATIEN.

11. 55th Divl. Artillery will take over 1st Divl. Artillery Ammunition Refilling Point at E.6.c.

12. Acknowledge.

11-9-16

Major,
Staff Officer to G.O.C.,R.A.,
IIIrd Corps.

SECRET.

Copy No 14

ADDENDUM NO. 1 to CENTRE GROUP D.A. No. B.M. 1636 dated 11/9/16.

---

1. Para. 3.     Aeroplane will also observe from 2.0pm to 4.0pm.

2. In order to identify howitzer batteries of 50th D.A. that are firing, aeroplane will send following ~~calls~~ :-

Objective of D/ 250 Bde. R.F.A.,    Call "D"

 "    "   "   251  "    "           Call "E"

 "    "   "   252  "    "           Call "F"

   4.5" How. batteries will fire 12 salvoes per hour at different times.

   Times will be as follows :-

| 250 Bde. | 251 Bde. | 252 Bde. |
|---|---|---|
| 10.0  | 10.5  | 10.2  |
| 10.7  | 10.10 | 10.9  |
| 10.11 | 10.15 | 10.12 |
| 10.17 | 10.20 | 10.18 |
| 10.22 | 10.24 | 10.21 |
| 10.26 | 10.29 | 10.27 |
| 10.31 | 10.34 | 10.32 |
| 10.36 | 10.37 | 10.35 |
| 10.39 | 10.42 | 10.40 |
| 10.44 | 10.47 | 10.45 |
| 10.49 | 10.53 | 10.51 |
| 10.55 | 10.58 | 10.56 |

and repeat at 11.0a.m., 2.0p.m., and 3.0p.m.


Distribution :-

   As for B.M. 1636.

Major R.A.,
B.M. 50th D.A.
11.9.16.

SECRET
\*\*\*\*\*\*\*\*\*\*\*\*

Headquarters, R.A.

IIIrd Corps.

Right Divl. Arty. Group.
Centre Divl. Arty. Group     "G.S" (for information)
Left Divl. Arty. Group.
------------------------

Addendum No.1 to Artillery Instructions No.70.

1. Attached find sunprint with trenches shown up to date.

2. Objectives are shown as follows:-

    1. First objective    Brown.

    2. Second objective    Green

    3. Third objective    Blue.

3. Dividing lines between Divisions are shown in chain dot in red.

    Dividing lines between Corps are shown in red.

4. Objectives for Divl. Arty. for 12th shown in red and marked with a letter as follows:-

| | | | | |
|---|---|---|---|---|
| Right Group | T. | K | H | |
| Centre Group | F | E | D | |
| Left Group | C | M | Z | A |

5. Between 10 a.m. and 12 noon and between 2 p.m. and 4 p.m. 12 salvoes per battery will be fired and observations will be given by aeroplane.

    Group Commanders will arrange that all batteries do not fire at the same time.

6. During remainder of the day a steady bombardment will be kept up.

7. Acknowledge.

12-9-16

Major,
Staff Officer to G.O.C.,R.A,
IIIrd Coprps.

## "A" Form.
### MESSAGES AND SIGNALS.
Army Form C. 2121.

Priority

TO  F A
    1 0

Sender's Number: *BM 962  
Day of Month: Sept 12  
AAA

Reference BM 1636 aaa Serial Number 6 and 10 aaa for M33c9980 and M33D9980 aaa

From: F.J  
Place:  
Time:

Major RA

Ref: 1/10,000 Trench Map.

SECRET.

Copy No. 14

BM 1636

## CENTRE GROUP DIVISIONAL ARTILLERY, IIIrd CORPS.

Programme from 6.0a.m. 12/9/16 till further orders.

1. Preliminary bombardment will start at 6.0a.m. to-morrow, 12th inst., and last till further orders.

2. By day, 4.5" howitzers will bombard from 6.0a.m. to 6.30p.m.

3. 18-pdrs. will take up fire at 6.30p.m. and prevent any repair or work being done on trenches which have been bombarded by day.

4. Howitzers will fire P.S. gas shell by night.

5. 18-pdrs. will not fire by day.

6. From 10.0a.m. to 12 mid-day an aeroplane will be up to observe but will only be able to send mostly short or mostly over. To assist aeroplane observation 4.5" Hows. will fire in salvoes as far as possible.

7. Zones of trench to be bombarded are shown roughly on attached tracing.

8. No guns are to be fired fast; every effort must be made by resting guns alternately to keep all guns in action.

9. Fire during day to be continuous.

10. Acknowledge by wire.

F. Brown
Major R.A.,
B.M. 50th D.A.

11. 9. 16.

Copies to :-

```
1 - 250 Bde. R.F.A.
2 - 251 Bde. R.F.A.
3 - 252 Bde. R.F.A.
4 - 253 Bde. R.F.A.
5 - Right Group D.A.
6 - Left Group D.A.
7, 8, 9, 10, H.Q. 50th Div.
11 - R.A. IIIrd Corps.
12 - IIIrd Corps H.A.
13 - War Diary.
14, 15, 16, 17 Spare.
```

CENTRE GROUP DIVISIONAL ARTILLERY, IIIrd CORPS.                SHEET 1.

Programme from 6.0a.m. 12/9/16 till further orders.

| Serial No. | Time. | Unit. | Objective. | Remarks. | |
|---|---|---|---|---|---|
| 1. | 6.0a.m. to 10.0am. | D/250 | Trench S.2.b.0.8. to S.3.a.0.8. | For first half hour 1 round per how. per minute; afterwards slow steady observed fire. | 560 BX. |
| 2. | 10.0a.m. to 12 noon & onwards to 3.30pm. | —do— | Trench u.33.c.0.6. to u.33.c.99.80. | As aeroplane observation is available; when not available return to (1) | |
| 3. | 12 mid-night. | —do— | Company H.Q. at u.32.d.2540. | 160 P.S. First ten rounds fast, remainder at 1 round per minute. | |
| 4. | 5.30pm to 6.0am | 353 Bde RFA 18-pdrs. | Trenches bombarded by howitzers in day time, also nest of trenches in u.32.d. | 1300 A and AX. | |

SHEET 2.

| Serial No. | Time. | Unit. | Objective. | Remarks. |
|---|---|---|---|---|
| 5. | 6.0a.m. to 10.0a.m. | D/251 | Trench S.3.a.0.8. to S.3.a.9980. | For first half-hour, 1 round per how. per minute; afterwards slow steady observed fire. } 560 BX. |
| 6. | 10.0am to 12 noon and onwards to 6.30pm | -do- | Trench H.32.c.9980 to H.33.c.5.5. to H.33.a.9980. | As aeroplane observation is available; when not available return to (5) |
| 7. | 12-mid night. | -do- | Battalion H.Q. at H.33.a.2.6. | 160 P.S. First ten minutes fast, remainder at 1 round per gun per 1½ minutes. |
| 8. | 6.30pm to 6.0am. | 251 Bde. RFA. 18-pdrs. | Trenches bombarded by howitzers in day-time. | 1200 A and AX. |

SHEET 3.

| Serial No. | Time. | Unit. | Objective. | Remarks. |
|---|---|---|---|---|
| 9. | 6.0a.m. to 10.0a.m. | D/252. | Trench S.3.a.9980 to S.3.b.9.8. | For first half-hour 1 round per hou per minute; afterwards slow steady observed fire. } 560 BX. |
| 10. | 10.0a.m. to 12 noon & onwards to 6.30pm. | —do— | Trench H.33.d.9980 to H.34.b.3.0. | As aeroplane observation is available; when not available return to (9). |
| 11. | 11.0p.m. to 12 midnight | —do— | Nest of trenches H.33.b.6.5. | 160 P.S. First ten rounds fast, remainder at 1 round per minute. |
| 12. | 6.30p.m. to 6.0a.m. | 252 Bde. RFA 18-pdrs. | Trenches bombarded by Hows. in day-time, also nest of trenches H.33.b.6.5. | 1200 A and AX. |

ORIGINAL DIS-
POSITIONS.

1.     The two assaulting Brigades at zero hour must be north of and including the O.G. 1 and 2 lines.

    The Reserve Brigade which will be fully equipped with sandbags, grenades, etc. will be distributed as follows :-

    1 Battalion MAMETZ WOOD.
    1     "     QUADRANGLE TRENCH.
    2 Battalions about SHELTER WOOD.

    At zero the Reserve Battalions of the assaulting Brigades will move forward out of the O.G. 1 & 2 lines and their places are taken by the two leading Battalions of the Reserve Brigade, the other two Battalions closing up to MAMETZ WOOD and QUADRANGLE TRENCH.

2.     If the trench round the North side of BAZENTIN-LE-PETIT is completed, C.T.s will be marked IN and OUT as follows :-

    IN     JUTLAND ALLEY.
            KERRY ALLEY.

    OUT     ARGYLE - SUTHERLAND ALLEY.
             Trench North BAZENTIN-LE-PETIT.

3.     Brigade H.Q. on the day of the assault will be :-

    149th.     QUARRY.     S.8.d.8.9.
    150th     O.G.1.     S.7.d.2.1.
    151st.     MAMETZ WOOD.     X.24.a.9.8.

4.     The total number of officers to accompany each Battalion is not to exceed 20.

5.     Conference of M.G. Company Commanders to discuss and decide the work of the Machine guns prior to the assault and after.

(1).

6. Battalion Commanders should move forward with the last of their Battalions. But as long as they have anything in hand their H.Q. should not move.

Should the whole of the Battalion not move forward it must be left to the discretion of the C.O. when he should go forward to see the situation from the information he receives.

He should always remember that when once he leaves his H.Q. he ceases temporarily to exercise command over the situation.

R. E. 7. Collection of R.E. material for consolidation in the hollow in rear of SWANSEA trench before the day of the battle.

The material to be taken up gradually.

8. In case of a further advance and even if the final objective is secured, it may be possible to bring vehicles up to the hollow behind SWANSEA TRENCH.

1 Field Company and 100 Pioneers to be detailed to make a route as soon as possible after the attack. Hurdles for bridging shell holes ?

9. C.T.s to be dug after the assault. One Company of Pioneers will be allotted to each Brigade for this purpose. They will not be sent forward until the Brigadier considers that they will have a reasonable chance of being able to do the work.

"Q". 10. Sandbagging of rations.

3,000 rations to be prepared in this way and placed in the forward dump the day before the battle.

These are exclusive of what is carried on the man

11. Water tanks should be placed about S.8.d.9.1. from which water will be carried forward in petrol tins.

How many tins should we have forward to start with.

COMMUNICATIONS. 12. Battalions and Brigades must have definite plans for visual signalling both before and after the assault.

Also everything should be ready to push forward telephone lines.

Pigeons will be employed. Ask O.C.Signals about this.

ARTILLERY. 13. Forward guns.

Liaison.

One Brigade will be grouped with each Infantry Brigade for any special situation which may arise after the assault takes place.

On no account must the original artillery programme be interfered with.

MEDICAL. 14. Cannot Ambulance wagons move up to S.14.b.8.9. This would enable bearer sub-division men to take over from Regimental stretcher bearers at the Regimental Aid Posts in front.

Ref: Map 1/40,000, Sheets 57c., 57d.,
62d., and Trench Map.

SECRET.

Copy No 10

## CENTRE DIVISIONAL ARTILLERY GROUP (PRELIMINARY) OPERATION ORDER NO. 35.

12. 9. 16.

1. (a) The Fourth Army in conjunction with the French and the Reserve Army is going to renew the attack on Friday 15th September.

   (b) The 50th Division will attack with the 47th Division on its right and the 15th Division on its left.

2. (a) The final objective of the 50th Division is a line from H.34.b.5.9. - H.33.a.4.8. - H.33.c.1.9. - H.32.d.7.8. - H.32.d.2.7.

   (b) This objective will be reached in three bounds.
   The first bound is to the line S.3.b.8.9. - H.32.d.9.4. - H.32.d.2.7.
   The Second bound is to the line H.34.b.3.1. - H.33.b.7.3. - H.33.c.8.9. - H.32.d.7.7. - H.32.d.2.7.
   The Third bound is to the line COPSE (H.34.b.5.8.) (inclusive) - H.33.a.9.8. - H.33.a.4.7. - H.33.c.1.9. - H.32.d.7.8. - H.32.d.2.7.
   Each line when captured will be consolidated and garrisoned.

3. (a) The 50th Division will attack with two brigades in the front line and one in Reserve.
   The 149th Infantry Brigade will be on the Right and the 150th Infantry Brigade on the Left, with the 151st Infantry Brigade in Reserve.
   The Boundary between the 149th Infantry Brigade and the 150th Infantry Brigade will be H.33.b.4.6. - H.33.d.0.8. - S.3.c.0.9.
   The 50th Divisional boundaries are as follows :-
   On Right (East) S.3.d.2.9. - S.3.b.Central - H.34.c.9.5. - H.34.b.5.9.
   On Left (West) S.2.a.3.1. - S.2.b.2.8. - H.32.d.3.0. - H.32.d.2.7.

   (b) The 151st Infantry Brigade will be situated prior to zero as follows :-
   A Battalion ... ... MAMETZ WOOD.
   B Battalion ... ... QUADRANGLE TRENCH.
   C and D Battalions ... SHELTER WOOD area.
   At zero these battalions will move :-
   A and B Battalions to O.G.1 and 2.
   C Battalion to MAMETZ WOOD.
   D Battalion to QUADRANGLE TRENCH.

   The 149th and 150th Infantry Brigades will arrange for the O.G.1 and 2 lines to be vacated at zero to allow the A and B Battalions 151st Infantry Brigade to occupy them.

4. WOUNDED. Wounded will be brought back as follows :-

   Right Brigade - To Advanced Collecting Posts at S.8.d.8.4. and S.8.d.8.8.

   Left Brigade - To Advanced Collecting Posts at S.8.a.1.4. and about X.12.c.9.5.

   At the Advanced Collecting Posts the personnel of the Field Ambulances will remove the lying down cases to the Advanced Dressing Stations at FLATIRON COPSE (S.14.c.5.2.) and CONTALMAISON.
   Walking cases will all go to CONTALMAISON.

## PAGE 2.

5.  Headquarters will be established as follows by 6.0pm on the 14th September :-

    | | |
    |---|---|
    | Advanced Div. H.Q. | RAILWAY COPSE. X.28.b.2.1. |
    | 149th Infantry Bde | QUARRY S.8.b.9.1. |
    | 150th Infantry Bde. | O.G.1., S.7.d.2.1. |
    | 151st Infantry Bde | MAMETZ WOOD, X.24.b.9.8. |

6.  Centre D.A. Group covering 50th Division will be :-

    251 Bde. R.F.A., (H.Q. F.6.a.4025) four 18-pdr Bty's & one 4.5" How. Bty.

    252 Bde. R.F.A., (H.Q. F.6.a.7.5.)    -do-    -do-    -do-

    253 Bde. R.F.A., (H.Q. X.29.d.5.7.)    -do-    -do-    -do-

    276 Bde. R.F.A., (H.Q. X.29.d.5.7.) Three 18-pdr Bty's & one 4.5" How. Bty.

6.  O.C., 251 Bde. will arrange to carry out all necessary reconnaissances and make preparations to move two 18-pdr and one 4.5" Howitzer batteries forward as soon as the situation permits.

7.  D.T.M.O. will make arrangements for placing three Medium Trench Mortar Batteries and two 9.45 Trench Mortars in action.

8.  Acknowledge by wire.

*F. Brown*

Major R.A.,
B.M. 50th D.A.

Issued at 8.0p.m.

Copy No. 1 - 250 Bde. R.F.A.
    2 - 251 Bde. R.F.A.
    3 - 252 Bde. R.F.A.
    4 - 253 Bde. R.F.A.
    5 - 276 Bde. R.F.A.
    6 - 50th D.T.M.O.
    7 and 8 - 50th Div.
    9 - R.A., 111rd Corps.
    10 - War Diary.
    11, 12, 13, 14 Spare.

B.M. 1636/

O.C., 251
252
253 Bde. R.F.A.
276

The following has been reported from No. 34 Squadron R.F.C. :-

Target "F".    Is fairly well knocked about; most damage done on the left.

Target "G".    Is very little knocked about up to the present.

Target "E".    Well knocked about.

13. 9. 16.

Major R.A.,
B.M. 50th D.A.

B.M. 1636/11.

O.C., 251
252   Bde. R.F.A.
253
276
_____

Reference B.M. 1636/6 - Artillery Programme for 18-pdrs.

Rates of fire are :-

Intense :-   3 rounds per gun per minute.

Decreased :- 2 rounds per gun per minute for 10 minutes, then 1 round per gun per minute.

14. 9. 16.

Major R.A.,
B.M. 50th D.A.

SECRET.

B.M. 1656/22.

O.C., 4 Bde S.R.F.A.

## WARNING ORDER.

1. The Fourth Army will renew the attack on the 21st instant in conjunction with the French.

2. The objective of the 3rd Corps is a line xxxxxx giving a good field of view across the spurs in M.26, M.27 M.28 and M.29.

3. A tracing is sent herewith shewing boundaries and objective of 50th Division and zones of Artillery Brigades.

4. A steady bombardment of the hostile position will commence at 7.0a.m. on the 20th and will be continued till 6.30; it will re-commence at 6.30a.m. on the 21st.

5. There will be no intensive fire previous to zero.

6. The fire of the artillery will be intense when the Infantry advance to the assault at zero.

7. Zero will probably be in the afternoon.

8. Acknowledge.

Major R.A.,
B.M. 50th D.A.

19. 9. 16.
12. 30pm.

**ARTILLERY INSTRUCTIONS**

O.C.,
A Brigade R.F.A.

1. From 10.0a.m. on the 19th instant the front occupied by 50th Division is as shewn in tracing.

2. Each Brigade will so distribute the fire of one 18-pdr Battery over their zone that this Battery is always available for a special task without making a gap in the barrage.

3. **Liaison Officers.** 252 Bde. will provide a Liaison Officer at the H.Q., 151st Infantry Bde. and one other who will be with whichever Battalion the G.O.C. Brigade desires.

    253 Bde. will provide one Liaison Officer with H.Q. of Infantry Brigade on our left. He is mainly for information.

4. Registration of zones, observation of barrages on STARFISH LINE and PRUE TRENCH to be carried out as soon as possible.

5. F.O.O.'s will take advantage of the advance of the Infantry to gain any better observation pos s that may be available.

19. 9. 16.

Major R.A.,
B.M. 50th D.A.

50th DIVISIONAL ARTILLERY - S.O.S. BARRAGES.

**252 Bde.**

M.29.c.2.0. to M.34.b.6.5. to M.34.b.2.5.

**251 Bde.**

M.34.b.2.5. to M.34.a.6.5.

**253 Bde.**

M.34.a.6.5. to M.34.a.0.6.

**276 Bde.**

M.34.a.0.6. to M.27.d.3.0. to M.27. Central.

---

O.C., Bde. R.F.A.

50th D.A.
B.M. 1631/3

Forwarded for action. These S.O.S. Barrages will come into force at once.

*4.5 Hows on c. To and roads at discretion of Brigade Commanders.*

Major R.A.,
B.M. 50th D.A.

19.9.16.

*Cancelled*

## 50TH DIVISIONAL ARTILLERY - S.O.S. BARRAGES.

The following S.O.S. Barrages will come into force at once.

| | |
|---|---|
| 252 Bde. | M.29.c.1.5. to M.28.d.8.8. |
| 251 Bde. | M.28.d.8.8. to M.28.b.1.2. |
| 253 Bde. | M.28.b.1.2. to M.28.c.2.8. |
| 276 Bde. | M.28.c.2.8. to M.27.d.3.9. |

4.5 Hows. on C.T's. and roads at discretion of Brigade Commanders.

50th D.A.
B.M.1631/4.

O.C.,

Bde. R.F.A.

Forwarded for action.

*Cancelled*

F. Brown
Major, R.A.
B.M. 50 D.A.

23rd September, 1916.

B.M. 1631/5.

50th Divisional Artillery - S.O.S. Barrages.

The following S.O.S. barrages will come into operation at once :-

| | |
|---|---|
| 252 Bde. | M.29.a.5.5.<br>to<br>M.28.b.8.8. |
| 251 Bde. | M.28.b.8.8.<br>to<br>M.28.b.2.9. |
| 253 Bde. | M.28.b.2.9.<br>to<br>M.28.a.6.9. |
| 276 Bde. | M.28.a.6.9.<br>to<br>M.28.a.0.9. |

Howitzers on roads and C.T.'s in rear.

Acknowledge.

25. 9. 16.
O.C., 4 Bde. R.F.A.

Major R.A.,
B.M. 50th D.A.

B.M. /1631/G.

O.C., A Bde. R.F.A.

Herewith tracing shewing zones of Brigades and S.O.S. Barrages.

S.O.S. barrages will be as follows, and will be brought into operation at once :-

252 Bde.     M.23.c.2.0.
             to
             M.23.c.0.2.  } lift 100×
             to
             M.22.d.4.0.  }

251 Bde.     M.22.d.4.0.  }
             to           } +100×
             M.28.b.0.9.  }

253 Bde.     M.28.b.0.9.  }
             to           } +100×
             M.28.a.6.9.  }

276 Bde.     M.28.a.6.9.  }
             to           } +100
             M.27.b.9.9.  }
             28.C.2!.

Howitzers on roads and C.T.'s in rear.

* * * *

Acknowledge by wire.

26. 9. 16.

Major R.A.,
B.M. 50th D.A.

B.M.1631/7.

O.C.

Bde. R.F.A.

## 50TH DIVISIONAL ARTILLERY.

### S.O.S. BARRAGES.

The following S.O.S. Barrages will come into operation forthwith.

| | |
|---|---|
| 252 Bde. | M.22.b.5.4. to M.22.b.2.4. |
| 251 Bde. | M.22.b.2.4. to M.22.a.8.5. |
| 253 Bde. | M.22.a.8.5. to M.22.a.4.5. |
| 276 Bde. | M.22.a.4.5. to M.22.a.0.5. |

Acknowledge.

27th September, 1918.

Major, R.A.
B.M. 50 D.A.

B.M.1631/7.

B.M.1831/7.

O.C.

4 Bde, R.F.A.

## 50TH DIVISIONAL ARTILLERY.
:ooo:

### S.O.S. BARRAGES.
oOo

The following S.O.S. Barrages will come into operation forthwith.

| | |
|---|---|
| 252 Bde. | M.22.b.5.4.<br>to<br>M.22.b.2.4. |
| 251 Bde. | M.22.b.2.4.<br>to<br>M.22.a.8.5. |
| 253 Bde. | M.22.a.8.5.<br>to<br>M.22.a.4.5. |
| 276 Bde. | M.22.a.4.5.<br>to<br>M.22.a.0.5. |

Acknowledge.

27th September, 1918.

Major, R.A.
B.M. 50 D.A.

B.M./1631/8.

## 50th DIVISIONAL ARTILLERY.

### S.O.S. BARRAGES.

The following S.O.S. barrages will come into operation at once :-

| | |
|---|---|
| 252 Bde. | M.22.b.5.0. to M.22.a.9.2. |
| 251 Bde. | M.22.a.9.2. to M.22.a.5.3. |
| 253 Bde. | M.22.a.5.3. to M.22.a.2.4. |
| 276 Bde. | M.22.a.2.4. to M.21.b.7.3. |

Howitzers on C.T.'s and roads in rear.

\* \* \* \*

Acknowledge.

28. 9. 16.

Major R.A.,
B.M. 50th D.A.

WAR DIARY 18/6

SECRET.

Copy No. 12

## 50th DIVISIONAL ARTILLERY OPERATION ORDER NO. 36.

27. 9. 1916.

1. 50th Division, in conjunction with 1st Division intend to take remainder of objective at zero hour this afternoon.

2. 50th Division will take from M.28.a.6.6. to M.28.b.3.7., and 1st Division from thence Eastwards.

3. Artillery bombardment programme of 50th Divisional Artillery assisted by 23rd Divisional Artillery is attached.

4. Zero hour will be 2.15 p.m.

5. Acknowledge.

Issued at 12.30p.m.

Major R.A.,
B.M. 50th D.A.

Copies to :-
        No. 1 - 251 Bde. R.F.A.
            2 - 252 Bde. R.F.A.
            3 - 253 Bde. R.F.A.
            4 - 276 Bde. R.F.A.
            5 and 6 - H.Q. 50th Div.
            7 - Right D.A. Group.
            8 - Left D.A. Group.
            9 - R.A., IIIrd Corps.
          10 - War Diary.
          11, 12, 13, Spare.

Issued with 50th D.A. Operation
Order No. 36.

## PROGRAMME OF BOMBARDMENT.

| Serial No. | Unit Bombarding. | Time. | Objective. | Rate of fire. | Remarks. |
|---|---|---|---|---|---|
| 1. | 252 Bde. | 0.00 to 0.20 | Trench M.22.d.5.0. to M.28.b.1.8. | 2 rounds per 18-pdr) per minute. 1 round per 4.5 How) | |
| 2. | -do- | 0.20 onwards | Trench M.23.c.4.3. to M.22.d.7.9. | -do- | Gradually decreasing. |
| 3. | 251 Bde. | 0.00 to 0.20 | Trench M.28.b.6.7. to M.28.b.1.6. | -do- | |
| 4. | -do- | 0.20 onwards | Trench M.23.c.0.5. to M.22.d.5.0. | -do- | Gradually decreasing |
| 5. | 253 Bde. One 4.5" How. Bty. One 18-pdr Bty. | 0.20 onwards. | M.22.d.5.5. to M.22.c.9.5. | -do- | Search backwards and forwards 200 yards from this line, gradually decreasing rate. |
| 6. | 276 Bde. One 4.5" How. Bty. One 18-pdr. Bty. | 0.00 to 0.02 | Trench M.28.a.1.8. to M.21.d.5.3. | 2 rounds per 18-pdr per minute. 1 round per 4.5 How per 2 mins. | |
| | | 0.02 onwards | | | Gradually decreasing. |
| 7. | 276 Bde. One 18-pdr Bty. | 0.00 onwards | OLD QUARRY to Cross Roads, M.22.d.4.1. to M.22.c.9.0. | 1 round per gun per minute till 0.20 then gradually decreasing. | 50% A. 50% AX. |

SHEET 2.

| Serial No. | Unit bombarding. | Time. | Objective. | Rate of fire. | Remarks. |
|---|---|---|---|---|---|
| A. | 1 Brigade, 23rd D.A. | 0.00 to 0.02 | ... | Intense. | |
|    |                     | 0.02 to 0.20 | Trench M.21.d.5.3. to M.22.a.2.1. | Slow. | |
|    |                     | 0.20 to 0.25 | ... | Intense. | |
|    |                     | 0.25 onwards | ... | Gradually decreasing. | |
| B. | 2 Brigades, 23rd D.A. | As in A. | Trench M.22.a.2.1. to M.22.b.3.1. | As in A. | |

S E C R E T.                                            COPY NO. 11

## RIGHT DIVISIONAL ARTILLERY GROUP OPERATION ORDER NO. 61.

Reference Map :- Fourth Army 1/10,000
Map No. 678 dated 19/9/16.

                                        24th. September 1916.

1. **INFORMATION.**

   (a) The Fourth Army is renewing the offensive tomorrow.

   (b) The New Zealand Division on our right is assaulting the line of the road from M.30.c.1.1. through M.30.d. and b. at Zero, and GOOSE ALLEY between our block and the Sunken Road in M.30.a. at 25 minutes after Zero. The 3rd. Brigade will arrange for a flag to be hoisted at our block in GOOSE ALLEY at Plus 30 minutes.

   (c) After capturing GOOSE ALLEY the New Zealand Division will put out a line of outposts from M.30.a.5.7. to connect with our right M.29.b.4.1.

   (d) The 3rd. Brigade will capture the FLERS front and support line (if this has not already been done) as far as the communication trench in M.29.d.4.9. inclusive. After reaching the objective the position will be consolidated and wired at once, and the trenches beyond will be filled in for a distance of at least 50 yards. A trench will also be dug from the FLERS line at about M.29.d.3.9. to connect with the new trench at about M.29.d.0.5.

   The attack of the 3rd. Brigade will be launched at 25 minutes after Zero.

   (e) When the New Zealand Division have captured their objectives they will take over from the 1st. Division the whole of GOOSE ALLEY and the FLERS Support line as far as M.29.d.5.9.

   (f) Should the objective mentioned in para 1 (d) be captured before the 25th. inst. the whole of these orders will hold good except para 1 (d).

2. **ARTILLERY ACTION.**

   The 47th. D.A. will open an intense barrage at plus 25 minutes on the line M.29.b.6.5. - 2.3. - 29.a.2.3.
   All fire will be directed in accordance with attached Time Table.
   After plus 40 minutes the Artillery fire will be directed by the G.O.C. 3rd. Brigade through the Artillery Liaison Officer.

3. Zero hour will be notified later.

4. Orders as regards synchronizing watches will be issued later.

H.Q. 47th. D.A.                          Major R.A.,
                                         Brigade Major,
24/9/16.                                 Right D.A. Group.

Issued to :-
   Copy No. 1. War Diary.              No. 8. 277 Bde. R.F.A.
           2. File.                         9. 1st. Division.
           3. 235 Bde. R.F.A.              10. 14th. D.A.
           4. 236 Bde. R.F.A.              11. 50th. D.A.
           5. 237 Bde. R.F.A.              12. IIIrd. Corps R.A.
           6. 238 Bde. R.F.A.              13. IIIrd Corps H.A.

SECRET.

THE TABLE of Fire - 4.5" Howitzers - to accompany Right Group R.A. Op. Order No. 61.

| UNIT. | TIME. | PROCEDURE. | OBJECTIVE. | REMARKS. |
|---|---|---|---|---|
| (1) D/235 | 6.30 a.m. | Bombardment. | GOOSE ALLEY - M.30.a.1.0. to M.24.c.8.3. | Stops firing at Zero plus 10 minutes on this objective. |
| (2) " | Zero plus 10 minutes. | " | Sunken road from M.23.d.3.9. to M.23.d.9.4½. but not S.E. of latter point. | Continues on this objective till further orders. |
| (3) D/275 | 6.30 a.m. | Bombardment. | GOOSE ALLEY - M.24.c.8.3. to M.24.b.3.3. | As in (2) but no fire to be South of M.24.c.8.3. after Zero plus 10 minutes. |
| (4) D/236 | 6.30 a.m. | " | FLERS line front and support from M.29.b.0.3. Southwards as far as safety permits. | Stops firing at Zero. N.B. This shoot is not to be carried out till further orders on the subject are issued. |
| (5) " | Zero | " | FLERS line front and support from M.29.a.9.5. to M.23.c.5½.2. | As in (2). |
| (6) D/277 | Zero. | Search. Bombardment. | 1 Section on trench from M.23.d.3.4½. to M.23.b.8.6½. 1 Section on Cross Roads at M.23.a.9.3. | As in (2). " |
| (7) D/238 (2 guns only). | Zero. | " | EAUCOURT L'ABBAYE. | As in (2). |

RATES OF FIRE FOR 4.5" HOWITZERS.

Up to Zero.  :  40 rounds per hour (D/235, D/275 and D/236).
Zero to plus 15  :  1 round per gun per minute.
Plus 15 to plus 40  :  1 round per gun per 2 minutes.
Plus 40 onwards.  :  1 round per gun per 4 minutes.

S E C R E T.

TIME TABLE OF FIRE - 18-POUNDERS - TO ACCOMPANY RIGHT D.A. GROUP OP. O. NO. 61.

| UNIT. | TIME. | PROCEDURE. | OBJECTIVE. | REMARKS. |
|---|---|---|---|---|
| (1) 235th. Bde. R.F.A. | Zero. | Barrage. | FLERS front and support line M.29.b.2.5. to M.23.c.5½.1½. | Continuous on this barrage until further orders. |
| (2) 236th. Bde. R.F.A. | " | " | M.29.b.6.5. to M.29.b.2.5. to M.29.a.2.3. | ditto. |
| (3) 277th. Bde. R.F.A. | " | " | FLERS front and support line M.23.c.5½.1½. to M.23.c.0.6½. | ditto. |
| (4) 275th. Bde. R.F.A. | " | Search with bursts of fire. | Square M.23.b. | ditto. |

RATE OF FIRE FOR 18-PDRS.

Zero to plus 15   —   3 rounds per gun per minute.

Plus 15 to plus 30   —   1 round per gun per minute.

Plus 30 onwards.   —   1 round per gun per 3 minutes.

S E C R E T.

ADDENDUM NO. 1 TO RIGHT DIVISIONAL ARTILLERY GROUP OPERATION
ORDER NO. 61 DATED 24/9/16.

1.     ZERO hour will be 12.35 p.m. Sept. 25th. and will only
be communicated to those whom it immediately concerns. It must
not be communicated by telephone.

2.     There will be no intense fire of any kind before Zero.

3.     Each Field Artillery Brigade of Right Divisional Artillery
Group will have a representative at 3rd. Infantry Brigade H.Qtrs.
at BAZENTIN - LE - GRAND at 7.0 a.m. Sept. 25th. for synchronization
of watches.

4.     In para 1 (d) of Right D.A. Group Op.O. No. 61, line 3 -
delete "at 25 minutes after Zero" and substitute "at Zero".

5.     In para 2, line 1 - delete words "at plus 25 minutes" and
substitute "at Zero".

6.     In para 2, line 5 - delete words "plus 40 minutes" and
substitute "plus 15 minutes".

H.Q. 47th. D.A.                    Major R.A.,
                                   Brigade Major,
24/9/16.                           Right D.A. Group.


Issued to all recipients of Right D.A. Group Op. O. No. 61.

B.M.1647/9.

O.C.,
    4 Bde. R.F.A.

## ARTILLERY INSTRUCTIONS 26/27th September, 1916.

(1) Allottment of ammunition same as for 25/26.

(2) Howitzers will bombard enemy front line trenches.

(3) 276 and 253 Brigades to bombard trench M.28.a.5.6. to M.21.d.5.3.

(4) 18 pdrs. except for special opportunity and three minutes intense fire on front line trenches ordered at 12.35 p.m. to be reserved for night work.

(5) P.S. targets for to night will be EAUCOURT L'ABBAYE. Further instructions will be issued later.

(6) Acknowledge.

26/9/16.

Major, R.A.
B.M. 50 D.A.

PROGRAMME OF BOMBARDMENT, NIGHT 26/27 SEPTEMBER.

| Serial No. | Unit bombarding. | Time. | Objective. | Rate of fire. | No. of Rds. | Remarks. |
|---|---|---|---|---|---|---|
| 1. | All 4.5" Howitzer Batteries. | 8.30p.m. | HAUCOURT L'ABBAYE. |  | 100 P.S. per Bty. | Fire to be intense for first ten minutes; then 1 round per Bty. per minute. Thermit shell will be fired by D/251 and D/252 as soon as P.S. is finished. Rate :- 1 round per gun per 1½ minutes. |
| 2. | D/251 and D/252. |  | As in 1. |  | 124 Thermit per Bty. |  |
| 3 | One 18-pdr Bty. per Brigade. | 11.10p.m. | S.O.S. Barrage of brigade lifted 200 yards. | 1 Rd. per gun per 4 minutes |  |  |
| 4 | One 18-pdr Bty., 276 Bde. | 11.10p.m. | Barrage M.22.c.2.9. to M.21.d.5.1. | 1 rd. per gun per 2 minutes. |  |  |
| 5 | One Howitzer, D/252 Bty. | 11.5p.m. | Trench Junction, M.23.c.0.6. | 1 round per 2 minutes. |  |  |
| 6 | One Howitzer, D/251 Bty. | 11.5p.m. | OLD QUARRY, M.22.d.3.1. | -do- |  |  |
| 7 | Two howitzers, D/276 Bty. | 11.5p.m. | Trench M.21.d.8.0. to M.21.d.5.4. | -do- |  |  |
| 8 | One Howitzer D/250 Bty. | 11.5p.m. | Trench junction M.22.a.2.0. | -do- |  |  |

NOTE :- Usual programme will be carried on with guns and ammunition available.

Major R.A.,
B.M. 50th D.A.

SECRET.

50th Divn.
G.546.

C.R.A.

1. Reference 50th Division Operation Order 55 dated 21st September, the attack will take place to-morrow the 25th Sept.

2. The final objective of the 111 Corps is the line M.29.d.5.9.- M.29.c.8.6. - M.29.c.0.1. - M.28.d.1.7. - thence along the track to M.27.d.0.5. - M.27.c.5.6. - M.27.a.4.0. - M.27.a.0.4. - M.26.b.0.9.

3. Any portion of this line not already occupied will be occupied at zero hour to-morrow and patrols pushed forward along the FLERS line, CRESCENT ALLEY and the C.T. in M.27.a.
   The whole line will then be consolidated and all Divisions will push out strong posts as far as possible with the object of gaining further ground and forming a jumping off line for the next assault.

4. The 150th Inf. Bde. will to-night (24/25) dig a continuous fire trench along the line mentioned above from M.28.d.1.7. to CRESCENT ALLEY and from M.28.d.1.7. to connect with the 1st Division at M.28.d.8.0.
   One Company Pioneers is allotted to the 150th Brigade to dig a C.T. from PRUE TRENCH about M.34.a.5.6. - M.28.c.8.0. - M.28.c.7.4. during the night 24/25 September.

5. At zero hour on 25th September the 18-pdrs. of the 50th Divisional Artillery will open an intense fire on the nearest enemy trenches until 0.03.

6. Flares will be called for by contact patrol at 0.30 and plus two hours.
   Please ensure that all advanced posts and flanks shew flares at these hours.

7. Zero hour will be notified later.
   Representatives of Infantry and Artillery Brigades will receive correct time from a Staff Officer of the Corps at FRICOURT FARM at Six hours before zero.

8. Acknowledge.

(sgd) H. KARSLAKE, Lt. Col.
General Staff,
50th Division.

4.15p.m.
24th September, 1916.

-2-

50th D.A.
B.M. 1647/7.

O.C.,
    Bde. R.F.A.

For information and action.

Reference Para. 7, on 25th September zero hour will be 12.35p.m.
Representatives will attend at FRICOURT FARM at 6.30a.m.

Acknowledge.

Major R.A.,
B.M. 50th D.A.

24. 9. 16.

**"A" Form.** Army Form C. 2121.

## MESSAGES AND SIGNALS.

SECRET

DRLS

TO CRA
CRE

Sender's Number: GB 249
Day of Month: 24/9/16

AAA

On 25 Septr ZERO HOUR will be Twelve Thirty Five PM AAA Representatives to attend at TRICOURT FARM at 6.30 AM 25th to Set watches with Corps representative AAA acknowledge by wire

From Fiftieth Division
Place
Time 4 0 PM

SECRET.
50th Division.
G.546.

| | |
|---|---|
| 149th Inf.Bde. | C.R.A. |
| 150th " " | C.R.E. |
| 151st " " | 1st Division. |
| 7th D.L.I. Pioneers. | 23rd Division. |
| Div. T.M. Officer. | III Corps. |

1.	Reference 50th Division Operation Order 55 dated 21st September, the attack will take place tomorrow the 25th September.

2.	The final objective of the III Corps is the line M.29.d.5.9. – M.29.c.8.6. – M.29.c.0.1. – M.28.d.1.7. thence along the track to M.27.d.0.5. – M.27.c.5.6. – M.27.a.4.0. – M.27.a.0.4. – M.26.b.0.9.

3.	Any portion of this line not already occupied will be occupied at zero hour tomorrow and patrols pushed forward along the FLERS line, CRESCENT ALLEY and the C.T. in M.27.a.
	The whole line will then be consolidated and all Divisions will push out strong posts as far as possible with the object of gaining further ground and forming a jumping off line for the next assault.

4.	The 150th Inf.Bde. will to-night (24th/25th) dig a continuous fire trench along the line mentioned above from M.28.b.1.7. to CRESCENT ALLEY and from M.28.d.1.7. to connect with the 1st Division at M.28.d.8.0.
	One Company Pioneers is allotted to the 150th Brigade to dig a C.T. from PRUE TRENCH about M.34.a.5.6.– M.28.c.8.0. – M.28.c.7.4. during the night 24th/25th September.

5.	At zero hour on 25th September the 18 prs. of the 50th Divisional Artillery will open an intense fire on the nearest enemy trenches until 0.03.

6.	Flares will be called for by contact patrol at 0.30 and plus two hours.
	Please ensure that all advanced posts and flanks shew flares at these hours.

7.	Zero hour will be notified later.
	Representatives of Infantry and Artillery Brigades will receive correct time from a Staff Officer of the Corps at FRICOURT FARM at six hours before zero.

8.	Acknowledge.

Lt-Col.
General Staff.
50th. Division.

4.15 p.m.
24th September 1916.

SECRET.
Copy No. 4.

FIFTIETH DIVISION OPERATION ORDER NUMBER 55

21st September, 1916.

1. (a) On a date to be notified later (probably the 23rd September) the Fourth Army will renew the attack in conjunction with the French.

   (b) The 15th Corps is to capture FACTORY CORNER and is to establish a line thence to the high ground in M.29.b. & d. and to join up with the 3rd Corps in FLERS support line at M.29.b.4.1.
   The 1st Canadian Division will be attacking the ZOLLERN GRABEN to the North of COURCELETTE.

2. The objectives of the III Corps are shown on the tracing already issued.

3. (a) The 50th Division will attack as its first objective the STARFISH LINE and PRUE TRENCH from M.34.b.7.9. to CRESCENT ALLEY inclusive (M.33.b.4.6).

   The 2nd objective will be the road from about M.28.d. 8.0. - M.28.d.1.8. - M.27.d.7.4. and thence to CRESCENT ALLEY inclusive.
   The general direction of the attack is due North.
   (b) On arrival at the 2nd objective patrols must be pushed forward at once on to the best line for constructing a defensive line.

   (c) Both the STARFISH LINE and PRUE TRENCH must have parties left in them to clear out dugouts and to garrison them.

   The final objective must be consolidated as quickly as possible.

4. The 50th Division will attack with the 149th Infantry Brigade with two Battalions of the 150th Infantry Brigade attached.

   The 150th Infantry Brigade less two Battalions will be in support and the 151st Infantry Brigade in Reserve.

5. The attack will be assisted by all available artillery, details of which will be notified later, including three 2" Trench Mortars.

   The 150th Light T.M. Battery will be placed at the disposal of the 149th Infantry Brigade for the preliminary bombardment.

O V E R

6. The Brigades will at zero hour be disposed as follows :-

149th Infantry Brigade and two Battalions 150th Infantry Brigade in the front line including MARTIN TRENCH, BOAST TRENCH and JACKSON TRENCH.

150th Infantry Brigade - HOOK TRENCH.

151st Infantry Brigade - 1 Battalion EYE TRENCH.
                           2 Battalions CLARKS and SWANSEA.
                           1 Battalion INTERMEDIATE LINE.

All troops will be in these positions two hours before zero.

7. A Communication trench will be dug joining up PRUE TRENCH, STARFISH Line and the jumping off trench as soon as possible.

One Company of Pioneers is allotted to the 149th Infantry Brigade for this purpose, and will be ordered forward when the B.G.C. considers it possible for them to work.

They will be accommodated prior to the attack by the 149th Infantry Brigade.

7a. There will be two Communication Trenches available
     BETHEL SAP - RUTHERFORD ALLEY   I N.
     JUTLAND ALLEY - CRESCENT ALLEY   O U T.

8. "C" Dump will be at junction of BETHELL SAP and CLARK'S TRENCH.

An Engineer dump will also be formed there.

9. Headquarters will be as under :-

Advanced Div.H.Q.     RAILWAY COPSE.
    149th Bde.H.Q. -  QUARRY.
    150th  "   "  -  O.G.Line.
    151st  "   "     MAMETZ WOOD.

10. Acknowledge.

*H. Hardcastle*
Lt-Col.
General Staff.
50th. Division.

Issued at 8.0 a.m.

Copy No. 1. 149th Inf.Bde.    11. Div. T.M.Officer.
        2. 150th  "   "     12. III Corps.
        3. 151st  "   "     13. 1st Division.
        4. C.R.A.             14. 23rd Division.
        5. C.R.E.             15. 47th Division.
        6. 7th D.L.I.Pioneers. 16. "Q".
        7. Div. Signal Coy.   17. War Diary.
        8. A.D.M.S.           18. Office.
        9. Div. Train A.S.C.  19. Office.
      10. A.P.M.

| | | "A" Form. | | Army Form C.2121 (in pads of 100). |
|---|---|---|---|---|
| | | **MESSAGES AND SIGNALS.** | | No. of Message........... |

| Prefix......Code......m. | Words | Charge | This message is on a/o of: | Recd. at.............m. |
|---|---|---|---|---|
| Office of Origin and Service Instructions. | | | | Date ..... |
| | Sent | | ...............Service. | From ..... |
| | At............m | | | |
| | To | | | By ..... |
| | By | | (Signature of "Franking Officer.") | |

| TO | IO | FU |
|---|---|---|
| | FA | RO |

| Sender's Number. | Day of Month | In reply to Number. | | A A A |
|---|---|---|---|---|
| B.M. A 11 | Sept 25 | | | |
| Programme | from | 11 am | 25th | to |
| 11 am | 26th | will | be | the |
| same | as | yesterday | see | IO |
| Bde. | in | addition | 100 R.S. | in |
| addition | as | acknowledge | | |

From F.J.R.
Place
Time 9.30 am

(Z) F. Bryan

B.M. 1647/8.

O.C., 4 Bde, R.F.A.

P. S. TARGETS FOR TO-NIGHT.

    Area    M.22.b.4.2.
            M.22.d.4.9.
            M.22.a.7.2.
            M.22.c.7.9.

Fire to open at 11.30p.m.

First 10 minutes intense. After this, one round per battery per minute.

2.     253 Bde. will fire A from 11.30 to 11.33 into this area.

    RATE :- One round per gun per minute.

3.     Acknowledge.

Major R.A.,
B.M. 50th D.A.

25. 9. 16.

B.M./1647/8.

O.C., 4 Bde.R.F.A.
───────────

Reference Serial No. 2 of Programme of
Bombardment forwarded with my B.M. 1647/4 dated
23rd September, for " As in 1", read :-

    "Trenches    M.28.b.0.5.
                     to
                 M.28.b.8.8.
                     to
                 M.29.a.2.3.

24. 9. 16.

                                       Major R.A.,
                                 B.M. 50th D.A.

B.M. 1647/4.

O.C.,
      Bde. R.F.A.

## ARTILLERY INSTRUCTIONS.

1.   The Fourth Army are continuing the attack on 25th September.

2.   The Reserve Army are attacking on 26th September.

3.   Artillery Programme for Centre Divisional Artillery Group will be as attached.

4.   Zero hour on the 25th will be notified later.

5.   Acknowledge.

              Major R.A.,
              B.M. 50th D.A.

23. 9. 16.

## PROGRAMME OF BOMBARDMENT.

| Serial No. | Unit bombarding. | Time. | Objective. | Rate of fire. | No. of rounds. | Remarks. |
|---|---|---|---|---|---|---|
| 1. | D/251. | 7.0am 24th to 6.30pm 24th. | Trenches M.28.b.8.8. to M.29.a.2.3. to M.39.b.1.1. | Slow bombardment. | 500 | |
| 2. | D/251. | 6.30am 25th to Zero 25th | As in 1. | -do- | 500 | |
|  |  | At 0.00 25th, | Cease fire ... | ... | ... | Continue ordinary programme. |
| 3. | All 18-pdrs of :- 252 Bde. 251 Bde. 253 Bde. 276 Bde. | 0.00 25th to 0.03 | Enemy front line trenches on own zone. | Intense | As required | |
|  |  | 0.03 | Cease fire | ... | ... | Continue ordinary programme. |

WAR DIARY 18/7

SECRET.

Copy No. 15

## 50th DIVISIONAL ARTILLERY OPERATION ORDER NO. 37.

28.9.16

1. 276 Bde. R.F.A. will be relieved on 28/29 September by 39th Bde. 1st D.A.; relief to be complete on afternoon of 29th. Guns will be taken over in situ.

2. O.C. 39th Bde. will arrange to move the batteries which relieve C/276 and D/276 to more forward positions as soon as possible after relief.

3. A., B., and C. Batteries, 250 Bde. R.F.A. (personnel only) will come out of action on afternoon of 29th and proceed to wagon-lines, handing over guns required to O.C. 39th Bde. Any guns which O.C., 39th Bde. does not require to make up his establishment of 6 guns will be handed over to the O.C. Brigade to which they were attached before relief.

4. 1st D.A.C. is relieving 55th D.A.C. at E.6.c. this afternoon, 28th; relief to be complete by afternoon of 29th.

5. All wire, maps, portable O.P.'s, wireless installations and Very pistols are to be handed over to incoming brigades of 1st D.A. by 55th D.A.

6. After each relief the Brigades and D.A.C. of 55th D.A. will take over the billets and bivouacs vacated by the 1st D.A.

7. Route to be followed by incoming brigades and D.A.C. of 1st Division :-

    28th Sept.  BAZIEUX - HENENCOURT - MILLENCOURT - ALBERT.
                Tail of column to be clear of MILLENCOURT by 12.30pm.

    29th Sept.  Same route. Tail to be clear of BEHENCOURT by
                10.45a.m. and clear of HENENCOURT by 12.30p.m.

    Route for out-going Brigades and D.A.C. of 55th D.A. :-

        28th, via LAHOUSSOYE and FRECHENCOURT.

        29th, via LAHOUSSOYE and FRECHENCOURT.

    "B" Echelon 55th D.A.C. will not go to billets of "B" Echelon 1st D.A.C. at BREBLE.

8. Echelons 55th Divl. Arty. will go out of action full. All ammunition dumped will be handed over. Amounts handed over to be reported to this office.

9. All details will be arranged between Lt-Cols. Comdg: Brigades.

10. 39th F.A. Bde. is billetted at FRECHENCOURT.

11. Completion of reliefs to be reported by wire to this office.

12. Acknowledge.

Issued at 10.0a.m.

Major R.A.,
B.M. 50th D.A.

Copies to -
1 - 250 Bde. R.F.A.
2 - 251 Bde. R.F.A.
3 - 252 Bde. R.F.A.
4 - 253 Bde. R.F.A.          10 - Right Group D.A.
5 - 276 Bde. R.F.A.          11 & 12 - H.Q. 50th Div.
6 - 50th D.A.C.              13 - 50th Div. Train.
7 - C.R.A. 1st Div.          14 - R.A. IIIrd Corps.
8 - C.R.A. 55th Div.         15 - War Diary.
9 - Left Group D.A.          16, 17, 18 - Spare.

B.M. 1647/10.

O.C., 4 Bdes R.F.A.

## ARTILLERY INSTRUCTIONS, 28/29th SEPTEMBER.

1. Zones of Brigades are shewn on attached tracing.

2. Allotment of ammunition, 12 noon 28th to 12 noon 29th, 1500 A and AX, and 400 BX per Brigade.

3. TASKS.
   During daylight bombard FLERS LINE on own zone with 4.5" Hows. 18-pdrs - any target of opportunity that may be seen.
   During night, 18-pdrs. on all roads, tracks, and C.T.'s on Divisional zone.

4. Acknowledge.

28. 9. 16.

Major R.A.,
B.M. 50th D.A.

"A" Form.
Army Form C. 2121.

## MESSAGES AND SIGNALS.

| Prefix | Code | m. | Words | Charge | This message is on a/o of: | Recd. at ......... m. |
| Office of Origin and Service Instructions. | | | Sent | | ............ Service. | Date .......... |
| | | | At ......... m. | | | From .......... |
| | | | To | | | |
| | | | By | | (Signature of "Franking Officer.") | By .......... |

TO { F.A.   R.O.
     I.O.   Div. T.M. Officer.
     F.H.

| Sender's Number. | Day of Month. | In reply to Number. | AAA |
| B.M.1121 | Sept 28. | | |

Following from LH begins AAA Both heavy and divisional artillery are going to bombard FLERS line from 5.30p.m. to 5.55p.m. to-day AAA Special concentration will be made on trench between M.22.a.4.1. and M.21.b.5.4. AAA Strong patrols should be held ready to push into FLERS line when bombardment ceases AAA Trench Mortars both light and medium should be up ready to assist AAA At 5.55pm the Divisional Artillery will put a barrage round the point of entry about M.22.a.6.0., M.22.a.7.5., M.22.a.5.6., M.21.b.6.6., M.21.b.4.5. AAA This barrage will be intense for two minutes and then become very light AAA ends AAA Acknowledge

From    F.J.R.
Place
Time

The above may be forwarded as now corrected.   (Z)

Censor.   Signature of Addressee or person authorised to telegraph in his name.

* This line should be erased if not required.

PROGRAMME OF BOMBARDMENT, FROM 5.30p.m. 29th SEPTEMBER 1916.

| Serial No. | Unit bombarding. | Time. | Objective. | Rate of fire. | Remarks. |
|---|---|---|---|---|---|
| 1. | D/252. Two 18-pdr batteries. | 5.30pm to 5.55pm. | M.22.b.5.1. to M.22.b.0.1. | 1 round per gun per minute. | |
| 2. | Two 18pdr batteries 252 Bde. | 5.55pm onwards | M.22.b.6.6. to M.22.b.2.7. | Intense for two minutes, decreasing to 1 round per gun per 4 minutes. | |
| 3. | D/251. | 5.30pm to 5.55pm | M.22.a.8.0. to M.22.a.2.1. to M.21.b.8.4. | 1 round per gun per minute. | |
| 4. | D/276 | 5.30pm to 5.55pm. | M.22.a.4.1. to M.21.b.8.4. | 1 round per gun per minute. | |
| 5. | 251 Bde. All 18-pdrs. | 5.55pm onwards | M.22.a.6.0. to M.22.a.7.3. to M.22.a.5.6. | Intense for two minutes then decrease to 1 round per gun per 4 minutes. | |
| 6. | 253 Bde. All 18-pdrs. | 5.55pm onwards | M.22.a.5.6. to M.21.b.6.6. | Intense for two minutes then decrease to 1 round per gun per 4 minutes. | ✗ |
| 7. | 276 Bde. All 18-pdrs. | 5.55pm onwards | M.22.a.2.3. to M.21.b.6.6. to M.21.b.5.5. | Intense for two minutes then decrease to 1 round per gun per 4 minutes. | ✗ |

SHEET 3.

| Serial No. | Unit bombarding. | Time. | Objective. | Rate of fire. | Remarks. |
|---|---|---|---|---|---|
| 8. | 252 Bde. Two 18-pdr guns. | 5.30pm to 5.57pm. 5.57pm onwards | HILL at M.32.b.0.5. | 1 round per gun per minute. 1 round per gun per 2 minutes. | AX only. |

B.M. 1647/11.    Copy No. 10

Copies to -  1 - 252 Bde. R.F.A.
            2 - 251 Bde. R.F.A.
            3 - 253 Bde. R.F.A.
            4 - 276 Bde. R.F.A.
            5 and 6 - H.Q. 50th Div.
            7 - Left D.A. Group.
            8 - Right D.A. Group.
            9 - War Diary.
            10, 11 - Spare.

ACKNOWLEDGE.

Major R.A.,
B.M. 50th D.A.

PROGRAMME OF BOMBARDMENT, FROM 5.30p.m. 29th SEPTEMBER 1916.

| Serial No. | Unit bombarding. | Time. | Objective. | Rate of fire. | Remarks. |
|---|---|---|---|---|---|
| 1. | D/252, Two 18-pdr batteries. | 5.30pm to 5.55pm. | M.22.b.5.1. to M.22.b.0.1. | 1 round per gun per minute. | |
| 2. | Two 18pdr Batteries 252 Bde. | 5.55pm onwards | M.22.b.6.6. to M.22.b.2.7. | Intense for two minutes, decreasing to 1 round per gun per 4 minutes. | |
| 3. | D/251. | 5.30pm to 5.55pm | M.22.a.8.0. to M.22.a.2.1. to M.21.b.8.4. | 1 round per gun per minute. | |
| 4. | D/276 | 5.30pm to 5.55pm. | M.22.a.4.1. to M.21.b.8.4. | 1 round per gun per minute. | |
| 5. | 251 Bde. All 18-pdrs. | 5.55pm onwards | M.22.a.6.0. to M.22.a.7.3. to M.22.a.5.6. | Intense for two minutes then decrease to 1 round per gun per 4 minutes. | |
| 6. | 253 Bde. All 18-pdrs. | 5.55pm onwards | M.22.a.5.6. to M.21.b.6.3. | Intense for two minutes then decrease to 1 round per gun per 4 minutes. | |
| 7. | 276 Bde. All 18-pdrs. | 5.55pm onwards | M.22.a.2.6. to M.21.b.6.6. to M.21.b.5.5. | Intense for two minutes then decrease to 1 round per gun per 4 minutes. | |

SHEET 2.

| Serial No. | Unit Bombarding. | Time. | Objective. | Rate of fire. | Remarks. |
|---|---|---|---|---|---|
| 8. | 252 Bde. Two 18-pdr guns. | 5.30pm to 5.57pm. | HILL at M.22.b.0.5. | 1 round per gun per minute. | AX only. |
|  |  | 5.57pm onwards |  | 1 round per gun per 2 minutes. |  |

B.M. 1647/11.   Copy No. 9

Copies to –
1 – 252 Bde. R.F.A.
2 – 251 Bde. R.F.A.
3 – 253 Bde. R.F.A.
4 – 276 Bde. R.F.A.
5 and 6 – H.Q. 50th Div.
7 – Left D.A. Group.
8 – Right D.A. Group.
9 – War Diary.
10, 11 – Spare.

ACKNOWLEDGE.

Major R.A.,
B.M. 50th D.A.

B.M. 1647/12.

O.C.,
Bde. R.F.A.

ARTILLERY INSTRUCTIONS.
6.0a.m. 30/9/16 to 6.0a.m. 1/10/16

1. Allotment of ammunition per Brigade :-

   1500 A and AX.

   | 251 Bde. | 500 BX. | 39 Bde.  | 200 BX |
   | 252 Bde. | 500 BX. | 253 Bde. | 200 BX. |

2. Howitzers during day-light, SUNKEN ROAD M.22.b.3.9. to M.16.c.1.4. on own zones.

   251 and 252 Bdes, Nest of trenches about M.22.a.6.9.

   39 and 253 Bdes., registration.

3. 18-pdrs., by day, registration where required and any target of opportunity.

   By night, roads and C.T.'s in Divisional zone.

   NOTE.

   A captured German document of very recent date states that we never shoot between 4.0 and 7.0a.m., and that valleys are always shot at, and spurs and high ground left untouched.

4. Acknowledge.

29. 9. 16.

Major R.A.,
B.M. 50th D.A.

WAR DIARY 18/8

B.M.1647/13.

O.C.,
4 Bde. R.F.A.
---------------

## WARNING ORDER.

1. 50th Division will continue the attack on 1st October.
2. Zero hour will be in the afternoon.
3. Brigades will cut wire on their own Zones today commencing at 11.0 a.m.
4. 151 Infantry Bde. has been warned.
5. Advantage will be taken of this to carefully register barrages by 18 pdrs on German front line so that it is completely and fully covered.
6. Barrages must be so arranged that the fire of one battery per brigade can be turned on to any target of opportunity without leaving gaps in barrage.
7. Allotment of ammunition for wire cutting is as required. O.C.Brigades will use whichever batteries of their brigades they consider most suitable.
8. Acknowledge.

30/9/16.

Major, R.A.
B.M. 50 D.A.

## "A" Form.
### MESSAGES AND SIGNALS.

Army Form C. 2121.

Office of Origin and Service Instructions: Priority

TO: ~~DG~~ CRA

Sender's Number: GA192/1
Day of Month: 29

AAA

In continuation of my GA192 there will also be a concentrated fire on trench between M22651 to M22601 ceasing at 5.55 p.m. to enable patrols to slip in along the road AAA Time will be sent through over the telephone at 12 noon AAA Addressed DG repeated CRA.

From: LM
Time: 10.45 a.m.

(Z) H. Randall Lt Col

# "A" Form.
## MESSAGES AND SIGNALS.

Army Form C. 2121.

Priority to
DG

TO ~~DG~~  ~~2nd Div~~  CRA

AAA

GA 192  29

Both heavy and divisional artillery are going to bombard FLERS line from 5.30 p.m to 5.55 p.m today AAA Special concentration will be made on trench between M22a 41 and M21 b 84 AAA Strong patrols should be held ready to push into FLERS line when bombardment ceases AAA Trench mortars both light and medium should be up ready to assist AAA At 5.55 p.m the Divisional artillery will put a barrage round the point of entry about M22a6 0 M22a 73 M22a 516 M21 b 66 M21 b 45 AAA This barrage will be intense for two minutes and then become very light AAA Addressed

From DG repeated 4th and 23 Div CRA
Place LM
Time 9.30 a.m

"A" Form.
**MESSAGES AND SIGNALS.**
Army Form C. 2121.

| Prefix | Code | Words | Charge | This message is on a/c of: | Recd. at ... m. |
| --- | --- | --- | --- | --- | --- |
| Office of Origin and Service Instructions. | | Sent At ... m. To ... By ... | | ... Service. (Signature of "Franking Officer.") | Date ... From ... By ... |

Priority

TO  3. Corps  CRA

Sender's Number: * GA195.  
Day of Month: 29  
In reply to Number:  
AAA

Re 3. Corps Artillery instructions N° 80 para 2(b) subpara 1 AAA Instead of putting 4·5" Hows on LE SARS may be put them on trenches which we hope to capture AAA Is this bombardment to take place today AAA Addressed 3. Corps repeated CRA

M 22 6 5·1
   22 6 0·1

From: 
Place: 30 D 4
Time: 9.45 a m

(Z) H Hanbek Lt Col

"A" Form.  Army Form C. 2121
**MESSAGES AND SIGNALS.**  No. of Message

| TO | T.Z. | F.U. |
| | F.A. | |
| | F.O. | |

| Sender's Number. | Day of Month. | In reply to Number. | AAA |
| M 1132/ | Sept. 30 | | |

(1) O.C. 50th Bde. will detail one section 18-pdrs. to keep the BUTTE DE WARLENCOURT in M.17.a. under fire at irregular intervals from 0.04 onwards until the line of outposts vide Para. 10 of Operation Order No. 38 is established AAA Ammunition allotted for this task:- 120 A and AX.

(2) Ref. 50th D.A. Operation Order No. 38 dated 30/9/16, zero hour on October 1st will be 3.15p.m. AAA

(3) Acknowledge.

From 50 D.A.
Place
Time 10.10p.m.

(Z) — Major R.A.

"A" Form.
Army Form C. 2121.

## MESSAGES AND SIGNALS.

| Prefix … Code … m. | Words | Charge | This message is on a/c of: | Recd. at … m |
|---|---|---|---|---|
| Office of Origin and Service Instructions. | | | | Date |
| | Sent | | …………… Service. | From |
| D. R. L. S. | At …… m. | | | |
| | To | | | |
| | By | | (Signature of "Franking Officer.") | By |

TO
- C. R. A.
- ~~C. R. E.~~
- 50th Div. Signals.
- ~~189th Inf. Brigade.~~
- ~~150th " "~~
- ~~151st " "~~

| Sender's Number. | Day of Month. | In reply to Number. | |
|---|---|---|---|
| G.B.366. | 29/9/16. | | A A A |

Correct clock time will be distributed to representatives of Infantry Brigades and Artillery Brigades at 47th Division Advanced Headquarters FRICOURT FARM, at TEN A.M. First October by Staff Officer of Third Corps AAA  Above is Greenwich mean Time not Summer Time AAA  The change from Summer Time to normal Greenwich time will take place at ONE A.M. on First October at which hour clocks will be put back one hour i.e. to 12.0 Midnight.

From: Fiftieth Division.
Place:
Time: 4.30 P.M.

Major
G.S. 50th Division.

# "A" Form.
## MESSAGES AND SIGNALS.

| Prefix ......... Code ......... m | Words | Charge | This message is on a/c of : | Recd. at .......... m |
| Office of Origin and Service Instructions. | | | | Date .......... |
| ................................ | Sent | | ........................ Service. | From .......... |
| ................................ | At .......... m | | | |
| ................................ | To | | | |
| ................................ | By | (Signature of "Franking Officer.") | By .......... |

TO — Third Corps.    Adv. Q.    D.L.
     G.O.C. 80th Div.    Y.M.    G.E.
     Hqrs 99th Bde.    C.R.A.    Box

| Sender's Number. | Day of Month. | In reply to Number. | A A A |

G.B.577.    30th.

Reference para. 9 of G.600 dated 29th September
the D Dump of L.M. owing to NON arrival of Tramway
Rails will be at M.34.b.0.6. and NOT at M.29.a.4.5.
AAA    The N.E. Dump will also be in PRUE TRENCH
about M.34.b.0.6.    AAA

From    L.M.
Place
Time

The above may be forwarded as now corrected.    (Z)

Censor.    Signature of Addresser or person authorised to telegraph in his name.    Major.

* This line should be erased if not required.

"A" Form.
Army Form C. 2121.

## MESSAGES AND SIGNALS.

| Prefix | Code | m. | Words | Charge | This message is on a/c of: | Recd. at | m. |
| Office of Origin and Service Instructions. | | | Sent | | | Date | |
| | | | At | m. | Service. | From | |
| | | | To | | | | |
| | | | By | | (Signature of "Franking Officer.") | By | |

TO  C.R.A.

| Sender's Number. | Day of Month | In reply to Number | AAA |
|---|---|---|---|
| *G.630. | 30th | | |

Third Corps wire G284 timed 11 p.m. 29th begins aaa Correction No. 1 to Third Corps Operation Order No. 140 begins aaa Delete third sub para of para. 4 and substitute the following aaa. The field artillery barrage will lift from the above line at plus 4 minutes and go back to 150 yards behind the GREEN line from M.22.B.5½.4½. Westwards aaa From that point Eastwards the barrage will lift on to a line 150 yards behind the FLERS support line and then rake back at the

## "A" Form.
### MESSAGES AND SIGNALS.

Army Form C. 2121.

rate of 30 yards a minute to 150 yards behind the GREEN line aaa Delete para. 5 and substitute the following aaa At plus 30 minutes the Artillery barrage will lift clear of the line M.22.B.4½.8.— M.16.C.1.3½. — M.15.D.7.8. when the 50th Division will push forward to the work in M.22.A.8.8. and the 23rd Division will push forward strong patrols into LE SARS and to the QUARRY in M.15.D.7.8 aaa acknowledge aaa ends.

From 50th Division
Place
Time 12.15 AM

BM1129

NDRE/4241.

C.R.A.

Report on road from BAZENTIN-LE-PETIT to
MARTINPUICH at 6.0a.m. to-day was :-

Road cleared to M.32.c.5.5. - can be used for
urgent traffic.
Holes filled in to S.2.c.9.3. and partially
filled in up to S.2.c.8.9.

(sgd) C.W.Singer, Lt. Col. R.E.,
C.R.E.

-2-

50th D.A.
B.M./1129

O.C., A Bde S R.F.A.

For information.

30. 9. 16.

Major R.A.,
B.M. 50th D.A.

SECRET.
50th Division.
G.609/2.

C.R.A.
149th Inf.Brigade.
150th  "      "
151st  "      "
_____

1. Para. 5 of 50th Division letter G.609/1 dated 29th September will be amended to read :-

"5. At "Plus Thirty minutes" the Barrage will lift "clear of the line M.22.b.4½.8. - M.16.c.1.3½. - "M.15.d.7.8.

"At this hour the 50th Division will push forward "to the work in M.22.a.8.8. and the 23rd Division will "push forward strong patrols into LE SARS and the "Quarry in M.15.d.7.8."

2. At the end of para. 4 of G.609/1 add :-
"Eastward of point M.22.b.5½.4½. the Barrage will "lift on to a line one hundred and fifty yards beyond "the FLERS SUPPORT LINE and then rake back at the rate "of thirty yards a minute to a line one hundred and "fifty yards beyond the green line".

H. Kandatte
Lt-Col.
General Staff.
50th. Division.

30th September 1916.

SECRET.
50th Division.
G.609/1.

C.R.A.
C.R.E.
149th Inf.Brigade.
150th  "      "
151st  "      "
50th Div.Signals.
A.D.M.S.
"Q".
Third Corps.
23rd Division.
47th Division.

---

1.     In continuation of 50th Division Letter G.609 dated 29th September 1916.

2.     The Artillery will begin deliberate bombardment of the objectives at 7.0 A.M. 1st October.
       The Infantry will advance to the attack at Zero, at which hour the Artillery Barrage will begin.

3.     This barrage will begin fifty yards short of the German front line, and will rake back at "Plus Two Minutes" on to the German front line.

4.     The Barrage will lift off the German front line at "Plus four minutes"; and will establish itself one hundred and fifty yards beyond an East and West line drawn through M.22.b.5½.4½.

5.     At "Plus Thirty minutes" the Barrage will lift clear of the line M.23.a.6.7. - M.23.a.2.8. - M.22.b.4½.8. - M.16.c.1.3½. - M.15.d.7.8.
       At this hour the 47th Division will push forward to the German Trenches in M.23.a.2.8. and 50th Division to the work in M.22.a.8.8.

6.     The 23rd Division will push forward strong patrols into LE SARS and to the QUARRY in M.15.d.7.8.

7.     At "Plus one hour and thirty minutes" the Artillery will lift on to the line of Trenches running North West from the BUTTE DE WARLENCOURT, and patrols will be pushed forward by 50th and 23rd Divisions due North; and an outpost line will be formed on the line M.23.a.2.8. - M.16.a.9.1. - Round the Village of LE SARS - QUARRY in M.15.d.7.8.

8.     A Contact Patrol will fly over the objective from Zero onwards. Yellow flares will be shown when called for at Four P.M., Five P.M., and Six P.M. on 1st October..

9.     All ground gained must be consolidated at once. The main line of resistance being from M.23.Central - Trenches in vicinity of M.23.a.2½.5. - round the MILL - thence to FLERS LINE.

10.     ACKNOWLEDGE by Telegram.

H. Karslake
Lt-Col.
General Staff.
50th. Division.

29th September 1916.

## "A" Form.
## MESSAGES AND SIGNALS.

Army Form C. 2121.

| Prefix | Code | m. | Words | Charge | This message is on a/c of: | Recd. at | m |
| --- | --- | --- | --- | --- | --- | --- | --- |
| Office of Origin and Service Instructions. | | | Sent | | Service. | Date | |
| | | | At | m. | | From | |
| | | | To | | (Signature of "Franking Officer.") | By | |
| | | | By | | | | |

TO ~~Brig. G.R.A. Thirty ~~~~ps.~~ A.D.M.S.~~
~~G.E. C.R.E. 23rd Div. 69th Div.Sigs.~~  **Z Z**

| Sender's Number. | Day of Month. | In reply to Number. | AAA |
| --- | --- | --- | --- |
| G.S.252. | 29th. | | |

Reference Letter G.609 ~~by special m.~~ to you to-day AAA Paragraph 3 of G.609 AAA D Divisional Dump will be established at end of the Tramline about N.22.a.4.5. and not at N.22.d.3.0. AAA

From L.M.
Place
Time 11.10 a.m.

The above may be forwarded as now corrected. (Z)

Major.

"A" Form.  Army Form C. 2121.
## MESSAGES AND SIGNALS.

| Prefix | Code | m. | Words | Charge | This message is on a/c of: | Recd. at ... m |
|---|---|---|---|---|---|---|
| SECRET. | | | Sent | | | Date |
| D.R.L.S. | | | At ... m. To By | | Service. (Signature of "Franking Officer.") | From By |

TO
- C.R.A. — 149th Inf. Bde. — 50th Div. Signals.
- C.R.E. — 150th " " — A.D.M.S.
- 7th D.L.I. — 151st " " — "Q".

| Sender's Number. | Day of Month. | In reply to Number. | |
|---|---|---|---|
| G.B.355. | Twenty ninth. | | AAA |

Reference G.609 AAA Zero Hour on First October is THREE FIFTEEN p.m.

From **Fiftieth Division.**

Place

Time **10.10 A.M.**

Major.
G.S.

SECRET.

50th Division.
G.609.

C.R.A.
C.R.E.
149th Inf. Brigade.
150th    "    "
151st    "    "
50th Div. Signals.
A.D.M.S.
"Q"
III Corps.
23rd Division.
47th Division.

1. (a) On October 1st (probably) the 50th Division will capture and hold the two lines of German trenches between M.22.b.3.4. and M.21.b.8.4.

   (b) The 47th Division will attack on the right and the 23rd Division on the left; their objectives are shown on attached tracing.

2. The 151st Inf. Brigade with one Battalion 149th Brigade will carry out the attack supported by the 149th Infantry Brigade less one Battalion, with the 150th Inf. Brigade in Reserve.

2a. The Artillery Programme will be issued later.

3. The Supporting Brigade will at zero hour be situated in PRUE TRENCH to JACKSON STREET and BOAST TRENCH both inclusive, and the Reserve Brigade between HOOK TRENCH and the INTERMEDIATE Line both inclusive.

4. As soon as the objective has been captured patrols will be pushed forward at once and an outpost line established on the line M.22.b.1.9. - M.16.a.9.1. - M.16.a.1.5. From this line patrols will be pushed forward at once due North to gain contact with the enemy. When once contact is gained it must never be lost, and every man must be on the alert to gain ground at any time so as to give the enemy no rest whatever.

5. The 7th D.L.I. (Pioneers) will work under the orders of Lt-Col. VAUX entirely on communication trenches.

6. The C.R.E. will detail the necessary R.E. personnel to carry forward the tramline as far as possible, and continue the repair of the road between the N.W.Corner of HIGH WOOD and MARTINPUICH.

7. The A.D.M.S. will arrange for an A.D.S. about M.27.b.7.2. evacuating through MARTINPUICH and BAZENTIN LE PETIT.

8. "D" Divisional Dump will be established at the end of the tramline about M.22.d.2.0.

An R.E.Dump will also be established at the same place if time admits of this being done.

9. Acknowledge. ackd BM/1121

29th September 1916.

H. Karslake
Lt-Col.
General Staff.
50th. Division.

WAR DIARY

## 50th DIVISIONAL ARTILLERY.

Programme from 12 noon, September 2nd, 1916 to 12 noon September 3rd, 1916.

| Time. | Unit. | Objective. | | Remarks. |
|---|---|---|---|---|
| 8.0pm to 6.0am. | 251 Bde. R.F.A. | Roads in R.30.c. and R.36.a. Buildings & Trenches in R.36.a. | 100 A and AX. 50 BX. | One or two rounds gun fire at uncertain hours at discretion of Bde. Commander. |
| 8.0pm to 6.0am. | 252 Bde. R.F.A. | Roads from S.W. of MARTINPUICH. | 100 A and AX 50 BX. | —do—   —do— |

NOTES :—

(1) Remainder of Programme detailed in Left Divisional Artillery Operation Order No. 55.

(2) Continuous Barrages as usual.

(3) Infantry Patrols will be out from 11.15p.m. to 1.15a.m.

WAR DIARY.

B.M. 1599/1.

3.9.16

## 50th DIVISIONAL ARTILLERY.

### BOMBARDMENT PROGRAMME.

| Serial No. | Time from Zero. | Unit. | Objective. | Remarks. |
|---|---|---|---|---|
| (1) | - 1. 35 to - 0. 40 | D/251<br>D/252 | Trenches S.2.a.40.45 to S.2.a.75.60.<br>Trenches S.2.a.75.60 to S.2.b.0.8. | } One round per gun per 1½ minutes. |
| (2) | - 0. 40 to ZERO. | D/251<br>D/252 | Trenches S.2.a.40.45 to S.2.a.75.60.<br>Trenches S.2.a.75.60. to S.2.b.0.8. | } 1½ rounds per gun per 1 minute. |
| (3) | 0. 00 to 0. 05. | 251 Bde. R.F.A.<br>252 Bde. R.F.A. | Trenches M.31.d.5.0. to M.31.d.15.30.<br>Trenches G.1.b.8.9. to M.31.d.5.0. | 18-pdrs 50 yards short of enemy trenches. 4.5" Hows. on trench.<br>Rate of fire :-<br>18pdrs. 3 rds. per gun per minute.<br>4.5" Hows. 2 " " " " |
| (4) | 0. 05 to 0. 07 | 251 Bde. R.F.A.<br>252 Bde. R.F.A. | Lift 300 yards | Rate as above. |
| (5) | 0. 07 | 251 Bde. R.F.A.<br>252 Bde. R.F.A. | Objective as in (3). | One salvo from each Battery, and stop firing; then return to normal barrages. |

WAR DIARY.

## 50th DIVISIONAL ARTILLERY.

Reference Map 1/10,000 Trench Map
of 47 D.A. corrected to 31.8.16.
Programme from 1.0p.m. 3rd September, to 12 noon, 4th September, 1916.

| Serial No. | Time. | Unit. | Objective. | Remarks. |
|---|---|---|---|---|
| 1. | Continuous. | 251 Bde. R.F.A. | Communication trenches, S.1.b.65.85. to M.32.c.1.4., and M.31.d.15.35. to M.32.c.00.55. | 1,200 rounds A and AX per 24 hours, two 18-pdr. batteries firing 400 rounds by night, 200 rounds by day each. Slow bombardment with occasional bursts. |
| 2. | Continuous. | 252 Bde. R.F.A. | Trenches S.1.b.7.9. to M.31.d.15.30. | 1 round per gun per 6 minutes by day, 6.0am to 8.0pm. 1 round per gun per 3 minutes by night, 8.0p.m. to 6.0a.m. Slow search every hour for 400 yards. Slow bombardment with occasional bursts. 2,000 A and AX per 24 hours. |
| 3. | 5.0pm | D/251 | Strong point X.6.a.25.90. | 100 rounds BX. Slow bombardment. |
| 4. | 1.0pm 3/9. to 12 noon 4/9. | 251 Bde.R.F.A. | Buildings and trenches in R.36.a. | 100 Rounds A and AX ) Bursts of fire<br>100 " BX. ) at uncertain<br>) intervals. |
| 5. | 7.0pm to 6.0am. | 252 Bde.R.F.A. | Road through centre of MARTINPUICH from M.32.a.8.1. to M.33.a.05.95. | 100 rounds A and AX ) Guns and Hows. to<br>200 " BX. ) fire together<br>) bursts at uncertain<br>) intervals. |

NOTE :-

(1) Infantry Patrols will be out between 10.30p.m. and 12.30a.m.

WAR DIARY

## 50TH DIVISIONAL ARTILLERY.

Programme from 12 noon, 4/9/16 to 12 noon, 5/9/16.

| Serial No. | Time. | Unit. | Objective. | Remarks. | |
|---|---|---|---|---|---|
| 1. | 7.0pm to 6.0am | 251 Bde. R.F.A. | Trench and road, M.52.a.6.5. to M.25.d.8.5. | 100 A and AX ) 150 BX. } | Bursts of fire at uncertain intervals. |
| 2. | 7.0pm to 6.0am | 252 Bde. R.F.A. | Trenches in M.31.b.85.00. to M.31.d.7.5. | 100 A and AX.) 200 BX. } | Bursts of fire at uncertain intervals. |
| 3. | 4.0pm to 6.0pm | D/251. | Buildings and trenches in R.36.a. | 50 BX. | Two salvoes at a time at uncertain intervals. |

NOTES :-

1) Continuous barrages as before.

(2) Infantry Patrols will be out between 12 mid-night and 2.0a.m.

B.M. 1552/19.

## 50th DIVISIONAL ARTILLERY.

Programme from 12 noon 5/9/16 to 12 noon 6/9/16.

| Serial No. | Time. | Unit. | Objective. | | Remarks. |
|---|---|---|---|---|---|
| 1. | 4.0p.m. to 7.0p.m. | D/251 | Buildings and trenches in K.36.a. | 50 BX. | Small bursts at uncertain intervals. |
| 2. | 8.0p.m. to 10.0p.m. | 251 Bde. R.F.A.; one 18-pdr Batt'y. | Trench and road M.32.a.6.5. to M.25.d.8.5. | 50 A and AX. | Two rounds gun fire at uncertain intervals. |
| 3. | 7.0a.m. to 12 noon. | 252 Bde. R.F.A. | MARTINPUICH. | 100 rds. A and AX. 200 rds. BX. | Guns and Hows. to fire together bursts at uncertain intervals. |
| 4. | 7.0a.m. to 12 noon. | 251 Bde. R.F.A. | COURCELETTE | 100 B.P.F. 50 A and AX. 50 BX. | } Bursts at uncertain } intervals. |

NOTES :- (1) Continuous barrages as before.

(2) Infantry patrols will be out between 10.15p.m. and 12.15a.m.

WAR DIARY

## 50th DIVISIONAL ARTILLERY.

Programme from 12 noon 6/9/16 to 12 noon 7/9/16.

| Serial No. | Time. | Unit. | Objective. | Remarks. |
|---|---|---|---|---|
| 1. | Continuous. | 252 Bde. R.F.A. | Trenches S.1.b.7.9. to M.31.d.15.30. | 1 round per gun per 6 minutes by day. 6.0a.m. to 8.0p.m. 1 round per gun per 3 minutes by night, 8.0p.m. to 6.0.am. Search every hour for 400 yds. slow bombardment with occasional bursts. 2,000 A and AX per 24 hours. |
| 2. | Continuous. | 251 Bde. R.F.A. | Area M.31.d.85.40. - M.32.c.0.3. to M.32.c.30.75. - M.32.c.45.80. | Search backwards and forwards at uncertain hours. Slow bombardment with occasional bursts. 1,000 A and AX; 200 BX and BPF per 24 hours. |
| 3. | Continuous. | 251 Bde. R.F.A. | Communication trenches S.1.b.MM.85 to 65. M.32.c.1.4. and M.31.d.15.35 to M.32.c.00.55. | Bursts of fire at uncertain intervals mostly at dusk and just after dawn. 200 A and AX per 24 hours. |
| 4. | 7.0pm to 10.0pm and 6.0am to 7.0am. | 251 Bde. R.F.A. | Valley from M.31.d.0.5. to M.31.b.8.0. | Search Valley backwards and forwards 100 A and AX; 200 BX. |
| 5. | 9.0pm to 11.0pm and 6.0am to 8.0am | 252 Bde. R.F.A. | N.E. of MARTINPUICH about M.27.c.2.2. to 2.5. to 1.2. | Bursts of fire at uncertain intervals. 100 A and AX; 200 BX. |

NOTE :-

(1) Infantry Patrols will be out between 11.30p.m. and 1.30a.m.

WAR DIARY

## 50th DIVISIONAL ARTILLERY.

Programme from 12 noon, 7/9/16 to 12 noon, 8/9/16.

| Serial No. | Time. | Unit. | Objective. | Remarks. |
|---|---|---|---|---|
| | | | Continuous barrages Nos. 1, 2, and 3 as from noon 6th to noon 7th. | |
| 4. | Continuous during daylight. | D/251. | Strong point X.6.a.25.90. | 20 rounds BX per hour. Fire to be very carefully observed. 103 Inf. Bde., also Inf. Bde. on left to be warned. |
| 5. | 12 noon to 6.0p.m. | 252 Bde. RFA. | TRWE O.P. at M.25.d.9.6. | 60 A and AX. Bursts of fire at uncertain intervals especially when enemy artillery is active on S.l.d. |
| 6. | 8.0p.m. to 11.0p.m. | 251 Bde. RFA. | Road Junction M.32.a.60.65. | 60 A and AX. 50 BX. |
| 7. | 2.0p.m. to 3.0p.m. | 251 Bde. RFA. | Buildings & Trenches in R.36.a. | 60 A and AX. 50 BX. Bursts of fire at uncertain intervals. |
| 8. | 9.0p.m. to 12 midnight. | 252 Bde. RFA. | Exit from MARTINPUICH at M.32.c.50.65. | 20 A and AX. 30 BX. |
| 9. | 10.0p.m. to 3.0a.m. | D/252 | COURCELETTE. | 20 BX one round at a time at intervals during night. Varying objective slightly at each round. |

NOTE :-

(1) Infantry Patrols will be out from 1.15a.m. to 3.15a.m.

"WAR DIARY" 9.9.16.

## PROGRAMME OF BOMBARDMENT.

| Serial No. | Unit bombarding. | Time. | Objective. | Rate of fire. | Remarks. |
|---|---|---|---|---|---|
| 1. | 252 Bde. R.F.A. | 0.00 to 0.02 | S.1.b.8.9. to M.31.d.20.25. | 18-pdrs, 3 rounds per gun per minute. 4.5" Hows. 2 rounds per gun per minute. | |
| 2. | -do- | 0.02 to 0.03 | Lift 150 yards. | -do- | |
| 3. | -do- | 0.03 | As in 1. | Fire one salvo and return to daily programme. | |

WAR DIARY

## PROGRAMME OF BOMBARDMENT. 9.9.16.

| Serial No. | Unit bombarding. | Time. | Objective. | Rate of fire. | Remarks. |
|---|---|---|---|---|---|
| 1. | D/251 | 0.00 to 0.03 | R.36.c.7.2. | 2 rounds per gun per minute. | See note. |
|  | -do- | 0.03 onwards | -do- | 1 round per gun per minute. |  |
| 2. | 251 Bde. R.F.A., three 18-pdr Batteries. | 0.00 to 0.03 | X.6.a.20.75. to R.36.c.7.2. | 3 rounds per gun per minute. | See note. |
|  |  | 0.03 onwards | X.6.a.95.70. to R.36.c.7.2. | 3 rounds per gun per minute, decreasing gradually to 1 round per gun per minute at 0.08. |  |

NOTE :- (1) Fire will be maintained at this rate till orders are received via Liaison Officer on left that fire is no longer required.

WAR DIARY

## 50th DIVISIONAL ARTILLERY.

Programme from 12 noon 9/9/16 to 12 noon 10/9/16.

| Serial No. | Time. | Unit. | Objective. | Remarks. |
|---|---|---|---|---|
| 1. | Continuous. | 252 Bde. R.F.A. | Trenches S.1.b.7.9. to M.31.d.15.30. | 1 round per gun per six minutes by day 6.0am to 8.0pm. 1 " " three " " night 8.0pm to 6.0am. Search every hour for 400 yards, slow bombardment with occasional bursts. 2000 A and AX. per 24 hours. |
| 2. | Continuous | 251 Bde. R.F.A. | Area M.31.d.85.40. – M.32.c.0.3. to M.32.c.30.75 – M.32.c.45.60. | Search backwards and forwards at uncertain intervals mostly at dusk hours; slow bombardment with occasional bursts. 1000 A and AX. 200 BX and SPF per 24 hours. |
| 3. | Continuous | 251 Bde.R.F.A. | Communication trenches S.1.b.65.85. to M.32.c.1.4. and M.31.d.15.35 to M.32.c. 00.55. | Bursts of fire at uncertain intervals mostly at dusk and just after dawn. 200 A and AX per 24 hours. |
| 4. | 12 noon to 8.0pm. | 252 Bde.R.F.A. | Tree O.P. at M.25.d.9.6. | 80 A and AX. Bursts of fire at uncertain intervals especially when enemy artillery is active on S.1.d. |
| 5. | 12 noon to 12 noon. | 251 Bde. R.F.A. | Buildings & Trenches in R.36.a. | 50 BX. 50 A and AX. One salvo from guns and hows. at uncertain intervals by day and night. |
| 6. | 8.0pm to 9.0pm. and 6.0am to 8.0am. | 252 Bde R.F.A. | Exit from MARTINPUICH at M.32.c.50.65. | 80 A and AX. 80 BX. |

NOTE :- Time that Infantry Patrols will be out will be ascertained by Liaison Officers.

Reference 1/10,000 Trench Map.

SECRET.

COPY NO. 11

## CENTRE GROUP DIVISIONAL ARTILLERY, IIIrd CORPS.

Programme from 12 noon 10/9/16 to 12 noon 11/9/16.

| Serial No. | Time. | Unit. | Objective. | Remarks. |
|---|---|---|---|---|
| 1. | Continuous. | 232 Bde. R.F.A. | | |
| | | 18-pdrs. | Trenches S.2.a.45.50. to S.2.b.2.8. | Search 400 yards every hour. 1200 A and AX. |
| | | 4.5" Hows. | Trenches in N.32.d. | 200 BX. Whole area to be searched and swept. |
| 2. | -do- | 237 Bde. R.F.A. | Trenches S.2.b.2.8. to N.32.d.7.1. | Search 400 yards every hour. 1200 A and AX. |
| 3. | -do- | 70 Bde. R.F.A. | | |
| | | 18-pdrs. | Trench S.2.b.70.95. to S.3.a.8.7. | Search 300 yards every hour. 1300 A and AX. |
| | | 4.5" Hows. | Trenches and roads in N.33.c. | 300 BX. Whole area to be searched and swept. |
| 4. | -do- | 72 Bde. R.F.A. | | |
| | | 18-pdrs. | Trenches S.3.a.8.7. to S.3.b.45.75. | Search 300 yards every hour. 1200 rounds A and AX. |
| | | 4.5" Hows. | Trenches and roads in N.33.c. | 200 BX. Whole area to be searched and swept. |

Slow bombardments with occasional bursts of fire.

SHEET 2.

| Serial No. | Time. | Unit. | Objective. | Remarks. |
|---|---|---|---|---|
| 5. | Continuous. | 238 Bde. R.F.A. | Trench from S.3.b.45.75. to S.3.b.85.75. then back to N.35.d.05.20. | Fire to sweep backwards and forwards along these two trenches. 1200 A and AX. Slow bombardment with occasional bursts of fire. |

NOTE :- Time of Infantry Patrols to be ascertained through Liaison Officers.

Copy No. 1 - 238 Bde. R.F.A.
2 - 237 Bde. R.F.A.
3 - 70 Bde. R.F.A.
4 - 72 Bde. R.F.A.
5 - 73 Bde. R.F.A.
6 - Right Group D.A.
7 - Left Group D.A.
8 - H.Q. 50th Div.
9 - R.A., IIIrd Corps.
10 - IIIrd Corps H.A.
11 - War Diary.
12, 13, 14 Spare.

B.M. 50th D.A.
Major R.A.,
10. 9. 16.

Reference 1/10,000 Trench Map.

SECRET.

Copy No. 10

## CENTRE GROUP DIVISIONAL ARTILLERY, IIIrd CORPS.

### Programme from 12 noon 11/9/16 to 12 noon 12/9/16.

| Serial No. | Time. | Unit. | Objective. | Remarks. |
|---|---|---|---|---|
| 1. | Continuous | 238 Bde RFA 18-pdrs. | Trench S.2.a.3.9. to M.32.d.1.2. M.32.c.9.1. - S.2.b.2.9. - M.32.d.5.3. | Search 200 yards every hour. 1300 A and AX. |
|  |  | 4.5" Hows. | Trench S.2.b.2.9. to M.32.d.3.3. | 200 BX. |
| 2. | -do- | 237 Bde RFA 18-pdrs. | Trench S.2.b.0.8. to S.2.b.7095. | 1300 A and AX. |
| 3. | -do- | 251 Bde RFA 18-pdrs | Trench S.2.b.7.8. to S.3.a.9.8. | 1300 A and AX. |
|  |  | 4.5" Hows. | M.G. Emplacement S.3.b.1585. | 100 BX. |
| 4. | -do- | 252 Bde RFA | Trench M.33.d.1.2. to M.33.d.4.6., thence to M.33.b.6.0. and M.33.d.9585. | 1200 A and AX. 200 BX. Slow continuous bombardment with occasional bursts. |
| 5. | 8.0pm to 10.0pm | 238 Bde RFA | N.E. end of MARTINPUICH. | 100 A and AX. 48 BX. Two rounds gun fire at uncertain intervals. |

SHEET 2.

| Serial No. | Time. | Unit. | Objective | Remarks. |
|---|---|---|---|---|
| 5. | 6.0am to 8.0am | 337 Bde RFA. | Square N.32.d. | 300 A and AX. Search and sweep at uncertain intervals. |
| 6. | 9.0pm to 11.0pm and 5.0pm to 8.0pm | 251 Bde. RFA. 18-pdrs. D/251 | Communication trench from N.33.a.2.0. to N.33.a.5.9. Battalion H.Q. at N.33.a.2.6. | 300 A and AX. Bursts of fire at uncertain intervals. 50 bX. Salvoes at intervals. |
| 8. | 8.30pm to 10.30pm | 252 Bde RFA | Valley from N.32.Central to N.33.c.5.0. | 100 A and AX. Occasional salvoes at 40 bX. varying ranges. S.S.2 |

NOTES :- (1) Particulars as to Infantry Patrols must be ascertained from Liaison Officers.

(2) Acknowledge by wire.

Copies to :—
1 — 338 Bde R.F.A.
2 — 337 Bde R.F.A.
3 — 251 Bde R.F.A.
4 — 252 Bde R.F.A.
5 — Right Group D.A.
6 — Left Group D.A.
7 — H.Q. 50th Div.
8 — R.A., IIIrd Corps.
9 — IIIrd Corps H.A.
10 — War Diary.
11, 12, 13 Spare.

Major R.A.,
B.... 50th D.A.
11. 9. 16.

Artillery Programme 15/9/16

Programme of Bombardment.

| Serial no. | Unit bombarding. | Time. | Objective. | Rate of fire. | Remarks. |
|---|---|---|---|---|---|
| 1.a. | 18-pdrs. of 37B bde. | 0.00 | 150 yards in front of our front line trenches. | Intense. | Objectives and brigade boundaries shown on tracing. Path 50 yards on each side of TANK track as shown in tracing to be kept free of fire; this is to be covered by D/35 bty., in case of mishap to tank as per special instructions. |
| 2.a. | | 30 Secs | Lift to enemy front line trench. | Intense. | |
| 3.a. | | 30 Secs to 0.02 | Remain on front line trench. | Intense. | Actual rate of fire not yet received from M.M., IIIrd Corps. |
| 4.a. | | 0.02 to 0.05 | Lift 50 yards per minute till a line 150 yards beyond first objective is reached. | Intense. | |
| 5.a. | | 0.05 to 0.08 | Remain as in 4.a. | Intense. | |
| 5.b. | | 0.08 | Lift 150 yards beyond trench S.2.b.9.7. to N.32.d.4.4. which will then be occupied by our Infantry. | | |
| 5.c. | | 0.08 to 1.00 | Remain as in 5.b. | Decreased. | |

"A" Form.  Army Form C.2121.
## MESSAGES AND SIGNALS.

| TO | F.A. | R.O. |
|----|------|------|
|    | I.O. |      |
|    | F.U. |      |

| Sender's Number. | Day of Month. | In reply to Number. | AAA |
|---|---|---|---|
| BM.58 | 14ᵗʰ | | |

Zero hour for 18 pr aeroplane registration to-day will be 1.30 pm instead of 1 pm aaa rate of two battery salvoes per minute AAA will be

From F.J.
Place
Time 9.48 am

E.H.Johnson Lt
for BM 50th DA

PROGRAMME OF BOMBARDMENT BY 4.5" HOWITZERS, 15/9/16.

| Serial. | Unit bombarding. | Time. | Objective. | Rate of fire | Remarks. |
|---|---|---|---|---|---|
| A. | D/252 | 6.0am to Zero. | Enemy front line in own zone. | 1 round per gun per minute. | |
| B. | -do- | 0.00 to 0.02 | Remain on front line trenches as in A. | -do- | |
| C. | -do- | 0.02 to 1.00 | Enemy second line trench N.34.a.3.1. to N.34.b.2.0. | 1 round per gun per 2 minutes. | |
| D. | -do- | 1.00 to 2.00 | Enemy third line trench in N.34.a.6.6. to N.34.b.7.8. | 1 round per gun per 2 minutes. | |
| E. | -do- | 2.00 onwards | Road in N.28.d.2.0. to N.28.d.9.9. | 1 round per gun per 3 minutes. | |

SECRET.

Copy No. 9

B.M. 1836/6.

1. Herewith

    Artillery Instructions.
    Programme of ~~Bombardment and~~ Aeroplane
      Registration for 14th Sept.
    Artillery Programme for 15th Sept.(18-pdrs. only).

2. Programme from 6.0a.m. 14th, will be same as from 6.0a.m. 13th, for all Brigades, except that aeroplane registration will be carried out as per attached tables.

3. 276 Bde. R.F.A. will carry out general registration and D/276 will bombard trenches within their barrage area in H.32.d.

4. Watches will be synchronised from 50th D.A. at 9.0a.m.

5. Acknowledge by wire.

                                                          Major R.A.,
Issued at 2.0a.m. 14.9.16.           B.M. 50th D.A.

Copy No. 1 - 251 Bde. R.F.A.
        2 - 252 Bde. R.F.A.
        3 - 253 Bde. R.F.A.
        4 - 276 Bde. R.F.A.
        5, 6, 7 and 8 - H.Q., 50th Division.
        9 and 10 Spare.

SECRET.

B.M. 1636/5.

O.C.,
  Bde. R.F.A.

<u>ARTILLERY INSTRUCTIONS.</u>

1. Herewith tracing shewing lines of barrage for 18-pdrs. also trenches for bombardment with 4.5" Hows.

2. Line of TANK is shewn in BLUE. O.C. 273 Bde. must arrange to leave a path 100 yards wide through his barrage for the passage of tank.

3. This gap will be covered by B/253 who must get registered on it and must have a F.O.O. watching the passage of tank so as to be able to fill the gap if anything should happen to stop the tank going on.

4. 251 Bde. and 252 Bde. will so arrange their barrage that the fire of one of their 18-pdr. batteries covers the whole front of barrage. These two batteries will then be able to turn their fire on to any special point where assistance is required without making a gap in the barrage.

5. Barrages by 18-pdrs. must be registered with balloon observation on 14th, and, after guns are registered, the entire barrage put up by each Brigade must be observed so as to ensure that no gaps are left in it and that it slightly overlaps the barrages on its right and left.

6. Bombardment of trenches by 4.5" Hows. :-

 (a) The enemy first and second line must be destroyed.

 (b) Communication trenches will be dealt with by 4.5" Hows. during the advance.

 (c) The third line system is to be bombarded as far as time and ammunition permits.

7. During the night preceding the attack, 18-pdrs. must thoroughly search the ground in front of and for 200 yards beyond the front line so that no repairs to trenches can be done and no rations or reliefs can get up.

8. All 18-pdr. batteries must register on enemy's front line trench with direct observation and ascertain exactly how much short of EYE trench it is safe for them to shoot.

9. It must also be borne in mind that men must have rest so that they are as fresh as possible for the day of attack.

10. Any F.O.O.'s and parties that go forward should take with them rations and water for at least two days so as to be prepared to hang on to forward observing posts.

           F. Brown
           Major R.A.,
13. 9. 16.         B.M. 50th D.A.

ARTILLERY PROGRAMME, 15/9/16.

| Serial No. | Unit bombarding. | Time. | Objective. | Rate of fire. | Remarks. |
|---|---|---|---|---|---|
| 6. | All 18-pdrs. of 251, 252, 253 and 276 Bdes. | 1.00 | Lift 50 yards per minute till a line 150 yards beyond second objective is reached. | Intense. | Actual rate of fire not yet received from R.A., IIIrd Corps. Objectives and Brigade boundaries shown on tracing. |
| 7. | | to 2.00 | When line of 6 is reached, remain on this. | Decreased. | |
| 8. | | 2.00 | Lift to third objective. | Intense. | |
| 9. | | 2.09 | Lift 300 yards beyond third objective and remain. | Gradually decrease. | |

ARTILLERY PROGRAMME. 159/16.

| Serial No. | Unit bombarding. | Time. | Objective | Rate of fire. | Remarks. |
|---|---|---|---|---|---|
| 1.a. | 18-pdrs. of 276 Bde. | 0.00 | 150 yards in front of our front line trenches. | Intense. | Objectives and Brigade boundaries shown on tracing. Path 50 yards on each side of TANK track as shown in tracing to be kept free of fire; this is to be covered by B/253 Bty., in case of mishap to tank as per special instructions. |
| 2.a. | | 30 Secs | Lift to enemy front line trench. | Intense. | |
| 3.a. | | 30 Secs to 0.02 | Remain on front line trench. | Intense. | |
| 4.a. | | 0.02 to 0.05 | Lift 50 yards per minute till a line 150 yards beyond first objective is reached. | Intense. | |
| 5.a. | | 0.05 to 0.08 | Remain as in 4.a. | Intense. | Actual rate of fire not yet received from R.A., IIIrd Corps. |
| 5.b. | | 0.08 | Lift 150 yards beyond trench S.2.b.9.7. to M.32.d.4.4. which will then be occupied by our Infantry. | | |
| 5.c. | | 0.08 to 1.00 | Remain as in 5.b. | Decreased. | |

## ARTILLERY PROGRAMME 15/9/16.

| Serial No. | Unit bombarding. | Time. | Objective. | Rate of fire. | Remarks. |
|---|---|---|---|---|---|
| 1. | All 18-pdrs. of 251, 252, and 253 Bdes, less B/253 Bty. | 0.00 | 150 yards in front of our front line trenches. | Intense. | Actual rate of fire not yet received from R.A., IIIrd Corps. |
| 2. | | 30 secs. | Lift to enemy front line trench. | Intense. | |
| 3. | | 30 secs. to 0.02 | Remain on front line trench. | Intense. | Objectives and Brigade boundaries shewn on tracing. |
| 4. | | 0.02 to 0.06 | Lift 50 yards per minute till a line of 200 yards beyond first objective is reached. | Intense. | |
| 5. | | 0.06 to 1.00 | Remain as in 4. | Decreased. | |

CENTRE DIVISIONAL ARTILLERY GROUP, IIIrd CORPS.

Programme for Aeroplane Registration, 14th September, 1916.

| Time. | Unit. | Objective. | Remarks. |
|---|---|---|---|
| 0.00 0.20 | D/252 | M.33.d.9930 to M.34.b.2.0. | Salvoes every two minutes. Call for this target will be "F". Aeroplane will give corrections mostly over, short, etc. |
| 0.20 0.40 | -do- | M.33.b.8530 to M.34.a.2500. | -do-   Call "B". |
| 0.40 1.00 | D/251 | M.33.d.4035 to M.33.b.6530. | -do-   Call "J". |
| 1.00 1.20 | D/250 | M.33.c.0065 to M.33.c.9980. | -do-   Call "D". |
| 1.20 1.40 | -do- | M.33.c.0570 to M.33.a.4580. | -do-   Call "O". |

NOTE :-   Zero time will be 10.0a.m.

PROGRAMME OF BOMBARDMENT BY 4.5" HOWITZERS. 15/9/13.

| Serial. | Unit bombarding. | Time | Objective. | Rate of fire. | Remarks. |
|---|---|---|---|---|---|
| M | D/250 | 3.0am to Zero. | Enemy front line in own zone, S.3.A.0075 to S.3.a.3585 | 1 round per gun per minute. | |
| N. | -do- | 0.00 to 0.02 | Remain on front line trench as in M. | 1 round per gun per minute. | |
| O. | -do- | 0.02 to 1.00 | Enemy second line trench, M.33.d.1575 to M.33.d.8.8. | 1 round per gun per 2 minutes. | |
| P. | -do- | 1.00 to 2.00 | Enemy third line trench M.33.A.6555 to M.33.A.9960. | 1 round per gun per 2 minutes. | |
| Q | -do- | 2.00 onwards | Communication trench M.27.d.5.0. to M.27.d.6099. | 1 round per gun per 3 minutes. | |

PROGRAMME OF BOMBARDMENT of 4.5" HOWITZERS, 15/9/18.

| Serial. | Unit bombarding. | Time. | Objective. | Rate of fire. | Remarks. |
|---|---|---|---|---|---|
| R. | D/276 | 3.0am to Zero. | Front line trench from S.2.d.4.9. to S.2.d.2.9. | 1 round per gun per minute. | |
| S. | -do- | 0.00 to 0.03 | As in R. | -do- | |
| T. | -do- | 0.03 to 1.00 | Enemy second line trench M.33.c.6.8. to M.33.c.2.7. and M.33.c.5.3. to M.33.a.3.0. | 1 round per gun per 2 minutes. | |
| U. | -do- | 1.00 to 2.00 | Enemy third line trench, M.33.a.9550 to M.33.a.5550 and M.33.b.0575 to M.33.a.7065. | 1 round per gun per 2 minutes. | |
| W. | -do- | 2.00 onwards | Sunken road M.27.c.2.2. to M.27.c.1575 | 1 round per gun per 3 minutes. | |

Artillery Programme 15/9

PROGRAMME OF BOMBARDMENT.

| Serial No. | Unit bombarding. | Time. | Objective. | Rate of fire. | Remarks. |
|---|---|---|---|---|---|
| 3. | All 18-pdrs. of 351, 353, 355, and 376 Bdes. | 1.00 | Lift 500 yards per minute till a line 150 yards beyond second objective is reached. | Intense. | Objectives and brigade boundaries shown on tracing. |
| 7. | | to 3.00 | When line of 3 is reached, remain on this. | Decreased rate. | |
| 5. | | 3.00 | Lift to third objective. | Intense. | |
| 6. | | 3.09 | Lift 500 yards beyond third objective and remain. | Gradually decrease. | Actual rate of fire not yet received from H.A., IIIrd Corps. |

B.M. 1636/7.

O.C.,
    Bde. R.F.A.

The following results of aeroplane registration on 14.9.16, as per programme issued under my No. B.M. 1636/6 dated 14. 9. 16 are forwarded for information.

| Unit. | Call. | Time. | Result. |
|---|---|---|---|
|  |  | a.m. |  |
| D/252 | F | 10.10 | Mostly 30 yds. short. |
| " | " | 10.20 | -do-    -do- |
| D/252 | B | 10.30 | Mostly 50 yards short. |
| " | " | 10.35 | -do-    -do- |
| D/251 | J | 10.46 | Mostly 20 yds. Short & 30 yds. Right. |
| " | " | 10.55 | Mostly 20 yds. Right. |
| D/250 | D | 11.6 | Mostly 10 - 20 yds. short. |
| " | " | 11.15 | Mostly 20 yds. short. |
| D/250 | O | 11.26 | Mostly 20 yds. Short. |
| " | " | 11.35 | -do-    -do- |

14. 9. 16.

Major R.A.,
B.M. 50th D.A.

B.M. 1636/7.

O.C.,
Bde. R.F.A.

The following results of aeroplane registration on 14.9.16, as per programme issued under my No. B.M. 1636/6 dated 14. 9. 16 are forwarded for information.

| Unit. | Call. | Time. | Result. |
|-------|-------|-------|---------|
|       |       | a.m.  |         |
| D/252 | F     | 10.10 | Mostly 30 yds. short. |
| "     | "     | 10.20 | -do-    -do- |
| D/252 | B     | 10.30 | Mostly 50 yards short. |
| "     | "     | 10.35 | -do-    -do- |
| D/251 | J     | 10.46 | Mostly 20 yds. Short & 30 yds. Right. |
| "     | "     | 10.55 | Mostly 20 yds. Right. |
| D/250 | D     | 11.6  | Mostly 10 - 20 yds. short. |
| "     | "     | 11.15 | Mostly 20 yds. short. |
| D/250 | O     | 11.26 | Mostly 20 yds. Short. |
| "     | "     | 11.35 | -do-    -do- |

14. 9. 16.

Major R.A.,
B.M. 50th D.A.

Dauja Mapi
50TH D.A.                                    SECRET

The positions selected for C & D Batteries of this
Brigade, in the event of their being ordered to move
forward are as follows:—
    C/251     SQ b 8.5
    D/251     SQ b 7.5½
The exact locality is recognizable by an old
telephone cast lying on the top of a bank about
10 feet high.
    C Battery would be on the top of the bank
with dug-outs & ammunition dumps below, &
D Battery would fire over the bank.
    Approach to the positions is by road as far
as SQ d 8.8, then across country. One trench
would have to be crossed viz. HIGH ALLEY
& this would require bridging over or filling in.
    The positions would not be suitable for occupation
so long as the high ground in M 32 c is in
the hands of the enemy.

                        D. K. Dauton Lt & Adjt
                for
                            Lieut Colonel
                    Commanding 251° (N) Bde R.F.A
13/9/16

SECRET.

B.M./1636/8.

Officer Commanding.
    251 (Northumbrian) Brigade. R.F.A.
------------------------------

251. Brigade must be prepared to move forward to a position about M.33.d.0.0. centre line on EAUCOURT L'ABBAYE.

Routes to be reconnoitred and arrangements made for crossing our trenches, Four trench bridges are being issued to-day from D.A.C.

All arrangements must be made for moving and horses kept harnessed on 15th instant. Move will be ordered by Corps.

F. Brown

14th September, 1916.

B.M., 50th D.A.    Major. R.A.

B.M. 1636/9.

SECRET.

O.C., 251
252
253  Bde. R.F.A.
276

1. When barrages are stationary, a certain proportion of AX is to be used. Maintain ammunition in hand at 25% AX and 75% A.

2. Moving barrages should be all A.

3. Rate of fire from 18-pdrs. must never exceed four rounds per gun per minute.

14. 9. 16.

F. Brown
Major R.A.,
B.M. 50th D.A.

1. Warn operators to be ready to receive LL messages and area calls on their respective area of trenches.

2. Brigades with masts should be warned to send through to Divisions all information about Infantry. Divisional masts may not get all signals.

3. LL = "Most important signal" and is only sent when enemy infantry is seen moving in large numbers in the open. If they are seen concentrating in the trenches the ordinary call is sent.

4. Enemy infantry attacking - LL is sent and smoke balls are dropped.

※※ ※※ ※※

50th D.A.
B.M. /1636/10.

O.C., 251
252
253 Bde. R.F.A.
276

Forwarded for information and action.

14. 9. 16.

Major R.A.,
B.M. 50th D.A.

B.M. 1636/13.

O.C., 251
252
253
276
Bde. R.F.A.

## COMMUNICATION BETWEEN AEROPLANES AND ARTILLERY.

1. If <u>Counter Attack</u> is seen by Aeroplane.

    i. Pilot comes down low and drops three smoke bombs over attackers, indicating flanks and centre of attack.

    ii. Sends LL. LL. KK. followed by a short message describing attack — Locality.
    e.g., Area Call "S.b.   S.4.a.6.5. — 8.5. Inf. Mass".

2. On receiving LL call <u>everybody</u>* opens fire on that area. Mast informs Brigade Commander who must inform Divisional Commander by telephone since latter has no mast.

3. LL. call also used for infantry in close formation in the open.

4. If Infantry seen concentrated in trenches only, then only the area call is sent and answered at discretion of Brigade Commander.

5. Brigades must inform wireless operator which calls to take.

    At present moment mast must be with <u>Brigade</u> because it is Stationary, takes area calls, which batteries cannot attend to.

    Afterwards on the move, batteries must have masts, which must be allotted at discretion of <u>Brigades</u> who must arrange for transference.

    \*\* \*\* \*\*

    \* This during the present programme would only refer to the batteries of 251 and 252 Brigades detailed by Para. 4 of Artillery Instructions, B.M. 1636/5 dated /3.9.16.

14. 9. 16.

F. Brown
Major R.A.,
B.M. 50th D.A.

## COMMUNICATION BETWEEN AEROPLANES AND ARTILLERY.

1. If Counter Attack is seen by Aeroplane.

    i. Pilot comes down low and drops three smoke bombs over attackers, indicating flanks and centre of attack.
    
    ii. Sends L.L. call G.L. followed by a short message describing attack - locality.
    e.g. Area call "C.B. H.4.a 6.5 - 6.1 Inf. Mass."

2. On receiving L.L. call everybody come fire on that area. Must inform Brigade Commander who must inform Divisional Commander by telephone since latter has no set. ✗

3. C.B. call also used for Infantry in close formation in the open.

4. If Infantry seen concentrated in trenches only, then only the area call is sent and answered at discretion of Brigade Commander.

5. Brigades must inform wireless operator which calls to take.

   At present pilot must rest with Brigade because it is stationary, takes area calls, which batteries cannot attend to.

   Afterwards on the move batteries must have posts, which is to be allotted at discretion of Brigades who must arrange for transference.

✗ This during the present programme would only refer to the batteries of 251 and 252 Brigades detailed by para 4 of Artillery Instructions B/M 1636/5 dt. 13.9.16.

## COMMUNICATION BETWEEN AEROPLANES AND ARTILLERY.

1. If <u>Counter Attack</u> is seen by Aeroplane.

    i. Pilot comes down low and drops three smoke bombs over attackers, indicating flanks and centre of attack.
    ii. Sends LL. LL. LL. followed by a short message describing attack - locality.
    e.g. Area Call "S.b.   S.4.a 6.5 - 8.5 Inf. Mass."

2. On receiving LL. call everybody opens fire on that area.  Mast informs Brigade Commander who must inform Divisional Commander by telephone since latter has no mast.

3. LL. call also used for infantry in close formation in the open.

4. If Infantry seen concentrated in trenches only, then only the area call is sent and answered at discretion of Brigade Commander.

5. Brigades must inform wireless operator which calls to take.

    <u>At present moment mast must be with Brigade</u> because it is stationary, takes area calls, which batteries cannot attend to.

    <u>Afterwards on the move</u> batteries must have masts, which must be allotted at discretion of <u>Brigades</u>, who must arrange for transference.

## COMMUNICATION BETWEEN AEROPLANES AND ARTILLERY.

1. If <u>Counter Attack</u> is seen by Aeroplane.

    i. Pilot comes down low and drops three smoke bombs over attackers, indicating flanks and centre of attack.
    ii. Sends LL. LL. LL. followed by a short message describing attack - locality.
    e.g. Area Call "S.b.  S.4.a 6.5 - 8.5 Inf. Mass."

2. On receiving LL. call everybody opens fire on that area. Mast informs Brigade Commander who must inform Divisional Commander by telephone since latter has no mast.

3. LL. call also used for infantry in close formation in the open.

4. If Infantry seen concentrated in trenches only, then only the area call is sent and answered at discretion of Brigade Commander.

5. Brigades must inform wireless operator which calls to take.

    <u>At present moment</u> mast must be with <u>Brigade</u> because it is stationary, takes area calls, which batteries cannot attend to.

    <u>Afterwards on the move</u> batteries must have masts, which must be allotted at discretion of <u>Brigades</u>, who must arrange for transference.

**"C" Form (Duplicate).**
**MESSAGES AND SIGNALS.**

Army Form C. 2123.
(In books of 50's in duplicate.)
No. of Message ................

|  | Charges to Pay. £ s. d. | Office Stamp. |

Service Instructions.

Handed in at ...... JA ...... Office 10.38 m. Received 10.38 m.

TO

| Sender's Number | Day of Month | In reply to Number | AAA |
| A107 | 14 | | |

Receipt of your BM/C 31/1 of
the 9th is ackd please

FROM PLACE & TIME    JA  10 45 am

SECRET

From

    Officer Commanding,
        253rd ( Northumbrian )Brigade R.F.A.

To
   Brigade Major R.A
        50th Division.

      Receipt of your B.M. 1636/14, dated 14-9-16. is acknowledged.

14-9-16.
                                     Capt R.F.A.
                                 for Lieut Col R.F.A.
             Commdg 253rd ( Northumbrian )Brigade R.F.A.

## "C" Form (Duplicate).
### MESSAGES AND SIGNALS.

Army Form C. 2123.
(In books of 50's in duplicate.)

No. of Message ..................

| | Charges to Pay. | Office Stamp. |
|---|---|---|
| Service Instructions. | £   s.   d. | |

Handed in at ..... 10 ..... Office 10.30 m. Received 10.46 m.

TO ..... FJR

| Sender's Number | Day of Month | In reply to Number | AAA |
|---|---|---|---|
| A14 | 14 | DM1E36/14 | |

Received ack

FROM ..... IO
PLACE & TIME ..... 10.35 PM

## "C" Form (Duplicate).
### MESSAGES AND SIGNALS.

Army Form C. 2123.
(In books of 50's in duplicate.)

No. of Message ................

| Charges to Pay. | Office Stamp. |
| £ s. d. | |

Service Instructions.

Handed in at ................ Office ........ m. Received ........ m.

TO

| Sender's Number | Day of Month | In reply to Number | A A A |
|---|---|---|---|
| | | | |
| 1636/14 received | | | |

FROM
PLACE & TIME    RD 8 26

B.M. 1636/14.

O.C., 251
      252  Bde. R.F.A.
      253
      276

ARTILLERY INSTRUCTIONS.

1. Zero day will be September 15th.
   Zero hour will be - 6.20a.m.
2. Each Brigade R.F.A. will send an officer to 47th Advanced Division H.Q. at FRICOURT FARM at 9.0p.m. to-day to synchronise watches.
3. Acknowledge.

F. Brown

Major R.A.,
B.M. 50th D.A.

14. 9. 16.

SECRET.
\*\*\*\*\*\*\*\*\*\*\*\*

Copy No. 5

ADDENDUM NO.2 to

ARTILLERY INSTRUCTIONS NO.71
BY
THE G.O.C., R.A., III Corps.

H.Q., R.A., III Corps.

1. Zero day will be - September 15th.

   Zero hour will be - 6.20 a.m.

2. Correct time will be distributed to representatives of Divisional Artilleries and Heavy Artillery by a Staff Officer of the IIIrd Corps at 47th Adv. Division H.Q. FRICOURT FARM at 9.0 p.m. to-day, 14th September.

3. For convenience of reference Tanks will be known by the following numbers:-

   | Route A | = | A.1 and A2. |
   | " B | = | B1 and B2 |
   | " C | = | C1 and C2 |
   | " D | = | D2 |
   | " E | = | E1 |

4. Acknowledge.

Issued at 2-45 pm

Staff Officer to G.O.C., R.A.,
Major,
IIIrd Corps.

Addressed all recipients Arty. Instructions No.71.

B.M. 1636/13.

O.C., 253 Bde. R.F.A.

COMMUNICATION BETWEEN AEROPLANES AND ARTILLERY.

1. If <u>Counter Attack</u> is seen by Aeroplane.

    i. Pilot comes down low and drops three smoke bombs over attackers, indicating flanks and centre of attack.

    ii. Sends LL. LL. KK. followed by a short message describing attack - Locality.
       e.g., Area Call "S.b.   S.4.a.6.5. - 8.5. Inf. Mass".

2. On receiving LL call <u>everybody</u>* opens fire on that area. Mast informs Brigade Commander who must inform Divisional Commander by telephone since latter has no mast.

3. LL. call also used for infantry in close formation in the open.

4. If Infantry seen concentrated in trenches only, then only the area call is sent and answered at discretion of Brigade Commander.

5. Brigades must inform wireless operator which calls to take.

    At present moment mast must be with <u>Brigade</u> because it is Stationary, takes area calls, which <u>batteries</u> cannot attend to.

    Afterwards on the move, batteries must have masts, which must be allotted at discretion of <u>Brigades</u> who must arrange for transference.

            ** ** **

    * This during the present programme would only refer to the batteries of 251 and 252 Brigades detailed by Para. 4 of Artillery Instructions, B.M. 1636/5 dated /3.9.16.

14. 9. 16.
                                                Major R.A.,
                                                B.M. 50th D.A.

**"C" Form (Duplicate).** Army Form C. 2123.
## MESSAGES AND SIGNALS. No. of Message...........

| | Charges to Pay. £ s. d. | Office Stamp. |

Service Instructions.

Handed in at................ Office............m. Received.......m.

TO  F JR

| Sender's Number | Day of Month | In reply to Number | A A A |
|---|---|---|---|
| KJH | | | |

BM 1636/15 and BM 1640/15

received

FROM  I O
PLACE & TIME  9.7 PM

SECRET.

B.M./1636/15.

O.C., 251 Bde. R.F.A.
3
267
HD 50 + 15 Division

Reference B.M. 1636/6 - Artillery
Programme, 18-pdr. barrages, Serial No. 6.

Alter to :-

"Lift 50 yards a minute till a line
200 yards beyond second objective is reached.

*F. Br*—

14. 9. 16.
Major R.A.,
B.M. 50th D.A.

SECRET.

B.M. 1636/16.

O.C., 252 Bde. R.F.A.

## PROGRAMME OF BOMBARDMENT.

Right Infantry Brigade will attack PRUE TRENCH from M.34.b.5.8. to M.33.b.7.5. at 7.30p.m. to-day.

**252 Bde.** Will bombard this trench with three 18-pdr. and 1 How. Batteries from 7.0 to 7.30pm on their own zone.
Rate :- 1 round per 18-pdr. per minute.
1 round per 4.5" How. per two minutes.
Lift at 7.30p.m., 200 yards. Increase rate to 2 rounds 18-pdr. per minute and 1 round per how. per minute.
One battery 18-pdr. will barrage from M.33.b.8.8. - M.33.b.5.8. Rate :- 1 round per gun per minute.

**251 Bde.** Will carry out same programme on their own zone except that one 18-pdr. battery will barrage from M.33.b.8.8. to M.33.b.5.8. Rate, 1 round per gun per minute.
Also one Sect. How's on C.T. M.33.b.8.8. and one Sect. How's. on C.T. M.33.b.5.9. Rate :- One round per how. per two minutes.

**253 Bde.**
Will barrage with one 18-pdr. battery within the limits of their zone from M.33.b.8.8. to M.33.b.1.9.
Rate :- As for 251 Bde.

**276 Bde.**
Will barrage from M.33.b.5.8. to M.27.c.7.2. with three 18-pdr. and 1 How. batteries.
Rate :- As for 251 Bde.

Acknowledge by wire.

15. 9. 16.

Major R.A.,
B.M. 50th D.A.

## PROGRAMME OF BOMBARDMENT. 17.9.16.

| Serial No. | Unit Bombarding. | Time. | Objective. | Rate of fire. | Remarks. |
|---|---|---|---|---|---|
| 1. | All available 4.5" Hows. | 5.0 to 5.30 | Area:- M.33.b.9.6. M.33.b.5.7. M.33.b.4.4. M.33.b.8.4. | 1 round per How. per minute. | |
| 2. | 255 Bde :- One Bty. 18-pdrs. | 5.0 to 5.30 | Area as in 1. | 1 round per gun per 2 minutes. | 50% A. 50% AX. |
| 3. | 255 Bde:- 2 Hows. 276 Bde:- 4 18-pdrs. | 6.0pm onwards | CRESCENT ALLEY North of point M.27.d.5.5. | Hows :- 1 round per how per 5 minutes. 18-pdrs - 1 round per gun per 2 minutes. | 100% AX. |
| 4. | 252 Bde:- All available guns and hows. | 8.30 to 8.40 | M.34.b.7.7. to M.34.a.6.6. | 18-pdrs - 2 rds. per gun per minute. Hows.- 2 rounds per how gun per minute. | 70% AX. 30% A. |
| 5. | 251 Bde:- All available guns and hows. | 8.30 to 8.40 | M.34.a.6.6. to M.34.a.0.6. | -do- | -do- |
| 6. | 253 Bde, less two 4.5" Hows. and two 18-pdrs. Empty Bty. | 8.30 onwards | M.33.b.9.9. to M.27.d.5.2. | -do- | -do- |
| 7. | All guns and hows. firing in 4, 5, and 6. | 8.40 | Lift 200 yards. | -do- | 75% A. 25% AX. |

ARTILLERY PROGRAMME. 50th DIVISIONAL ARTILLERY.

Commencing night 16/17 at 8.0p.m.

| Serial No. | Unit bombarding. | Objective. | Remarks. |
|---|---|---|---|
| 1. | 252 Bde. 1 Sect. 18-pdrs. | M.28.d.5.4. | |
| 2. | -do- -do- | COPSE. M.34.b.3.9. | 1 round per gun, and 1 round per howitzer per four minutes. |
| 3. | -do- Remaining 18-pdrs. | M.34.b.5.8. – M.34.a.6.6. | |
| 4. | -do- How. Bty. | SUNKEN ROAD, M.29.d.7.8. – M.28.d.5.6. | |
| 5. | 251 Bde. 18-pdrs. | M.34.a.6.6. – M.34.a.2.6. – M.35.b.9.9. | Will not fire unless called for, except 1 Bty. at rate of 1 round per gun per four minutes on M.34.a.6.6. – M.34.a.2.6. and 1 Sect. Hows. at rate of 1 round per how. per four minutes. |
| 6. | -do- How. Bty. | O.T. M.27.d.5.1. – M.27.d.5.4. | |
| 7. | 253 Bde. 18-pdrs. | M.33.b.9.9. – M.27.d.6.1. – M.27.d.2.1. | Will not fire unless called for. |
| | -do- How. Bty. | –ditto– | |
| 8. | 275 Bde. 18-pdrs. | M.27.d.2.1. – M.27.c.6.4. | Will not fire unless called for except 1 Sect. How's at rate of 1 round per HOW for four minutes. |
| 9. | -do- How. Bty. | O.T. M.27.d.5.4. – M.27.b.6.0. | |

O.C., Bde. R.F.A.

Forwarded for action.
Acknowledge by wire.

16.9.16.

50th D.A.
B.M. 1653/17.

Major R.A.,
B.M. 50th D.A.

ARTILLERY PROGRAMME. 50th DIVISIONAL ARTILLERY.

Commencing night 16/17 at 8.0p.m.

| Serial No. | Unit bombarding. | Objective. | Remarks. |
|---|---|---|---|
| 1. | 252 Bde. 1 Sect. 18-pdrs. | M.28.d.5.4. | |
| 2. | —do— | COPSE. M.34.b.3.9. | 1 round per gun, and 1 round per howitzer per four minutes. |
| 3. | —do— Remaining 18-pdrs. | M.34.b.5.8. — M.34.a.6.6. | |
| 4. | —do— How. Bty. | SUNKEN ROAD, M.28.d.7.8. — M.28.d.5.8. | |
| 5. | 251 Bde. 18-pdrs. | M.34.a.6.6. — M.34.a.2.6. — M.35.b.9.9. | Will not fire unless called for, except 1 Bty. at rate of 1 round per gun per four minutes on M.34.a.6.6. — M.34.a.2.6. and 1 Sect. Hows. at rate of 1 round per how. per four minutes. |
| 6. | —do— How. Bty. | O.T. M.27.d.5.1. — N.27.d.5.4. | |
| 7. | 255 Bde. 18-pdrs. | M.33.b.9.9. — M.27.d.6.1. — M.27.d.2.1. | Will not fire unless called for. |
|  | —do— How. Bty. | —ditto— | |
| 8. | 276 Bde. 18-pdrs. | M.27.d.3.1. — M.27.c.6.4. | Will not fire unless called for except 1 Sect. How's at rate of 1 round per How for four minutes. |
| 9. | —do— How. Bty. | O.T. M.27.d.5.4. — M.27.b.6.0. | |

O.C., Bde. R.F.A.

Forwarded for action.
Acknowledge by wire.

16. 9. 16.

50th D.A.
B.M. 1038/17.

Major R.A.,
B.M. 50th D.A.

SECRET.

COPY OF TELEGRAM.

G. 56.   16th. AAA   WARNING ORDER NO. 131 AAA  Fourth
Army has made further progress to-day and will continue the
attack on 18th Sept. in conjunction with French AAA  14th
Corps attacking MORVAL LES BOEUFS and 15th Corps
GUEUDECOURT and GROVE ALLEY AAA 3rd Corps will attack
the FLERS LINE  up to EAUCOURT L'ABBAYE inclusive, the
enemy's trenches from M.23.c.1.5. to M.27.c.8.3. and the
trenches from M.27.c.0.4., M.28.b.8.2. to M.26.a.2.0.

     Exact boundaries between Divisions will be notified
later AAA

     Divisions will prepare plans for this operation
without delay AAA As many tanks as possible will be allotted
to Divisions for use during the attack.

     Night firing and counter battery work will be
continued vigorously and the bombardment of the objectives
will be commenced to-morrow under instructions now being
issued by B.G.R.A.

     The Bombardment will be continuous from 6.30a.m.
on the 18th.

     Zero will probably be in the afternoon AAA

     Addressed all Divisions 3rd Corps, H.A. and O.C.
4 Section, D. Co. Heavy Section M.G. Corps.

From 3rd Corps.
11.40pm BY S.D.R.                                (sgd) B. BATTYE Major G.S.

-2-

50th D.A.
B.M. 1836/18.

O.C., 4 Bde.S R.F.A.

For information.

17. 9. 16.

Major R.A.,
B.M. 50th D.A.

SECRET.

B.M. 1636/19.

O.C., A Bde. R.F.A.
_____

Please arrange to comply with programme attached.
Acknowledge receipt by wire.

*[signature]*

Major R.A.,
B.M. 50th D.A.

17. 9. 16.

## PROGRAMME OF BOMBARDMENT. 17.9.16.

| Serial No. | Unit Bombarding. | Time. | Objective. | Rate of fire. | Remarks. |
|---|---|---|---|---|---|
| 1. | All available 4.5" Hows. | 5.0 to 5.30 | Areas:- M.33.b.9.c. M.33.b.5.7. M.33.b.4.4. M.33.b.6.4. | 1 round per How. per minute. | 50% A. 50% AX. |
| 2. | 255 Bde:- One Bty. 18-pdrs. | 5.0 to 5.30 | Area as in 1. | 1 round per gun per 2 minutes. | 100% AX. |
| 3. | 255 Bde:- 2 Hows. 276 Bde:- 4 18-pdrs. | 6.0pm onwards | CRESCENT ALLEY North of point M.27.d.6.3. | Hows :- 1 round per how. per 3 minutes. 18-pdrs - 1 round per gun per 2 minutes. | 70% AX. 50% A. |
| 4. | 252 Bde:- All available guns and hows. | 8.30 to 8.40 | M.34.b.7.7. to M.34.a.6.6. | 18-pdrs - 2 rds. per gun per minute. Hows.- 2 rounds per how. per minute. | --do-- |
| 5. | 251 Bde:- All available guns and hows. | 8.30 to 8.40 | M.34.a.6.6. to M.34.a.0.0. | --do-- | --do-- |
| 6. | 255 Bde, less two 4.5" Hows. | 8.30 onwards | M.33.b.9.9. to M.27.d.3.2. | --do-- | --do-- |
| 7. | All guns and hows. firing in 4,"5. | 8.40 | Lift 200 yards. | --do-- | 75% A. 25% AX. |

B.M. 1636/20.

PROGRAMME OF BOMBARDMENT.    NIGHT 18/19th SEPTEMBER, 1916.

| Serial No. | Unit bombarding. | Time. | Objective. | Rate of fire. | Remarks. |
|---|---|---|---|---|---|
| 1. | 252 Bde. 18-pdrs. | | M.34.b.8.7. to M.34.a.6.6. | | Drop 200 yards and search back 400 yards at intervals. |
| 2. | 252 Bde. Two 4.5" Hows. Two 18-pdrs. | | on SUNKEN ROAD in M.29.d. | | Searching at intervals. |
| 3. | 251 Bde. 18-pdrs. | 8.0p.m. to 8.0a.m. | M.34.a.6.6. to M.34.a.0.6. Search back to M.28.c. Central. | One round on each objective every five minutes. | |
| 4. | 251 Bde. One 18-pdr. gun. | | CRESCENT ALLEY, North of M.27.d.5.0. | | |
| 5 | 253 Bde. 1 Howitzer. 1 18-pdr. | | CRESCENT ALLEY North of M.27.d.5.0. | | |
| | 1 18-pdr of B/253. | | Enfilade SUNKEN ROAD M.28.d.5.4. to M.29.a.4.4. | | |
| 6. | 276 Bde. 1 Battery 18-pdrs. | | Trench M.27.b.7.0. to M.29.a.0.2. | | |

C.C.,    Bde. R.F.A.
+-------------

Please arrange to comply with the above.
Acknowledge receipt by wire.

[signature]
Major R.A.
B.M. 50th D.A.
18.9.16.

B.M. 1836/20.

PROGRAMME OF BOMBARDMENT.   NIGHT 18/19th SEPTEMBER, 1916.

| Serial No. | Unit bombarding. | Time. | Objective. | Rate of fire. | Remarks. |
|---|---|---|---|---|---|
| 1. | 252 Bde. 18-pdrs. | | M.34.b.3.7. to M.34.a.d.6. | | Drop 200 yards and search back 400 yards at intervals. |
| 2. | 252 Bde. Two 4.5" Hows. Two 18-pdrs. | | On SUNKEN ROAD in M.28.d. | | Searching at intervals. |
| 3. | 251 Bde. 18-pdrs. | 8.0p.m. to 8.0a.m. | M.34.a.d.6. to M.34.a.0.6. Search back to M.28.c. Central. | One round on each objective every five minutes. | |
| 4. | 251 Bde. One 18-pdr. gun. | | CRESCENT ALLEY, North of M.27.d.5.0. | | |
| 5 | 255 Bde. 1 Howitzer. 1 18-pdr. 1 18-pdr of B/253. | | CRESCENT ALLEY North of M.27.d.5.0.<br>Enfilade SUNKEN ROAD M.29.d.5.4. to M.29.a.4.4. | | |
| 6. | 276 Bde. 1 battery 18-pdrs. | | Trench M.27.b.7.0. to M.28.a.0.2. | | |

O.C., ......... Bde. R.F.A.

Please arrange to comply with the above.

Acknowledge receipt by wire.

Major R.A.
B.M. 50th B.A.
18.9.16.

SECRET.

B.M. 1636/23.

O.C., 251 / 252 / 253 / 276 Bde. R.F.A.

1. At 8.0p.m. to-night a bombing attack will be made by 151st Infantry Brigade on THE CRESCENT and thence down the STARFISH LINE and PRUE TRENCH.

2. Serial Nos. 9, 11, 13, 14, 15, and 16 of Programme of Bombardment, 10.0a.m. 19/9/16 to 10.0a.m. 20/9/16 are cancelled.

3. All registration on PRUE TRENCH and STARFISH LINE must cease at 7.50p.m.

4. At 8.0p.m. and onwards till further orders, a light barrage will be put on the line :-

| | | | |
|---|---|---|---|
| 252 Bde. | 18-pdrs. | M.29.c.3.1. to M.28.d.5.0. | |
| 251 Bde. | 18-pdrs. | M.28.d.5.0. to M.28.c.8.0. | Rate of fire one round per gun per two minutes. |
| 253 Bde. | 18-pdrs. | M.28.c.8.0. to M.34.a.0.9. | |
| 276 Bde. | 18-pdrs. | M.34.a.0.9. to M.27.d.3.0. to M.27. Central. | |

5. These will be the S.O.S. barrage for to-night.

6. Serial Nos. 10 and 12 will continue as ordered.

7. 4.5" Howitzers will fire at a slow rate on roads and C.T.'s at longer range than the 18-pdr barrage at the discretion of Brigade Commanders. Ammunition allotted, 50 RX per battery.

8. Acknowledge.

Major R.A.,
B.M. 50th D.A.

19.9.16.

PROGRAMME OF BOMBARDMENT, 10.0am 19.9.16 to 10.0am 20.9.16.

| Serial No. | Unit bombarding. | Time. | Objective. | Rate of fire. | Remarks. |
|---|---|---|---|---|---|
| 1. | 252 Bde. | to be completed before 5.0pm. | STARFISH LINE, M.34.b.5.0. to M.34.a.8.0. | | Careful registration. |
| 2. | | | PRUE TRENCH, M.34.b.8.7. to M.34.b.4.7. | | |
| 3. | 251 Bde. | | STARFISH LINE, M.34.a.8.0. to M.34.a.5.0. | | Careful registration. |
| 4. | | | PRUE TRENCH, M.34.b.4.7. to M.34.a.7.6. | | |
| 5. | 253 Bde. | As required; | STARFISH LINE, M.34.a.5.0. to M.34.a.1.1. | | Careful registration. |
| 6. | | | PRUE TRENCH, M.34.a.7.6. to M.34.a.0.6. | | |
| 7. | 276 Bde. | | STARFISH LINE, M.34.a.1.1. to M.33.b.8.2. | | Careful registration. |
| 8. | | | XXXXXXXXXXXXXXXXXXX CRESCENT ALLEY North of M.27.d.5.0. | | |

## SHEET 2.

| Serial No. | Unit bombarding. | Time. | Objective. | Rate of fire. | No. of rounds. | Remarks. |
|---|---|---|---|---|---|---|
| ~~9.~~ | 252 Bde. | | M.34.b.8.7. to M.34.a.6.8. | Occasional bursts. | 100 A and AX. | Drop 200 yards and search back 400 yards. |
| 10. | 252 Bde. Two 4.5 Hows. Two 18-pdrs. | | On SUNKEN ROAD in M.28.d. | Various. | 50 BX. 100 A and AX | Searching at intervals. |
| ~~11.~~ | 251 Bde: 18-pdrs. | | M.34.a.6.6. to M.34.a.0.6. Search back to M.28.c.Central. | Various. | 100 A and AX. | |
| 12. | One 18-pdr. gun of B/253 | | Enfilade SUNKEN ROAD M.29.d.5.4. to M.29.a.4.4. | Single rds. at uncertain intervals. | 50 A and AX. | |
| ~~13.~~ | 252 Bde. | 8.0p.m. onwards | As in 1 and 2. | slow, steady fire. | 50 BX. 200 A and AX. | |
| ~~14.~~ | 251 Bde. | --do-- | As in 3 and 4. | --do-- | --do-- | |
| ~~15.~~ | 253 Bde. | --do-- | As in 5 and 6. | --do-- | --do-- | |
| ~~16.~~ | 275 Bde. | --do-- | As in 7 and 8. | --do-- | --do-- | |
| 17. | 251 Bde; One 18-pdr gun. | | Enfilade ~~CRESCENT~~ ALLEY North of M.7.d.5.0. | Single rds. at uncertain intervals. | 50 A and AX. | |

O.C., Bde. R.F.A.

1. Please arrange to comply with the above.
2. Acknowledge receipt by wire.

Major R.A.,
B.M. 50th D.A.

19: 9: 1916:

50th D.A.
B.M. 1632/21.

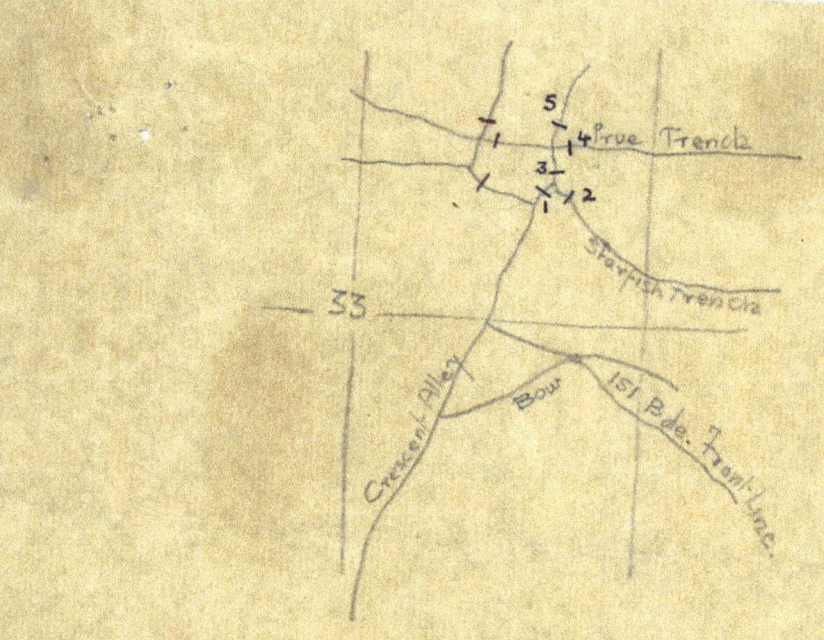

SECRET.
G.201.

Commanding Officer,
   8th Bn. Durham L.I.
50th Division (For information).
149th Inf. Brigade,   "
69th Inf. Brigade.   "
, C.R.A.

Reference attached sketch.

**Suggested plan for Bombing Attack on THE CRESCENT.**

1. Party to consist of 1 Officer and 3 Bombing Squads.

2. ZERO - 7 p.m.

Procedure.

3. Party move up trenches as far as point X, then leave trench and move North-west until inner flank is clear of O.T. Then move N.N.E. with O.T. as right guide and strike objective at point Y. Party will in addition be guided by flares fired from 150th Brigade BLOCKS parallel with and along German trenches.

Party crawl from shell hole to shell hole till within throwing distance of German trench, then at a given signal all throw bombs and leap in when they burst.

The whole then turn to the Right and move to junction with CRESCENT ALLEY, the leading squad establishing Block 1 if there is any resistance. If there is no resistance in that part of the trench, the leading squad should proceed to bomb down STARFISH, there if opposed establishing Block 2. 2nd squad move as rapidly as possible to PRUE TRENCH and bomb down it; if opposed apply Block 4. Block 3 should be applied if squad cannot reach PRUE TRENCH. 3rd squad proceed up O.T. and apply Block 5.

The 1st and 3rd squads will be responsible for gaining touch with 150th Brigade Blocks.

4. The operations will be preceded by a bombardment by 2" Trench Mortars and Stokes Guns. The bombardment will lift at ZERO, at which hour the party will be in position to assault.

The bombardment will creep gradually from point Y to Block 5 and then travel down PRUE TRENCH and STARFISH TRENCH.

5. "Pass words" will be arranged for as follows:
Should a man of the 8th D.L.I. challenge a man of the 150th Brigade, the answer will be "YORK". In the reverse case the answer would be "DURHAM".

6. Party will be supported in case of need by 2 Vickers guns situated about X.28.d.5.7. also by those of 150th Brigade Blocks.

                         Captain,
                         Brigade Major,
                         151st Infantry Brigade.

19.9.1916.

SECRET.
G.202.
19.9.16.

Commanding Officer,
    8th Bn. Durham L.I.
50th Division.    (For information).
149th Inf. Brigade.  "    "
69th Inf. Brigade.  "    "
C.R.A.              "    "

### Addenda and Corrigenda to Programme for Bombing Attack on the CRESCENT.

Delete para. 1 and substitute:

    "Party to consist of 1 Officer and 3 Bombing Squads, 8th D.L.I., with 1 Officer and 2 Bombing Squads 8th D.L.I. in Support".

Para. 2.  For 7 p.m. read 8 p.m.

Paras 3, 5, and 6.  For 150th Brigade read 69th Brigade.

Delete para. 4 and substitute the following:

    Para. 4 (a)  From 4 p.m. to 8 p.m. the Heavy Artillery will bombard PRUE TRENCH from M.34.a.0.6 to M.35.a.0.7 and STARFISH TRENCH from M.34.a.0.2 to M.34.b.2.1, also point M.34.b.5.1.

    (b)  From 4 p.m. to 8 p.m. 2 guns 151st T.M.B. will bombard STARFISH TRENCH from M.33.b.6.4 to about M.34.a.5.2.

    (c)  1 Stokes Gun 69th T.M.B. from 69th Brigade Blocks in THE CRESCENT will, starting at 8 p.m., enfilade PRUE TRENCH Eastwards from point M.33.b.7.6 and STARFISH TRENCH Eastwards from M.33.b.6.4.

Add para. 7:  At 8 p.m. a patrol will be sent out by the Left forward Company of the 8th D.L.I. and one from the Centre forward Company of the 8th D.L.I. to watch the proceedings of the Bombers Raid and look for opportunities to assist its operations by stamping over the open down into STARFISH TRENCH.

                              Captain,
                            Brigade Major,
19.9.1916.                151st Infantry Brigade.

SECRET.

B.M. 1636/24.

O.C.,
  Bde. R.F.A.
------------------------

Please arrange to comply with attached programme.
Acknowledge receipt by wire.

               *F. [signature]*
                Major R.A.,
20. 9. 16.            B.M. 50th D.A.

PROGRAMME OF BOMBARDMENT, 10.0a.m. 20/9/16 to 10.0a.m. 21/9/16.

| Serial No. | Unit bombarding. | Time. | Objective. | Rate of fire. | No of rounds. | Remarks. |
|---|---|---|---|---|---|---|
| 1. | All Brigades. | | PRUE TRENCH. STARFISH LINE. | As required. | | Careful registration. After registration 100 rds. BX per Bty to be fired to check. |
| 2. | 252 Bde. Two 4.5" Hows. Two 18-pdrs. | | Sunken Road in M.28.d. | Uncertain intervals. | 100 BX. 200 A and AX. | Continuous, searching at intervals. |
| 3. | 251 Bde. 18-pdrs. | | Barrage line M.34.b.2.5. to M.34.a.6.5. | -do- | 200 A and AX. | Search back for 600 yards. |
| 4. | 276 Bde. One 4.5" How. One 18-pdr. | | CRESCENT ALLEY M.33.b.5.9. to M.27.b.6.0. | Uncertain intervals. | 50 BX. 100 A and AX. | Continuous searching. |
| 5. | 276 Bde. One 4.5" How. One 18-pdr. 3 | | C.T. M.33.b.7.5. to M.27.d.9.0. | Uncertain intervals, principally at night. | 50 BX. 100 A and AX. | Continuous searching. |
| 6. | 252 Bde. Two 4.5" Hows. Two 18-pdrs. | | Cross roads M.22.c.9.0. | | 50 BX. 200 AX. | Continuous. |
| 7. | All Brigades. | 9.0p.m. to 8.0a.m. | Any C.T.'s and roads in their own zone. | Stray rounds at uncertain intervals. | 50 BX. 200 A and AX. | This is in addition to selected targets and objectives are at discretion of Bde. C.O.'s. |

PROGRAMME OF BOMBARDMENT. 10 a.m. 21/9/16 to 10 a.m. 22/9/16.

| Serial No. | Unit bombarding | Time | Objective | Rate of fire | No. of rounds | Remarks. |
|---|---|---|---|---|---|---|
| 1. | All 4.3" How. Bty's. | | STARFISH LINE PRUE TRENCH on own Zone. | Slow bombardment | 400 BX per battery 150 BX per battery | |
| 2. | 252 Bde. 9/18 pdrs. | 10.0 a.m. to 7.0 p.m. | SUNKEN ROAD in M.28.d. | Uncertain intervals. | 130 A 150 AX | Continuous searching at intervals. |
| 3. | 276 Bde. One 4.5 How. | | CRESCENT ALLEY M.33.B.5.7. to M.27.d.6.3. | Slow bombardment | 80 BX | |
| 4. | One 4.5 How. | | C.T.M.33.b.7.5. to M.27.d.6.6. | Slow bombardment | 80 BX | |
| 5. | All Bdes. 18 pdrs. | 7.0 p.m. to 10.0 pm | Objectives bombarded during daytime and C.T's. & roads in own Zone. | Bursts of fire at uncertain intervals. | 600 A and AX per battery. | |
| 6. | D/252 Bde. | 10.0 pm | SUNKEN ROAD from M.29.d.5.4. to M.29.a.2.0. | One round every 20 secs. | 80 PS | If wind is suitable. |

Acknowledged by wire.

(signed) Major R.A.,
H.Q. 50th D.A.

B.M. 1656/25.

B.M. 1647/2.

O.C., A Bde. R.F.A. *[handwritten annotation]*

PROGRAMME FOR NIGHT 22/23rd SEPTEMBER, 1916.

1. All trenches where work is reported going on that were fired on in daylight to be fired on at intervals during the night.

2. Roads and C.T.'s in each Brigade zone will also be fired on at intervals.

3. LE SARS will be fired at with P.S. from 9.0 to 11.0pm by D/250 and D/256 - 144 rounds per Battery.

4. Allotment of ammunition for the night 8.0p.m. to 8.0a.m., - 600 A and AX per Brigade.

5. As soon as it is light enough on morning of 23rd all opportunities of engaging visible targets to be seized immediately.

6. S.O.S. Barrages will be as notified in my B.M.1647/1 of to-day's date, till further orders.

7. Acknowledge.

22. 9. 16.

Major R.A.,
B.M. 50th D.A.

PROGRAMME OF BOMBARDMENT.    11.0a.m. 22/9/16 to 11.0a.m. 23/9/16.

| Serial No. | Unit bombarding. | Time. | Objective. | Rate of fire. | No. of rounds. | Remarks. |
|---|---|---|---|---|---|---|
| 1. | 251 Bde. | | Trenches M.23.b.3.3. to M.28.b.2.5. | Slow bombardment. | 400 BX. 400 AX. | Only to be fired at with direct visual observation after position of our own infantry is known. |
| 2. | | | LE SARS, M.16.c. | Bursts of fire at intervals. | 400 BX. | |
| 3. | 253 Bde. | | Trench M.28.b.2.5. to M.33.a.3.6. | Slow bombardment. | 800 A and AX. | Only to be fired at with direct visual observation after position of our own infantry is known. |
| 4. | | | LE SARS, M.16.d. | Bursts of fire at intervals. | 400 BX. | |
| 5. | 276 Bde. | | Trench M.28.a.4.4. to M.21.d.5.3. | Slow bombardment. | 800 A and AX. | |
| 6. | 252 Bde.; B and C Batteries. | | Trench M.23.c.5.2. to M.23.c.2.2. | Slow bombardment. | 800 A and AX. | |

O.C., Bde.    NOTES :-  (1) Any fleeting opportunity is to be seized at once with the roving battery of each brigade. } 400 A and AX per brigade.

(2) Provisional S.O.S. barrages are attached.

(5) Acknowledge.

B.M. 1647/5.

Major R.A.,
B.M. 50th D.A.

SECRET.

50th Divn.
G.546.

C.R.A.

1. Reference 50th Division Operation Order 55 dated 21st September, the attack will take place to-morrow the 25th Sept.

2. The final objective of the III Corps is the line M.29.d.5.9. - M.29.c.8.6. - M.29.c.0.1. - M.28.d.1.7. - thence along the track to M.27.d.0.5. - M.27.c.5.6. - M.27.a.4.0. - M.27.a.0.4. - M.26.b.0.9.

3. Any portion of this line not already occupied will be occupied at zero hour to-morrow and patrols pushed forward along the FLERS line, CRESCENT ALLEY and the C.T. in M.27.a.
   The whole line will then be consolidated and all Divisions will push out strong posts as far as possible with the object of gaining further ground and forming a jumping off line for the next assault.

4. The 150th Inf. Bde. will to-night (24/25) dig a continuous fire trench along the line mentioned above from M.26.d.1.7. to CRESCENT ALLEY and from M.28.d.1.7. to connect with the 1st Division at M.28.d.8.0.
   One Company Pioneers is allotted to the 150th Brigade to dig a C.T. from PRUE TRENCH about M.34.a.5.6. - M.28.c.8.0. - M.28.c.7.4. during the night 24/25 September.

5. At zero hour on 25th September the 18-pdrs. of the 50th Divisional Artillery will open an intense fire on the nearest enemy trenches until 0.03.

6. Flares will be called for by contact patrol at 0.30 and plus two hours.
   Please ensure that all advanced posts and flanks shew flares at these hours.

7. Zero hour will be notified later.
   Representatives of Infantry and Artillery Brigades will receive correct time from a Staff Officer of the Corps at FRICOURT FARM at Six hours before zero.

8. Acknowledge.

(sgd) H. KARSLAKE, Lt. Col.
General Staff,
50th Division.

4.15p.m.
24th September, 1916.

-2-

50th D.A.
B.M. 1647/7.

O.C., 4 Bde R.F.A.

For information and action.

Reference Para. 7, on 25th September zero hour will be 12.35p.m.
Representatives will attend at FRICOURT FARM at 6.30a.m.

Acknowledge.

Major R.A.,
B.M. 50th D.A.

24.9.16.

B.M. 1647/3.

O.C.,
    Bde. R.F.A.

ARTILLERY INSTRUCTIONS.    NIGHT 23/24th SEPT. 1916.

1. D/276 and D/250 will each fire 144 rounds P.S. into LE SARS commencing at 11.0p.m.  Fire for first 10 minutes to be as intense as possible, afterwards one round every one minute from each Battery.

   During the first 10 minutes one 18-pdr Battery, 276 Bde., and one 18-pdr Battery 253 Bde. will fire A into LE SARS, after this, occasional salvoes of A and AX will be fired into LE SARS throughout the night.

2. D/251 and D/252 will also fire P.S. and S.K. shell into EAUCOURT L'ABBAYE at 11.15p.m.  In the same manner one 18-pdr Battery of 252 Bde and one 18-pdr Battery of 251 Bde. also firing shrapnel as in 1.

3. Ammunition allotted during the past 24 hours has not been fired.  Every effort must be made to render the life of the German absolutely unbearable;  all roads and approaches by which rations and reliefs can come up to be kept under fire at intervals throughout the night.

   To be communicated to all batteries.

4. Acknowledge.

                                Major R.A.,
                            B.M. 50th D.A.

B.M. 1647/3.

O.C.,
    Bde. R.F.A.

ARTILLERY INSTRUCTIONS.    NIGHT 23/24th SEPT. 1916.

1.  D/276 and D/250 will each fire 144 rounds P.S. into LE SARS commencing at 11.0p.m.    Fire for first 10 minutes to be as intense as possible, afterwards one round every one minute from each Battery.

    During the first 10 minutes one 18-pdr Battery, 276 Bde., and one 18-pdr Battery 253 Bde. will fire A into LE SARS, after this, occasional salvoes of A and AX will be fired into LE SARS throughout the night.

2.  D/251 and D/252 will also fire P.S. and S.K. shell into EAUCOURT L'ABBAYE at 11.15p.m.    In the same manner one 18-pdr Battery of 252 Bde and one 18-pdr Battery of 251 Bde. also firing shrapnel as in 1.

3.  Ammunition allotted during the past 24 hours has not been fired.    Every effort must be made to render the life of the German absolutely unbearable;    all roads and approaches by which rations and reliefs can come up to be kept under fire at intervals throughout the night.

    To be communicated to all batteries.

4.  Acknowledge.

                                            Major R.A.,
                                            B.M. 50th D.A.

PROGRAMME OF BOMBARDMENT, 11.0a.m. 24/9/16 to 11.0a.m. 25/9/16.

B.M./1647/5.

| Serial No. | Unit bombarding. | Time. | Objective. | No. of rounds. | Remarks. |
|---|---|---|---|---|---|
| 1. | 252 Bde :— Hows. | Day. | All new work in zone seen or reported. | 500 BX. 100 PS | |
| | 18-pdrs | Night | Enemy works, roads, & C.T.'s. | 1500 A and AX. | |
| 2. | 251 Bde :— Hows. | Day. | Special task already ordered. | 500 BX. 100 PS. | |
| | 18-pdrs. | Night. | Enemy works, roads & C.T.'s. | 1500 A and AX. | |
| 3. | 253 Bde:— Hows. | Day. | All new work in zone seen or reported. | 500 BX. 100 PS. | |
| | 18-pdrs. | Night. | Enemy works, roads, & C.T.'s. | 1500 A and AX. | Special attention to be given at night to slip of ground between Road and Bank in M.22.c. and d. |
| 4. | 276 Bde :— Hows. | Day. | As above. | 500 BX. 100 PS. | |
| | 18-pdrs. | Night. | | 1500 A and AX. | |

NOTES :—
(1) Targets for P.S. will be given later.
(2) All working parties, etc., seen to be fired on at once.
(3) Special attention is drawn to Para. 3 of B.M. 1647/3 of 25.9.16.
(4) Acknowledge.

O.C., ........ Bde. R.F.A.

Major R.A.,
B.M. 50th D.A.

B.M. 1647/6.

O.C., 251
~~252~~ Bdes. R.F.A.
~~253~~
276.

P. S. shell will be fired to-night as follows :-

At 9.30p.m.

1. D/251 will fire at OLD QUARRY, M.22.d.5.1.

2. ( D/250    Will fire at slip of ground between road
   ( D/276    and bank from M.22.d.1.1. to M.22.d.2.7.

3. Rate of fire for first 10 minutes intense; afterwards one round per battery per minute.

4. 253 Bde. will fire A at a rapid rate at same targets from 9.30 to 9.33p.m.

5. Acknowledge.

24. 9. 16.

*[signature]*
Major R.A.,
B.M. 50th D.A.

B.M.1647/13.

O.C.,
    Bde. R.F.A.

## WARNING ORDER.

1. 50th Division will continue the attack on 1st October.

2. Zero hour will be in the afternoon.

3. Brigades will cut wire on their own Zones today commencing at 11.0 a.m.

4. 151 Infantry Bde. has been warned.

5. Advantage will be taken of this to carefully register barrages by 18 pdrs on German front line so that it is completely and fully covered.

6. Barrages must be so arranged that the fire of one battery per brigade can be turned on to any target of opportunity without leaving gaps in barrage.

7. Allotment of ammunition for wire cutting is as required. O.C.Brigades will use whichever batteries of their brigades they consider most suitable.

8. Acknowledge.

30/9/16.

                          Major, R.A.
                          B.M. 50 D.A.

M 21 d 5.3
M 21 b.7.4
21 b.6.8
15 d 8.8
10 central

S E C R E T.   COPY NO. 12

RIGHT DIVISIONAL ARTILLERY GROUP OPERATION ORDER NO. 63.

Reference Map :- Fourth Army
1/10,000 Trench Map No. 694.           30th. September 1916.

1.
INFORMATION.   (a)   The attack will be resumed on the 1st. October.

(b)   The infantry of 47th. Division will move forward to the attack of the objective allotted to them (shown in green on attached map) at ZERO hour.

The 141st. Infantry Brigade will carry out the attack.
The whole of this Brigade will be in front of the SWITCH LINE before daylight on the 1st. October.

(c)   The objectives and boundaries of the Divisions on the flanks of the 47th. Division are shown on attached map.

(d)   The New Zealand Division is attacking on the Right and the 50th. Division on the Left of the 47th. Division.

The New Zealand Division is attacking in a north-westerly direction and will direct its attack on the line Strong Point M.23.b.7.4. - M.23.d.5.8 crossing the track running across M.24.c. and a. at ZERO plus 10 minutes.
They will also co-operate by attacking at ZERO along the FLERS SUPPORT LINE as far as the line of the road at M.29.b.4.2.

The 50th. Division will attack as their first objective the front and support FLERS LINE; at ZERO plus 30 minutes they will push forward to the enemy's work in M.22.a.8.8. and at the same time the 23rd. Division will push forward strong patrols into the Southern portion of LE SARS.
At ZERO plus 1 hour 30 minutes the 23rd. Division will push patrols to the Northern portion of LE SARS.

(e)   The main line of resistance for 47th. Division will be the green line shown on the attached map, and posts will be pushed forward approximately to the points shown on the attached map.
In pushing forward posts the great importance of securing favourable points for observation must be born in mind.

(f)   Two Tanks will co-operate under orders which will be issued by the lllrd. Corps.
The route and starting points for the Tanks will be notified later.

(g)   The 34th. Squadron R.F.C. will detail a contact patrol aeroplane to fly over the objective from ZERO onwards.
Yellow flares will be shown when called for, at 4 p.m., 5 p.m. and 6 p.m.

2.
ARTILLERY
ACTION.      Divisional Artillery 4.5" Howitzers in conjunction with the Heavy Artillery will begin a regular bombardment of the objective and EAUCOURT L' ABBAYE defences at 7.0 a.m.
At ZERO the Divisional Artillery will cover the advance of the Infantry as per attached programme.
The creeping barrage will start 200 yards from the German front line (FLERS LINE) at ZERO and lift back 50 yards each minute till ZERO plus 3 minutes when it will lift on to the Support line.

P.T.O.

(2)

The fixed barrage will commence at ZERO on the front line and at ZERO plus 4 minutes lift also on to the Support line

At ZERO plus 5 the combined barrage will start creeping back 50 yards each minute till it arrives 150 yards beyond the line of posts on the attached map in which position it will become stationary.

It must be borne in mind that the left of the New Zealand attack at ZERO plus 14 minutes will have reached point N.23.b.8.4., its objective.

3. SYNCHRONIZATION OF WATCHES.

A representative from each Brigade 47th. D.A. and 25th. Brigade R.F.A., 1st. Division will be at 47th. Division Advanced H.Q. at FRICOURT FARM at 10 a.m. October 1st. to synchronize watches with a Staff Officer of lllrd. Corps.

N.B. All times are normal GREENWICH time. The change from present summer hour to normal GREENWICH time will take place at 1 a.m. on October 1st. at which hour clocks will be put back one hour, i.e. to 12 midnight.

4. ZERO HOUR.

ZERO hour will be 3.15 p.m.

map not attached

H.Q. 47th. D.A.

30th. Sept. 1916.

Major R.A.,
Brigade Major,
Right D.A. Group.

Issued to :-

Copy No.
1. War Diary.
2. File.
3. 25th. Brigade R.F.A.
4. 235th. Brigade R.F.A.
5. 236th. Brigade R.F.A.
6. 237th. Brigade R.F.A.
7. 238th. Brigade R.F.A.
8. 47th. D.A.C.
9. D.T.M.O. 47th. Division.
10. 47th. Division.
11. 14th. D.A.
12. 50th. D.A.
13. lllrd. Corps R.A.
14. lllrd. Corps H.A.

SECRET.

FIRE TIME TABLE - 4.5" HOWITZERS. (To accompany Right D.A. Group Op.O. No. 63.)

| UNIT. | TIME. | OBJECTIVE. | PROCEDURE. | REMARKS. |
|---|---|---|---|---|
| D/236 | 7 a.m. to 2 p.m. | Communication trench - K.23.d.0.0. to K.23.d.4½.8½. | Bombardment. | At 2 p.m. changes on to FLERS front line. |
| " | 2 p.m. to Zero plus 2 minutes. | FLERS front line - K.29.a.9½.8. to K.23.c.4½.2½. | Bombardment. | At plus 2 minutes lifts on to FLERS support line. |
| " | Plus 2 minutes to plus 4 minutes. | FLERS support line - K.29.a.9½.8½. to K.23.c.6.3½. | Bombardment. | At Zero plus 4 minutes lifts on to road. |
| " | Zero plus 4 minutes onwards. | Road from K.23.t.5.8. to K.18.c.4.6½. | Bombardment. | |
| D/25. | 7 a.m. to 2 p.m. | Small communication trench at K.23.c.9.5½. and communication trenches running North-West from EAUCOURT L'ABBAYE in K.23.a. | Bombardment. | At 2 p.m. changes on to FLERS front line. |
| " | 2 p.m. to Zero plus 2 minutes. | FLERS front line - K.23.c.4½.2½. to K.23.c.0.7. | Bombardment. | At Plus 2 minutes lifts on to FLERS support line. |
| " | Zero plus 2 minutes to plus 4 minutes. | FLERS support line from - K.23.c.6.3½. to K.23.c.1.8. | Bombardment. | At Plus 4 creeps back by one 50 yard lift per minute till line K.17.c.4.0. to K.23.b.0.9½. is reached.— about Zero plus 20. |
| " | Zero plus 20 onwards. | Track from K.17.c.7½.3½. to K.17.c.8.0. | Bombardment. | |

P.T.O.

(2)

| UNIT. | TIME. | OBJECTIVE. | PROCEDURE. | REMARKS. |
|---|---|---|---|---|
| D/238 | 7 a.m. to 2 p.m. | Small communication trenches about K.23.c.2.9½.; K.23.a. 1.½. and K.22.b.9.2½. | Bombardment. | At 2 p.m. changes on to FLERS front line. |
| " | 2 p.m. to Zero plus 2 minutes. | FLERS front line - K.23.c.0.7.; to K.22.b.3.1½. | Bombardment. | At plus 2 minutes lifts on to FLERS support line. |
| " | Zero plus 2 minutes to plus 4 minutes. | FLERS support line - K.23.c.1½.8½. to K.22.b.4½.4. | Bombardment. | At Zero plus 4 creeps back by one 50 yard lift per minute till the line K.17.c.4½.0. to K.16.d.6½.1. is reached - about Zero plus 20. |
| " | Zero plus 20 onwards. | Road from K.17.c.4.1½. to K.17.c.0.8. | | |

(1) No fire to be East of North and South line through K.23. central after Zero plus 4 minutes.

(2) Rate of fire - 4.5" Howitzers :-  
    7 a.m. to 2 p.m.    -    50 rounds per hour per Battery.  
    2 p.m. to Zero    -    50 rounds per hour per Battery.  
    Zero to Zero plus 4    -    2 rounds per gun per minute.  
    Zero plus 4 onwards.    -    1 round per gun per minute.

S E C R E T.

FIRE TIME TABLE - 18-POUNDERS.   (To accompany Right D.A. Group OP.O. No. 23).

| UNIT. | TIME. | OBJECTIVE. | PROCEDURE. | REMARKS. |
|---|---|---|---|---|
| 235th. Bde. R.F.A. | Zero to Zero plus 1 minute. | M.23.c.0.2. to M.23.d.3.7. | Barrage. | At Zero plus 1 creeps back at rate of 50 yards per minute for 3 mins. |
| | Zero plus 3 minutes to plus 5 minutes. | FLERS support line - M.23.c.0.7. to M.22.b.3½.1½. | Barrage. | At Zero plus 5 creeps back by 50 yards per minute to line M.17.c.6.0. to M.16.d.6½.1½. and continues on this objective till further orders. |
| | No fire to be East of a North and South line through M.23. central at any time. | | | |
| 236th. Bde. R.F.A. | Zero to zero plus 1 minute. | M.29.a.6½.6½. to M.23.c.0.2. | Barrage. | At Zero plus 1 creeps back at rate of 50 yards per minute for 3 mins. |
| | Zero plus 3 minutes to plus 5 minutes. | FLERS support line - M.23.c.9.2. to M.23.c.2.8½. | Barrage. | At Zero plus 5 creeps back by 50 yards per minute to line M.23.b.f.8½ to M.17.c.f.0. and continues on this objective till further orders. |
| | No fire to be East of a North and South line through M.23. central at any time. | | | |
| 238th. Bde. R.F.A. | Zero to plus 4 minutes. | FLERS front line from - M.29.a.7½.9½. to M.23.c.0.6½. | Barrage. | At Zero plus 4 minutes jumps on to FLERS support line. |
| | Zero plus 4 minutes to plus 5 minutes. | FLERS support line from - M.23.c.8½.1½. to M.23.c.1.8. | Barrage. | At Zero plus 5 minutes creeps back by 50 yards per minute to line M.23.b.5½.8. to M.17.c.5.0. and continues till further orders. |
| | No fire to be East of a North and South line through M.23. central at any time. | | | |

(2)

| UNIT. | TIME. | OBJECTIVE. | PROCEDURE. | REMARKS. |
|---|---|---|---|---|
| 25th. Bde. R.F.A. | Zero to plus 4 minutes. | FLERS front line from N.23.c.0.6½. to N.23.b.3.1. | Barrage. | At Zero plus 4 minutes jumps on to FLERS support line. |
| | Zero plus 4 mins. to plus 5 minutes. | FLERS support line from N.23.c.2.8. to N.23.b.4.4. | Barrage. | At Zero plus 5 minutes creeps back by 50 yards per minute to line - N.17.c.5.0. to N.16.d.6½.1. and continues till further orders. |

No fire to be East of a North and South line through N.23. central at any time.

RATE OF FIRE - 18-POUNDERS:-

Zero to plus 4 minutes = 3 rounds per gun per minute.
Plus 4 to plus 5 = 2 rounds per gun per minute.
Plus 5 onwards = 1 round per gun per minute.

### Diary of Information received on 15th. September 1916.

**253rd (NORTHUMBRIAN) BRIGADE, R.F.A.**

| Time | Information from | |
|---|---|---|
| 6-20 a.m. | O.P. S 1 d 9 5 | Bombardment started. |
| 6-23 a.m. | " " | Infantry have gone over bags. |
| 6-28 a.m. | " " | Strong hostile barrage on front line, especially on our right. |
| 6-40 a.m. | " " | Our tanks were seen to go over in good time before infantry started. |
| 6-43 a.m. | " " | Shelling especially heavy. Lancs. trench where O.P. Officer had gone forward has had to move back. |
| 6-45 a.m. | Liaison Officer | Our infantry have taken first line trenches: Germans retiring. |
| 7-0 a.m. | O.P. S 1 d 9 5 | Some prisoners have been taken and are being brought back. |
| 7-8 a.m. | " " | Estimated about 200 prisoners have been brought in. |
| 7-9 a.m. | " " | Our men can be seen north-west of MARTINPUICH presumably 45th. Brigade, 15th. Division. |
| 7-31 a.m. | Liaison Officer | Shelling bursting too high. |
| | | Ordered all batteries to lengthen Corrector. |
| 7-33 a.m. | Liaison Officer | Tanks have instructions not to return to place of assembly until they have instructions to do so. |
| 7-36 a.m. | O.P. S 1 d 9 5 | Another batch of prisoners being brought in. |
| 7-40 a.m. | O.P. S 15 d 3 9 | Large cloud of smoke 6 deg. left of HIGH WOOD: looks like a mine exploded. |
| | D/250 Bty. On duty | Wounded and returned states he saw two tanks go over German front line firing hard. |
| 7-50 a.m. | O.P. S 15 d 3 9 | Our men in HOOK TRENCH being bothered from HIGH WOOD, by machine gun fire. |
| 7-58 a.m. | O.P. S 1 d 9 5 | Third batch of prisoners brought in. |
| | Liaison Officer | Reports second objective gained. |
| 8-5 a.m. | F.O.O. with 4th. E. Yorks. | Shells still bursting high and are short. |
| | | Ordered batteries to add 100 and lengthen Corrector. |
| 8-30 a.m. | O.R.A. | Received verbal instructions re barrage required 3 hours after zero: informed him no priority message had been received. |
| 8-30 a.m. | B/253 Bty. | Two enemy 'planes have been over very high up since 8-0 a.m. |
| 8-35 a.m. | O.C. 253 Bde. | O.C. went to see Colonel of 276 Bde. re new barrage. |
| 8-55 a.m. | " | Returned from Headquarters 276 Bde. |

2.

| | | |
|---|---|---|
| 8-55 a.m. | | O.C. instructed batteries re new barrage. |
| 9-10 a.m. | B.M. | Instructions from B.M. to increase rate of fire 2 rounds per gun per minute. |
| | | Instructed batteries accordingly. |
| 9-10 a.m. | Liaison Officer | One advanced tank stranded at M 33 c 7 4 approximately. |
| | " | Another tank stranded at S 3 a 4 8, neigher being shelled. |
| | " | Enemy barrage on SWANSEA TRENCH and communication trench: also on captured ground. |
| | " | Heavy enemy barrage on line of first objective already captured. |
| 9-15 a.m. | " | Reports third objective is said to have been gained and is being consolidated. |
| 9-18 a.m. | " | The first tank reported stranded is now coming back to our lines. |
| 9-25 a.m. | F.O.O. | Enemy balloon brought down in flames right of HIGH WOOD. |
| 9-30 a.m. | Wounded men | Wounded men passing report 27th. London Battln. have taken HIGH WOOD and Anzacs are in front of them on the right. N.B. This has not been confirmed. |
| 9-55 a.m. | C.R.A. | Instructs reduction of rate of fire if situation permits. After consultation with General Price reduced to one round per gun per minute. |
| 10-0 a.m. | Liaison Officer | Machine guns at MILL north of MARTINPUICH giving trouble. Effort to turn fire but this was considered too dangerous as our infantry were reported close up. |
| 10-26 a.m. | " | Hostile Shelling on captured ground against reported direction of fire from N.E. from JUTLAND ALLEY and SWANSEA TRENCH. |
| √ 10-42 a.m. | Aeroplane | Wireless from aeroplane, hostile gun fire at M 21 c 6 5. |
| | | Advised B.M. of wire. |
| √ 10-50 a.m. | " | Hostile firing from M 21 b 3 5. |
| 11-0 a.m. | C/253 Bty. | Reports 3 guns out of action, one permanently; the other two they hope to start with again shortly |
| 11-5 a.m. | | Instructed all batteries to rest one gun at a time and continue barrage with three at one round per gun per minute. |
| 11-50 a.m. | O.P. Officer | At S 1 d 9 5 reports our men seen to have got through MARTINPUICH: enemy barraging heavily S and S.W. of village. |
| | " | At S 15 d 3 9 O.P. Officer reports situation quiet only intermittent shelling. One of our tanks a casualty lying on its side on the right of the wood. |
| | Liaison Officer | Reports definite information second objective consolidated, but nothing definite about third objective known. |
| 11-43 a.m. | B/253 Bty. | Enemy field guns shelling transport and wagon lines about X 23 central. |
| 12-3 p.m. | O.P. S 15 d 3 9 | Reports seeing tank returning midway between HIGH WOOD and MARTINPUICH. |
| 12-22 p.m. | Wireless | Signals, hostile batteries firing at M 21 b 2 5, M 23 a 2 5, M 21 c 6 5, M 21 b 6 7 to 6 6. Passed on to B.M. |
| 12-23 p.m. | F.O.O. | B Bty. F.O.O. returned and reports difficulty in observing passage of tank owing to smoke. |

3.

| | | |
|---|---|---|
| 12-50 p.m. | D/250 Bty. | Forward from F.O.O. of 47th. Division stating that FLERS has been taken. |
| 12-55 p.m. | O.P. S 15 d 3 9 | Reports batch of 100 prisoners coming from HIGH WOOD across open, and he states have been dribbling in for last hour. |

15/9/16    (Sgd) *illegible* Bde R.A.    Lieut Col R.A.

## DAILY DIARY OF INFORMATION

253rd (NORTHUMBRIAN) BRIGADE, R.F.A.

From 14th. Sept. to 10-30 p.m. 15th. September 1916. (cont'd from No. 1)

| Time | Information from: | |
|---|---|---|
| 1-20 p.m. | Liaison Officer | Reported that East Yorks are held up by machine gun fire from Windmill, N. of MARTINPUICH. Heavies are shelling the Windmill: infantry are experiencing difficulty in getting up stores for consolidating purposes. |
| 1-55 p.m. | General | Verbal instructions from General to move A and B batteries to positions approximately S 8 b this afternoon. |
| | | Instructed Battery Commanders to reconnoitre and move their guns forthwith, register if possible to-night or first thing in the morning and to outline by compass bearing the centre of their zone 28 Central, but be prepared to fire on present barrages. |
| 2-8 p.m. | C Bty. F.O.O. | Enemy are attacking in open formation from LE SARS, map reference approximately M 21 d. |
| | | Reported verbally to General C.R.A. |
| 2-30 p.m. | | A and B advised that C/251 would collect Trench Bridge and bring to Headqrs. about 4-30 p.m. |
| 2-35 p.m. | Aeroplane | Wireless report, hostile guns firing at M 21 c 6 5. |
| | | Reported to B.M. |
| 2-40 p.m. | F.O.O. | Reports from Infantry Hqrs. that HIGH WOOD has been definitely taken. |
| 2-45 p.m. | | Advised B.M. by wire. |
| 3-55 p.m. | C.R.A. | Instructions from C.R.A. to put all 18-pr. battys. on new barrages, B/253 M 33 b 5 6 to 9 6 from 4-15 to 4-45 two rounds per gun per minute. D/250 on junction of STARFISH LINE and CRESCENT ALLEY. |
| 4-5 p.m. | Aeroplane | Enemy troops advancing in pairs or single file. Head of column M 18 d 0 0, tail end LE BARQUE. |
| 4-10 p.m. | 253 Bde. | Passed on by telephone to B.M. |
| 4-10 p.m. | C.R.A. | Instructions for C/253 and D/250 to move up to-night to same square S 8 b after finishing the 4-45 shoot. |

5.

4-17 p.m.   Telephoned
~~Asked~~ B.M. that had put two 18-pr batteries (+ one How Battery) on new barrages in accordance with instructions, but in consequence of broken wire was unable to give instructions to the other batteries.

4-30 p.m.   Acknowledged instructions by wire for moving forward of C/253 and D/250.

4-50 p.m. Liaison Officer  Our troops had been withdrawn from Prue trench
5-0 p.m.   B.M.           Instructions received from C.R.A. to continue the barrage on the 4-15 to 4-45 line at a reduced rate of fire. The old barrage line is cancelled.

5-10 p.m.   Instructed B/253 to barrage M 33 b 5 6 to 9 6, and D/250 to resume firing on junction of STARFISH LINE and CRESCENT ALLEY.

5-14 p.m. Liaison Officer  Reported the 150 Infantry Bde. were pushing patrols up MARTIN ALLEY into PRUE TRENCH and thence from left to right along trench.
Asked that Artillery fire be arranged accordingly.

5-18 p.m.   Instructed B/253 and D/250 to stop shooting on their targets at M 33 b 5 6 to 9 6 and M 33 b 5 5.

Reported this to B.M.

253rd (NORTHUMBRIAN) BRIGADE, R.F.A.

| Time | Source | Entry |
|---|---|---|
| 5-25 p.m. | Aeroplane | Hostile guns firing from M 31 d 6 7. |
| 5-30 p.m. | Observer from H/d Bns | One of our Balloons came down: occupant descended by parachute. |
| 5-35 p.m. | B/253 Bty. | Reported having selected position at S 8 d 7 2. |
| 5-40 p.m. | A/250 Bty. | Reported having selected position at S 8 d 5 7½. |
| 6-5 p.m. | Aeroplane | Hostile guns firing from M 21 c 6. |
| 6-20 p.m. | B.M. | B.M. agreed to B/250 raising range 200 beyond line M 33 b 5 6 to 9 6. |
| | | Instructed Battery accordingly. |
| 6-35 p.m. | OP Officer Ridge ~~Liaison Officer~~ 149 Bde. | Reported enemy advancing in parties of 30 strong in section M 27 c to M 22 d from LE SARS direction. O.C. 149 Bde. sent request by F.O.O. D/250 returning from trenches that MARTINPUICH should have me more punishment from our guns. |
| 7-0 p.m. | B.M. | Written instructions B.M. 166/16 for shoot to-night received. |
| | | Informed B/250. |
| 7-20 p.m. | Liaison Officer | Reports that 6th. Camerons intend attacking ridge 150 contour N.E. of MARTINPUICH. |
| | General Price | Asked what support N.E. of MARTINPUICH was available. |
| | 253 Bde. | Given particulars through Liaison Officer. |
| | General Price | General Price thereupon requested that barrage should be lengthened, to which C.R.A. agreed. |
| | | Instructed batteries to add 200 on programme which was to start at 8 p.m. instead of 7-30 p.m. originally intended. |
| | C/253 Bty. | Reports unable to select position to-night. |
| | | Informed C.R.A. |
| | D/250 Bty. | Reports having selected position in S 14 b 3 7, but too late to occupy to-night. |
| | O.C. 253 Bde. | Agreed to his doing so to-morrow and ~~instructed~~ informed C.R.A. |
| 7-40 p.m. | | To-night's programme postponed to 8-30 p |
| | | Informed B/250 accordingly. |
| 8-18 p.m. | B/250 Bty. | Reported guns placed in newly selected position. Infantry attack again postponed till 9-40 p.m. Barrage to commence 9.35 p.m. Instructed batteries accordingly. Agreed to O.P. in S 15 being abandoned. |
| 9-40 p.m. | C.R.A. | C.R.A. decided that B.C's of C/253 and A D/250 must reconnoitre position to-night and occupy early to-morrow. |
| | | Issued instructions accordingly. |
| | B.M. | B.M. suggested that a position might be found in the valley through which SWANSEA and CLarks ~~are~~ trenches run. |
| 10-30 p.m. | B.M. | B.M. reduced rate of fire for B/250 to one round per gun per minute. |

7.

253rd
(NORTHUMBRIAN)
BRIGADE, R.F.A.

| | | |
|---|---|---|
| 11-30 p.m. | C.R.A. | Instructions to continue firing with B/250 on barrage with one section only and to warn all batteries in the event of S.O.S. to barrage from M 27 d 6 1 to M 27 c 6 5. |
| | | Instructed batteries accordingly. |
| 7-25 a.m. 16/9/16. | B.M. | Infantry attack this morning commences at 9-35. |
| 8-0 a.m. | Liaison Officer | Reports 15th. Division dug in N.E. of MARTINPUICH. Right rests on junction of Martin Trench and Prue Trench M 33 a 4 9. 150th. Bde. hold Martin Alley and Starfish Line as far as Crescent and have some men in Prue trench. |
| | Aeroplane | Later Aeroplane reports flares from our men at M 33 b 6 3, M 33 d 7 8, M 33 d 6 8, M 33 d 5 8, M 33 b 9 8, M 35 a 8 5. |
| 8-0 a.m. | B.M. | Written instructions with regard to Infantry attack previously mentioned by B.M. received, artillery barrage to commence at 9-10. |
| | | Batteries warned accordingly. |
| 8-20 a.m. | | Advised B.M. re Liaison Officer's report 8-0 a.m. |
| 8-53 a.m. | B/253 | Report having found new position at S 8 b 9 6 and a good O.P. at approximately M 33 c 9 1; asks permission to occupy new position. |
| | | Instructed him not to move till after attack at 9-35 a.m. |
| 9-8 a.m. | B.M. | Advised infantry advance will commence 9-25; artillery barrages to commence from 9-10 to 9-25, and intense firing to continue to 10 minutes after 9-25. |
| | | Batteries advised accordingly. N.B. D/250 and C/253 were not ready so were not included in barrage. |
| 10-15 a.m. | B/253 | Reports a premature from one of his guns resulting in one or two casualties among infantry thronging road over which one gun shoots. |
| | | Instructions to stop firing with that gun. |
| | B/253 | Captain Hllerns after careful investigation finds that the premature was unavoidable. No carelessness of detachment or neglect of supervision occurred. |
| 11-0 a.m. | D/250 | D/250 started firing one section on communication Trench from M 27 d 5 3 to M 27 b 6 0. |
| 11-10 a.m. | Liaison Officer: | Present position is as follows:- We have joined up from M 27 c 0 8 to M 33 a 6 8 and from thence to M 33 b 5 5. We hold strong point M 35 a 0 5; are now busy joining up from that point to M 33 b 5 5. Infantry are strongly dug in between M 33 d 2 7, 9 4, also trench in front M 33 d 5 8, 7 8. |
| | | Passed on by wire to C.R.A. |

8.

| | | |
|---|---|---|
| 11-42 a.m. | B/250 | Reports prematures from his right section shooting over road past Cemetry. |

N.B. This is the same road as Capt. Hllems reports his prematures have caused casualties.

Instructions given to stop firing with that section, not again to shoot on the line of the road in question.

Investigation by O.C. B/250 discloses no lack of care or supervision; no carelessness on the part of the detachment.
No previous prematures from this battery have occurred since in action at present position. The ground is stocked with guns behind them, and there were several prematures by other 18-pr. batteries.

| | | |
|---|---|---|
| 11-50 a.m. | Aeroplane | Reports Motor Transport M 9 c 2 6 to M 12 b 6 7. |
| 11-50 A.m. | B.M. | Given permission to stop B/253 firing and move that battery to new position at S 8.b 9 6. |

Battery instructions accordingly.

*[signature]*
Lt. Col.
Commanding 253rd (Nbn) Bde. R.F.A.

Report No. 3.   DAILY DIARY OF INFORMATION from 16th. September (noon) to noon 17th. 1916.

> 253rd (NORTHUMBRIAN) BRIGADE, R.F.A.
> No. ..........
> Date. ..........

| Time | From | |
|---|---|---|
| 12-38 p.m. | B.M. | Instructed O.O. to vary rate of fire at his discretion. |
| | | After conversation with Infantry Headquarters, reduced rate of fire by half. |
| 1-15 p.m. | | Ordered batteries to knock off one section entirely and carry on with remaining section at half rate. |
| 1-50 p.m. | | Requested C.R.A. for permission to inspect new gun positions and O.P's. |
| | C.R.A. | Not conceded at present. |
| 2-18 p.m. | B.M. | For the present the normal Intelligence Report could cease. |
| 3-40 p.m. | O.P. S 3 a 9 9 | Reported Transport and Infantry on road N 1 a 9 9 to N 1 c 1 2; beyond 18-pr. range. Tried to get more definite information, but owing to temporary breakdown of lines, failed. |
| 5-30 p.m. | O.O. | As more definite information was not available, above as it stands transmitted to B.M. |
| 6-40 p.m. | ~~Aeroplane~~ | Ascertained movement of movement reported in above to be from N. to S. |
| | | Reported to B.M. |
| 7-0 p.m. | Aeroplane | Hostile guns firing from M 20 b 7 7. |
| | C.R.A. | Asked if we knew of any point from which enemy's trench opposite Prue Trench could be seen. Wishes us to ascertain if General Price wishes barrage to be kept up all night. |
| 7-18 p.m. | O.C. | Informed him that General Price would do without barrage on his front for the night. |
| 7-30 p.m. | D/250 | Reports one gun registered. |
| 8-10 p.m. | | Instructed batteries to stop firing; that there would not be any further firing to-night, but to arrange for special alertness for S.O.S. |
| 8-15 p.m. | | Instructed B/250 to supply Liaison Officer for right Battalion to-night. |
| 9-10 p.m. | | Instructed A/253 in conjunction with C/253 to re-man the O.P. S 1 d 9 5; to look out for S.O.S. and to warn batteries promptly if it occurred. |
| 9-15 p.m. | O.C. | Reported our O.P's and registration as follows:- "Following O.P's have been reconnitred AAA S 3 a 9 9 This will be permanently occupied from dawn to-morrow, good view of squares M 16, 17, 22,23, 28,29. AAA B/253, B/250, have registered from there to-day AAA M 33 d central good view obtainable of same area AAA S 4 c 6 7 likely position for O.P. fuller report of view obtainable after further reconnaisance in morning AAA Shall permanently occupy the best two O.P's to-morrow AAA Guns registered as follows:- B/253 three guns, D/250 one gun, B/250 four guns AAA C and A Batteries of this Bde. not yet registered but lines carefully obtained by compass bearing ready to fire on S.O.S. just received from you AAA Officer who reconnitred |

Report No. 3 (continued)

253rd (NORTHUMBRIAN) BRIGADE, R.F.A.

| | | |
|---|---|---|
| | | HIGH WOOD reports seeing two tanks stranded just inside S.W. boundary not badly damaged AAA |
| 9-10 p.m. | | Acknowledged receipt of Artillery programme commencing 16/17 from 8 p.m. |
| 9-30 p.m. | C.R.A. | Rang up instructing special vigilance. |
| 9-10 p.m. | | Advised batteries by telephone of their target, in the event of S.O.S. |
| 10-45 p.m. | B.M. | Infantry report short shooting on Starfish Line. |
| | O.C. | Asked for further details. |
| | | Asked C.R.A. if any other battery was shooting on this point. His reply "No; not this Brigade." |
| 11-45 p.m. | B.M. | States possible attack at 3-0 a.m. |
| | O.C. | Warned batteries to stand by at 1-30 a.m. two Officers to be at the Battery and guns sparsely manned. |

14/9/16.

| | | |
|---|---|---|
| 3-0 a.m. | Liaison Officer | Ascertained from Liaison Officer that everything was quiet. |
| | | Reported to B.M. Asked for permission to reduce detachments. |
| | B.M. | Obtained permission to release one Officer only, small detachments to remain. |
| 4-50 a.m. | 251 Bde. | Reported S.O.S. |
| | | Told batteries to stand by. |
| 5-5 a.m. | B.M. | Ascertained false alarm. |
| 5-7 a.m. | Liaison Officer | Infantry no information with regard to S.O.S. |
| | | Informed batteries and told them not to fire. |
| 6-25 a.m. | B.M. | Conceded reduction of detachments of guns. |
| | | Informed all batteries. |
| 7-5 a.m. | Batt. Liaison Officer | Reports short shooting by 18-pr. batteries on Starfish Line. N.B. Our guns were not firing. This proves that we were not responsible for yesterday's short shooting. |
| 7-35. | O.C. | Informed B.M. |
| 7-40 a.m. | | Ascertained position of short shooting to be west end of trench, but map location not available: about 8 or 9 shots in all. |
| | | Informed B.M. |
| 10-0 a.m. | Liaison Officer | Germans bombing Starfish Line and Prue Trench from S 33 b 5 5. |
| | | Opened barrage with 3 18-pr. 1 How. on barrage 1636/17. |
| | | Informed B.M. |
| 11-25 a.m. | | Stopped barrage. |
| 11-35 a.m. | | Instructed B/253 to put one section on M 33 b 8 7 to 4 9; short bursts at irregular intervals. |

Report No. 4.   DAILY DIARY OF INFORMATION from 12 noon 17th. Septr.
                to 12 noon 18th. September 1916.

253rd (NORTHUMBRIAN) BRIGADE. R.F.A.

| Time 17/9 | Information from: | |
|---|---|---|
| 1-5 p.m. | B.M. | Instructions received re new barrage transmitted to batteries. M 33 b 7 5, M 27 d 2 1 for 18-prs: Howitzers left to O.C's discretion. |
| | | Instructed 18-prs. accordingly, and Howitzers to lay lines for shooting on M 33 b 5 5 to M 27 d 5 6 along Crescent Alley. |
| | D/250 | Reports shelling of HIGH WOOD and right of thereof by 4.2 battery. |
| 1-40 p.m. | 150 Infantry Bde. | Turned B/253 on to M 33 b 5 5 to 2 6, one round per gun per minute. |
| | | Informed General Price and advised C.R.A. |
| 1-50 p.m. | | Instructed all batteries to lay lines on M 33 b 7 5 to M 27 d 2 1, ready to shoot at short notice. |
| 2-15 p.m. | D/250 | Report lines laid on M 27 d 5 1 to M 27 d 6 6 ready to shoot at short notice. |
| 3-25 p.m. | Liaison Officer | Asks for concentrated fire on Prue Trench: Lines to all batteries down, ascertained 251 Bde already on it. |
| 4-10 p.m. | B.M. | Received orders re shoot from 5 p.m. onwards. |
| | | Transmitted to Batteries. |
| 4-55 p.m. | B.M. | Written orders received and acknowledged. |
| | | Transmitted to batteries by Orderly as all lines still down. |
| 6-10 p.m. | A/253 | Report their Officer unable to find where German trench in front of Prue Trench could be seen: will try again in the morning. Reported three guns carefully registered. |
| 6-30 p.m. | C/253 | Reported vain attempts to register from HIGH WOOD O.P.: line repeatedly broken, and ultimately shelled out. |
| | | Ascertained that batteries received message by Orderly re 5 o'clock shoot in good time, and commenced firing in accordance with instructions. |
| 6-55 p.m. | General Price | Asked for concentrated barrage on M 33 b 8 7, M 33 b 2 9. |
| | | Turned on A/253 and B/253 and B/250. Told them this must not interfere with 8-30 shoot as per programme. |
| 7-20 p.m. | B/253 | Reports S.O.S. going up three times from our zone. Subsequent enquiry pointed to these signals either being from THIEPVAL direction or Bosche imitations. |
| 7-30 p.m. | O.C. | Decreased rate of fire of 18-prs. on M 33 b 8 7 to 2 9, to one round per gun per minute. |
| 8-0 p.m. | | Stopped one section of each battery firing on above barrage. |

Report No. 4 (continued)

| Time | From/To | Message |
|---|---|---|
| 8-30 p.m. | | Started new barrage on programme. |
| 8-55 p.m. | O.C. | Reported to C.R.A. result of search for O.P's completion of registration with the exception of C/253 who had been shelled out of O.P.; also failed to locate German trench in front of Prue trench. |
| 9-30 p.m. | O.C. | Instructed all batteries to reduce rate of fire on barrage by one half, firing in bursts at irregular intervals; to be ready to go to "intense" on receipt of S.O.S. |
| | C.R.A. | Conversation re firing P.S. shells into LE SARS. |
| | | Arranged for three wagons to be brought from wagon lines, and for D/250 to fire from one gun for five minutes as quickly as possible, and then reduce fire to one round per gun per minute until P.S. ammunition exhausted. |
| 11-30 p.m. | B.M. | Reduced rate of fire to one round per gun per two minutes. |
| | | Advised batteries. |

18/9/16.

| Time | From/To | Message |
|---|---|---|
| 2-55 a.m. | Captain Cawston. | Reported short shooting. |
| | | Lengthened barrage 100 yds. |
| 5-25 a.m. | B/253 | Reported S.O.S. This not confirmed from O.P. Took no action. |
| 5-26 a.m. | Liaison Officer | Reported all quiet. |
| 6-58 a.m. | C.R.A. | Enquired if barrage still on. |
| | | Informed him of position. |
| 7-0 a.m. | B.M. | 150th. Brigade said barrage could be reduced but not taken off. C.R.A. informed. |
| 7-10 a.m. | C.R.A. | Sanctioned reduced rate to all batteries one round per gun per four minutes: How. cease fire. |
| | | Lines down: warned batteries by Orderly. |
| 7-20 a.m. | BM | Warning order not effective to-day. Rest all detachments to economise ammunition as much as possible. |
| 7-55 a.m. | | All wires down: instructions transmitted to batteries by Orderly to knock off one section per battery and keep other on one round per gun per four minutes in bursts. |
| 8-30 a.m. | Liaison Officer | Reported attack by 151 Infantry Brigade failed. Exact position is uncertain: are said to hold old line from M 33 b 7 2 to M 34 c 5 9 with strong point of 34 central. A battery has been shooting in that portion of Prue Trench held by the 150 Bde.* Have consolidated Prue Trench as far as strong point about M 33 b 5 6. A Bosche attack starting at 5 a.m. was repulsed at 6 a.m. two machine guns captured with bolts removed. Our own machine guns have been put in their emplacements. |
| | | Reported to C.R.A. by wire. |

* = Read barrage stopped

Report No. 4 (continued)

10-0 a.m.   A/253   F.O.O. reported result of attempt to view German
                    trench opposite Prue which is visible from
                    Martin Alley. It appears to run from M 33 b 4 9
                    for 150 yards parallel to Prue then bears off in
                    a northerly direction to MARTINPUIC main road.

                    Informed R.A.

10-15 a.m.          Stopped A/253 & other batteries firing on barrage: other lines down.

11-15 a.m. Liaison Officer  Reports short shooting in M 33 d 4 7 by 18-prs.

                    Rep reported to C.R.A.

---

Report No. 4.   DAILY DIARY OF INFORMATION
                from 12 noon 18/9/16 to 12 noon 19/9/16.

| Time | Information from: | |
|---|---|---|
| 12-0 p.m. | O.C. | Stopped all other batteries firing on barrage, serial 6, programme of bombardment dated 17th. |
| 12-5 p.m. | Batt. Liaison Officer. | Reports that Bosche prisoners state enemy demoralised. |
| 2-35 p.m. | C.R.A. | Wishes all Howitzers to register carefully Starfish Line M 34 a 5 0 to M 34 a 1 1. |
| | O.C. | Instructed D/250 accordingly. |
| 3-15 p.m. | S.C. | Stated no further supply of A ammunition obtainable from D.A.C. |
| 4-5 p.m. | B.M. | Asked for information re wireless. |
| | O.C. | Told him we had a wireless installation on the high ground behind Headquarters from which we were receiving Aeroplane messages. |
| | B.M. | Instructions to arrange with 276 Bde. to have the use of this.
N.B. This Station flooded out; operator making arrangements to return in the morning. |
| 4-30 p.m. | C.R.A. | Again impressed urgency of registration by Howitzers on Starfish Line. |
| | | Informed D/250. |
| 5-5 p.m. | Liaison Officer | Reports 151 Infantry Brigade has been stopped by machine guns in M 33 b 8 5 on three occasions when trying to bomb up Crescent Alley to extend their front along Prue Trench. General Price would like these machine guns knocked out. They also report machine guns in Prue Trench between M 33 b 5 6 and M 34 a 2 6. They say that these machine guns can be seen from their Company Headquarters from M 33 b 4 5. General Price said that during this wet weather, enemy Infantry advancing from EAUCOURT L'ABBAYE must use the sunken road, and would like this shelled systematically during the night. |
| | O.C. | Reported this to C.R.A. |
| 6-35 p.m. | O.C. | Instructed our Liaison Officer to report to 23rd. Division at VILLA WOOD at 6 a.m. |
| 7-15 p.m. | D/250 | Reports conditions of platforms and light have rendered it impossible for him to register Starfish Line this afternoon; hopes to do so early to-morrow. |
| | | Informed C.R.A. |
| 8-45 p.m. | B.M. | 1636/21 programme received and acknowledged. |
| 9-0 p.m. | Liaison Officer | Reported seeing photos confirming the presence of German of German trench in front of Prue. |

Report No. 4. (continued)
19/9/16.

| | | |
|---|---|---|
| 7-20 a.m. | Liaison Officer | Reports very quiet night. Has seen the General, 69th. Brigade and who will be glad of his assistance, but has no accommodation for him at their Headquarters. |
| | O.C. | Instructed Liaison Officer to remain where he is and keep in telephonic communication with the 69th. Brigade. |
| 8-40 a.m. | B.M. | Instructs to register Starfish Line and Prue Trench with 18-prs. and Howitzers any time after 10 a.m.<br>Re expenditure of ammunition: try and increase in proportion A.X; 40% A.X. and 60% A. |
| | O.C. | Informed batteries. |
| 10-15 a.m. | | Informed Colonel Topping that he was at liberty to use the wireless Station for our Headquarters as the C.R.A. thought it would be more convenient for him than the one at 262 Bde. which he is using at present. |
| 11-10 a.m. | Liaison Officer | Stated General Price would like a telephone communication with a good O.P. |
| | O.C. | I replied we should only too pleased if he cared to connect up with our O.P. at S 3 a 9 9. |

Report No. 5.    DAILY DIARY OF INFORMATION from noon 19/9/16
                                   to 20/9/16.

                                                    [Stamp: 253rd (NORTHUMBRIAN) BRIGADE, R.F.A.]

Time           Information from:

1-10 p.m.      B.M.                Operation Orders 1636/21 received and
                                   acknowledged.
                                   Instructs not to fire on Starfish Line or
                                   Prue Trench between 4 and 5.

2-18 p.m.      F.O.O.              Reports bombing attack from Prue Trench from
                                   the Crescent. F.O.O. who had line ready to
                                   register had to to retire to S 3 a 9 9.

3-0 p.m.       "                   Reported seeing Bosches in Prue trenches
                                   with bayonets fixed ready to attack.

3-30 p.m.                          Captain Law reported wounded.

3-55 p.m.      O.C.                Instructed B/253 to fire on the Crescent
                                   Alley from point M 33 b 5 8 northwards, and
                                   D/250 to do the same.

               Liaison Officer     Asked for assistance from 23rd. Brigade Div.
                                   Instructed C.R.A. Informed C.R.A.

4-10 p.m.      O.C.                Instructed D/250 and B/253 to lift 200.

4-40 p.m.      Liaison Officer     Reports bombing attack unsuccessful, Bosches
                                   defeated; can stop firing.

               O.C.                Instructed batteries accordingly.

5-30 p.m.      F.O.O. 267 Bde.     Reported that a further bombing attack had
                                   been made from the Crescent and had gained
                                   120 yds. of Prue and 150 yds. of Starfish
                                   Line.

6-50 p.m.      B.M.                Received and acknowledged Operation Order
                                   1636/22.

               O.C.                Sent on to Batteries by Orderly.

7-30 p.m.      C.R.A.              Variation for two Howitzers at M 34 a 6 2
                                   to start at 7 5 p.m. shoot at M 34 a 6 2 in
                                   switches of 50 yds. up to 34 b 4 1.

               O.C.                Transmitted instructions through B/250 to
                                   D/250.

7-55 p.m.      B/253               S.O.S. signals reported between HIGH WOOD and
                                   MARTINPUICH.
                                   Received same report from O.P. S d 9 5.
                                   Started firing from all batteries.

               O.C.                Informed C.R.A.

9-20 p.m.      O.C.                Stopped B/253 and D/250 except on programme,
                                   other batteries firing one round per gun per
                                   minute; also on programme 1636/22 one round
                                   per gun per minute.

9-20 p.m.      O.C.                Reduced rate of fire to one round per gun per
                                   two minutes.

9-40 p.m.      C.R.A.              Rang up, anxious about ammunition situation.

9-45 p.m.      O.C.                Reduced all guns to one round per gun per
                                   four minutes.

10-30 p.m.     C.R.A.              Asked for information.

Report No, 5 (continued)

| Time | From | Message |
|---|---|---|
| 10-30 p.m. | O.C. | Ascertained from Capt. Cawston that Infantry thought S.O.S.'s were enemy barrage signals and 23rd. Division are trying to recover portions of Prue ~~Line to~~ Trench lost this afternoon. Reports going to make an attack on Starfish Line and Prue Trench to their zone, ~~and 51st~~ |

151st Bde.

| | | |
|---|---|---|
| 10-34 p.m. | C.R.A. | Registration of Starfish Line and Prue Trench unsatisfactory.; did not consider it reliable, though ~~their~~ our Battery Commanders have done their level best. |

Continue efforts to-morrow.

| | | |
|---|---|---|
| 11-5 p.m. | O.C. | Instructed D/250 to cease firing and be ready in case of S.O.S. |
| 11-10 p.m. | C.R.A. | Agreed to other batteries continuing all night as ordered above. |
| 12-35 p.m. | O.P. | Officer from O.P. reports 23rd. Division have retaken trenches to M 33 a 8 7. |
| | O.C. | Informed C.R.A. |

20/9/16.

| | | |
|---|---|---|
| 6-28 a.m. | C.R.A. | Instructed cease all firing except on road and O.T's: programme 1636/22 postponed: carry on registration of trenches. |

Passed on to Batteries.

| | | |
|---|---|---|
| 7-30 a.m. | D/250 | Two sections start firing as follows:- one round per gun per three minutes, M 28 c 1 3½, M 28 d 1 7, M 28 a 3 6½, M 22 d 3 1. |
| 7-50 a.m. | B.M. | Further instructions later re programme 1636/22. |
| 8-30 a.m. | O.C. | Instructed B/253 to continue ~~firing~~ enfilading road in M 28 d and 29 a. |
| 9-15 a.m. | O.C. | Informed B.M. what firing was going on. |
| 9-30 a.m. | B.M. | Instructed to stop Hows. firing on road in 28 a and turn it on to O.T. 33 b 7½ 4 to 8½ d. |
| | O.C. | Instructed D/250 accordingly. |
| 10-55 a.m. | C/253 | Reported three guns out of action; two could be quickly repaired, the other would have to go to I.O.M. |
| | Liaison Officer | Reports 151 Bde. did not attack owing to muddy weather. |

Report No. 6.   DAILY DIARY OF INFORMATION from 12 noon 20th. Sept.
                to 12 noon 21st. September 1916.

| Time | Information from: | |
|---|---|---|
| 12-5 p.m. | B.M. | 1636/24 orders for firing received. |
| 12-10 P.m. | O.C. | Instructed two 18-prs. of B/253 to carry out serial 6, and two Hows. D/250 the same. |
| 12-45 p.m. | S.C. | Advised that Fricourt dump for ammunition would not be opened till surplus from old dump was exhausted. |
| 1-10 p.m. | C.R.A. | Spoke about our carefully watching ammunition expenditure and avoiding wastage by imaginary S.O.S's. |
| 2-20 p.m. | B/253 | Complained of the condition of road. |
|  | O.C. | Passed on complaint to S.C. |
| 2-45 p.m. | Signalling Office | Informed by Signalling Office of the location of our central telegraph exchange going through to all batteries to be X 20 a 3 4. |
| 3-30 p.m. | S.C. | Pointed out that arrangements for road control were imperative to stop blocking of traffic and irregularities of watering orders. |
|  | B.M. | Suggested that our Liaison Officer should act also as Liaison Officer between 276 Bde. R.F.A. and 69th. Infantry Brigade. |
|  | O.C. | Approved. Instructions given to Liaison Officer accordingly. |
| 4-45 p.m. | B.M. | Asked for map references of O.P's for registering Prue and Starfish lines. |
|  | O.C. | These were given as follows:- S 4 d 2 7, S 4 b 8 4, and 70th. Avenue. |
| 7-30 p.m. | B/253 | Reports having found an admirable O.P. at S 4 b 2 3½ which he proposes to occupy. Cannot however identify Prue and Starfish Line, though he can see the roads in this area; instructing if impossible to register on the actual trenches, the next best thing would be to register the roads. |
| 9-10 p.m. | B/253 | Reported S.O.S.; and the fact that they have started on the barrage. |
|  | O.C. | Stopped them firing. |
|  | Liaison Officer | Reports that two Red lights seen right of 50th. Division: shelling normal: practically no rifle fire. |
| 9-30 p.m. |  | Above report confirmed by 69th. Brigade. |
| 10-35 p.m. | B.M. | Reported short shooting at M 33 d 4 6. |
|  | O.C. | Explained the impossibility of being our batteries as our nearest guns were firing fully 1,000 away from this point. Informed all Warned all batteries to be very careful. |
| 21/9/16. 12-10 a.m. | F.O.O. | Officer at O.P. S 1 d 9 5 reported heavy firing by 18-prs: two red lights had gone up over MARTINPUICH and four over COURCELETTE. Spoke to Liaison Officer who reported all quiet on the 69th. Brigade front. |

Report No. 6. (continued)

| | | |
|---|---|---|
| 2-10 a.m. | B/253 | Reported barrage of gas shells due east of their position; distance difficult to estimate. |
| 2-30 a.m. | 253 H.q. | Wagon lines arrived in new position having been held up 8½ hours on the road. |
| 11-0 a.m. | B.M. | Programme 1636/25 for to-day and this evening received and acknowledged. |

Report No. 7.    Daily Diary of Information from 12 noon 21/9/16
                      to 12 noon 22/9/16.

| Time | Information from: | |
|---|---|---|
| 12-0 noon | | All wires down to front. |
| 12-15 p.m. | | C.E. wire up. |
| | B.M. | Orders received from B.M. to shell Starfish Line and Prue trench, slow bombardment. |
| 12-20 p.m. | | H.W. (Forward Exchange) up. |
| 12-45 p.m. | B/250 | Reports Prue trench well registered. |
| 1-0 p.m. | | Signalling Officer C.E. re clearing line. |
| 1-30 p.m. | M.N. | Reports Prue and Starfish Line well registered. |
| 2-50 p.m. | D.E. | One gun out of action. |
| 3-25 p.m. | B.M. | In reply to enquiry, said, objectives were trenches; also informed us that situation on the whole front was better. |
| 3-30 p.m. | Lt. Shaw, C.R.A. Signals: | Promised to lay two lines in his trench to our Forward Exchange. |
| 3-30 p.m. | Linesman | Reports balloon wire from 251 Brigade cut to pieces. |
| | O.C. | Instructed him to try and pick it up near the balloon, and tap in. |
| 5-30 p.m. | B.M.R.A. | Requested no firing on Starfish trench after 7-30 p.m. |
| | O.C. | Informed batteries. |
| 7-0 p.m. | O.C. | Informed B.M. and batteries, 1st. Division have now a strong point at M 34 b 4 0. |
| 7-5 p.m. | C.R.A. | Ordered no firing on Starfish line. All 18-prs. to be turned on S.O.S. barrage in front of Prue trench. |
| 6-45 p.m. | O.C. | Wired B.M. enemy firing wind-testing shell along front. |
| 7-30 p.m. | O.C. | Asked B.M.R.A. to advise 276 Brigade not to shoot on line south-west of M a 0 10 to M 27 d 6 6 at request of infantry. |
| 8-30 p.m. | C.R.A. | Lift 200 yards north of Prue trench. |
| | O.C. | All batteries advised. |
| 9-30 p.m. | | Informed C.R.A. patrols from 149 Brigade are in Starfish; patrols from 151 Bde. are also in Starfish, and enemy has retired. |
| 10-40 p.m. | B.M. | Re large fire to the west. Spoke to B.M. who informed O.C. this was a British ammunition dump. |

22/9/16.

| Time | Information from: | |
|---|---|---|
| 7-0 a.m. | B.M. | 18-prs. fall short. Instructing all 18-pr batteries to lift 100 yds. Please confirm. |
| 7-25 a.m. | C.R.A. | Instruct at 7-40, lift barrage 200 yds. beyond second objective. |
| | O.C. | Advised batteries. |
| 7-30 a.m. | | All wires except D.E. down. |
| 8-5 a.m. | B.M. | Ordered rate of fire same as during the night. |
| 9-50 a.m. | 150 Bde. | Patrols from 150 th. Bde. report no sign of enemy at 9-15. |
| 9-55 a.m. | B.M. | Orders received to cease firing. |
| 10-35 a.m. | | No enemy can be seen between our front and EAUCOURT l'ABBAYE. |
| 11-0 a.m. | | Infantry report digging in on second objective. It is doubtful whether further advance will be made at present. |

Report No. 7 (continued)

| | | |
|---|---|---|
| 11-20 a.m. | O.C. | Arranged with Lieut. Hutchinson to take over Brigade O.P. to keep look out for *[illegible] target* & *[illegible] on* B/150 (*this morning battery*) *promptly* |
| 11-45 a.m. | C.R.A. | Instructed that when 150th. Bde. relieve to-night, we supply as before Liaison Officer but no Battalion Liaison Officers. |

22nd.

From Officer Commanding
         253rd. (Northumbrian) Bde. R.F.A.

To Brigade Major, R.A.,
         50th. Division.

---

         Liaison Officer reports enemy machine guns are said to be situated as under:-
         The Mound approximately M 34 a 6 5; in a Copse approximately M 34 a 9 9; in a trench M 33 b 9 7.

         These guns have been causing casualties in our front line.
         You will notice from German tracing machine guns are reported at M 29 a 8 6 and M 29 a 7 8 or 8 9½. The latter will sweep down the valley to M 28 c 8 0.
         This is reported as a very steep valley, and our advancing Infantry will be certain to wish to hand on it.
         General Price is sending certain points which he wants specially attended to during the advance.
         In the advance of the ----- the jumping off place is to be line from M 33 d 5 9 to 34 c 9 8. General Price would like to be certain that the **Crescent trench** from M 33 b 6 8 to 27 d 5 5 is absolutely obliterated so that the enemy may be driven across the open where our machine guns may catch them. He also wishes the sunken road across M 28 d effectively strafed by continuius fire.

                                             Captain,
                     Adjutant, 253rd. (Northn.) Bde. R.F.A.
                         for O/c 253" Bde RFA

21/9/16.

Report No. 8.          Daily Diary of Information from 12 noon 22/9/16
                              to 12 noon 23/9/16.

---

Time           Information from:

12-30 p.m.     B.M.            Asked if Hows. shooting: replied, No; asked
                               for confirmation.
               O.C.            Obtained it, and informed him.
               B.M.            Daily programme B.M. 1647/1 received, acknow-
                               ledged, and transmitted to batteries, by
                               Orderlies.

12-50 p.m.     O.C.            Reported to S.C., continued congestion of road
                               owing to watering orders.

1-25 p.m.      B.M.            With reference to his 1647/1 serial 3, instructing
                               not to shoot unless, and until visual observ-
                               ation possible and certainty of safety of own
                               Infantry.

1-50 p.m.      O.C., D/250     Reports hostile aeroplanes and balloons up; also
                               shelling on area S 8 b.
               O.C.            Reported to S.C. names of two NEW ZEALAND
                               Drivers, scrambling down cliff N. of Headqtrs.

2-30 p.m.      O.P. S 4 a 9 7½ Enemy parties seen at M 24 c 2 3: fired on
                               with effect.

               O.C.            Reported to C.R.A.

3-30 p.m.      253 H.Q.        Got connected with balloon for registration.
                               Started registering when communication with
                               batteries broke down.

6-0 p.m.       "               Re-established communication: continued
                               registration: not completed when light failed.

7-10 p.m.      Liaison Officer Requested no firing south of central line
                               passing through 27, 28, and 29.

7-15 p.m.                      Reported gas-alert and S.O.S. from M 21 B 4.2.
                               Central. Gun firing started, but no gas came
                               over.

10-0 p.m.      C.R.A.          Instructed gradual reduction of ammunition at
                               guns to 400 per 18-pr., and 300 per Howitzer.

23/9/16.       O.C.            Advised batteries.

2-0 a.m.       F.O.O.          Reports noticable absence of Vary Lights on
                               Divisional front. Few there are, seem to be
                               very distant.
                               This seems to confirm retirement of enemy to
                               EAUCOURT l'ABBAYE lines.

8-50 a.m.      B.M.            Advised programme from 11-0 a.m. 23rd. to 11-0 a.m
                               24th. same as yesterday.

               O.C.            Transmitted to batteries.

9-50 a.m.      O.C.            From 12 noon B/253 instructed to act as "Roving
                               Battery" for next 24 hours.

---

11-15 a.m.     B.M.            Reports Prue trench line held by 50th. Division;
                               that posts over the road through 28 c up to 28
                               d 1 7. Asks for identification from O.P's of
                               post at S 3 b 1 9.

12-0 noon      O.P's           Think pole visable. Wishes confirmation by
                               man standing at pole.

Report No. 9.    Daily Diary of Information from 12 noon 23/9/16 to
                 12 noon 24/9/16.

| Time | Information from: | |
|---|---|---|
| 12-0 noon | O.C. | Asked B.M. to arrange for Red or White flag on pole at S 3 b 1 9. |
| 12-20 p.m. | B.M. | New barrages for S.O.S. (1631/4) received, acknowledged, and transmitted to batteries. |
| 12-25 p.m. | O.C. | Asked batteries for report on Dial Sights. |
| 4-25 p.m. | O.P. | Reports large fire in enemy's line 10 degrees right from THILLOY Church; taken from S 3 a 9 9. |
| 5-30 p.m. | B/253 | Report enemy transport seen and shelled at M 24 c 1 2: wagons abandoned. |
| 5-55 p.m. | F.O.O. | Reports heavy barrage on line N.E. of MARTINPUICH |
|  | O.C. | Reported to B.M. |
| 7-20 p.m. | B.M. | B.M. 1647/3 received, acknowledged, and transmitted to batteries. |
| 7-45 p.m. |  | Front line trench at M 25 a & b heavily shelled by 4.2. Reported to B.M. |
| 7-50 p.m. | Liaison Officer | Machine gun at M 29 a 7 8, bothering working party on Sunken Road; also in Prue and Starfish. |
|  | O.C. | Reported to B.M. |
| 10-45 p.m. | O.R.A. | Suggested firing on 29 a 9 9 to 4 6. |
|  | O.C. | Instructed B/250 to do so. |
| 11-55 p.m. | 276 Bde. | Asked if we could postpone shoot till 1-0 a.m. |
|  | O.C. | Informed them we had already started firing. We had carried out a programme starting at 11 pm. |
| 24/9/16. |  |  |
| 2-30 a.m. | O.P. S 3 a 9 9 | Reported 4 Red rockets on front of zone. Told them not to fire, as probably German. No reports of S.O.S. from elsewhere. |
| 10-30 a.m. | B.M. | B.M. 1647/5 received and acknowledged. D/250 instructed by telegram re day's programme. |
|  | B.M. | B.M. 1647/4 received and acknowledged. |

Report No. 10.    Daily Diary of Information from noon 24/9/16 to
                  12 noon 25/9/16.

253rd (NORTHUMBRIAN) BRIGADE, R.F.A.

| Time | Information from: | |
|---|---|---|
| 3-0 p.m. | | 149 Brigade have relieved 150th. Brigade. |
| 3-30 p.m. | Liaison Officer | Reports that Brigade on our left have taken trench running through M 27 a and d: they are going for trench 26 b and 26 c at 5-36 p.m. They state that quarry in 22 d is very strongly fortified. Reports position on our right is as follows:- M 28 d 8 0, 35 a 5½ 9 to 29 d 0 5. |
| 7-32 p.m. | Liaison Officer | Reports short shooting at M 27 d 6 4. None of our batteries shooting. |
| 8-0 p.m. | B.M. | Informed us S.O.S. barrage unchanged. |
| 8-45 p.m. | F.O.O. | Reports bombing attack. |
| 9-10 p.m. | F.O.O. | Reports bombing and also heavy shelling in front of O.P. |

25/9/16.

| Time | Information from: | |
|---|---|---|
| 12-5 a.m. | I.O.M. | Condemned gun No. 10899, and ordered that a new one be indented for. |
| 6-20 a.m. | D/250 | Premature reported at D/250 battery: 6 men wounded. |
| 6-40 a.m. | F.O.O. | Reports bombardment intense on our right. |
| 9-0 a.m. | B.M. | Hows. did not join in bombardment. |
| 10-10 a.m. | B.M. | Programme from 11-0 to 11-0 a.m. 26/9/16 same as yesterday, received. |
| | O.C. | Batteries advised. |
| | O.C. | Telegram to batteries: if any wires in Crescent Alley are not properly fixed to trench will be cut out. |
| | Liaison Officer | Our Infantry are trying for trenches M 29 b 1 2, 29 a 2 3, 28 b 8 8, 28 b 0 5, 28 a 4 4. Watch carefully if any hostile movement; especially watch the quarry. |
| 11-40 a.m. | C.R.A. | Enquired if had any Thimit. |
| | O.C. | Said we had not. |

Report No. 11.        Daily Diary of Information from 12 noon 25/9/16
                                to 12 noon 26/9/16.

| Time | Information from: | |
|---|---|---|
| 2-55 p.m. | | B/253 registering by balloon on new targets from 2-55 p.m. to 4-15 p.m. |
| 3-20 p.m. | F.O.O. | Reports shelling at M 28 d 2 8 to 8 0. |
| 4-45 p.m. | C.R.A. | Orders received from C.R.A. to fire 100 B X on enemy lines in our zone. |
| 4-50 p.m. | F.O.O. | Reports large fire in EAUCOURT l'ABBAYE said to have been caused by our heavies. |
| 6-0 p.m. | F.O.O. | Hows. reported falling short at new trenches. At this time ours were all firing on the back line about M 22 Central. |
| 6-15 p.m. | D.E. | O.C., D.E. reports from O.P. that the barrage put up at 12-35 was beautifully distributed, with very few bursts too high. |
| 7-25 p.m. | O.C. | Reported to B.M. that a party of the enemy at 4-30 were engaged at M 23 d 5 8: they were scattered. Small parties were also fired on at M 18 c 0 3 who proceeded to double across the tract through M 18 Central. These parties were also engaged, but light gave out. It is evident that roads running through M 23 a 9 2½ to M 24 c 1 3, also M 23 a 9 2½ to M    a 0 3 are much used. |
| 12-10 a.m. | D/250 | Aeroplane reported flying low over S 8 d 6 9. midnight. |
| 11-40 p.m. 26/9/16. | C.R.A. | Wired there are not likely to be further operations to-night. |
| 5-45 a.m. | F.A. | Complained of short shooting. Asked for times. |
| 7-0 a.m. | O.C. | Informed F.A. target my batteries were shooting at. |
| | O.C. | Asked R.O. for location of his new gun positions as I might have to take them over. |
| 7-45 a.m. | O.C. | Given S.C. full particulars of dispositions of Dial Sights. |
| 9-30 a.m. | O.C. | Arranged with C.R.A. to have maps marked up-to-date. |

Report No. 12.    Daily Diary of Information from 12 noon 26/9/16 to 12 noon 27/9/16.

*253rd (NORTHUMBRIAN) BRIGADE, R.F.A.*

| Time | Information from: | |
|---|---|---|
| 12-10 p.m. | O.C. | Asked No. 3 Kite Balloon to report on the shooting of Hows. at M 28 a 3 6 to M 21 d 5 3. |
| 12-55 p.m. | Balloon | Balloon reports How. shells dropping well, and about the right place. |
| | O.C. | Informed M.N. |
| | Balloon | Balloon also reports that 18-pr. barrage on enemy front seems more satisfactory. |
| 1-30 p.m. | O.C. | Reported to O.P. that hostile guns at M 21 b 2 3, M 23 c 5 9. |
| 1-45 p.m. | O.C. | Advised batteries of new S.O.S. barrage. |
| 2-45 p.m. | | Wire received that COMBLES has been taken by the French. |
| 4-20 p.m. | F.O.O. | Reports large parties of enemy Infantry passing in an easterly direction through wood M 3 Central and MM 4 Central. |
| 5-0 p.m. | O.C. | Reported to C.R.A. on his visit to possible forward positions. |
| 6-0 p.m. | S.C.R.A. | Telephoned that all guns must be handed over complete on relief, and any Dial Sights short must be indented for. |
| 7-10 p.m. | O.C. | The following correction was sent in to C.R.A. in O.C's letter re positions: para. 5, line 4, instead of S 9 a 8 5 read S 9 b 8 5; please correct. |
| 8-30 p.m. | O.C. | Instructions given to M T for ~~not~~ firing 200 yds. behind S.O.S. barrage. |
| 10-40 p.m. & 10-50 p.m. | O.C. | Instructions issued to M T and D E to move a section of the batteries at dawn to forward position. |
| 11-40 p.m. | B.M. | Asked if our F.O.O. had noticed a S.O.S. signal. |
| | O.C. | Informed him, No. Probably his enquiry referred to red Infantry flares. |
| 27/9/16. 2-10 a.m. | B.M. | 1097 received and acknowledged. |
| 5-0 a.m. | C.R.A. | By telephone, drop barrage 100 yds. |
| | O.C. | A/253 advised. |
| 7-40 a.m. | B.M. | Instructed barrage to continue until further orders. |
| 8-40 a.m. | ~~M.N.~~ O.C. | M N advised to use S K in lieu of P S when latter is not available. |
| 9-20 a.m. | O.C. | K D instructed to take over duties of roving battery from 12 noon, for 24 hours. |
| 9-55 a.m. | O.C. | All batteries informed ammunition to be used as required by situation, 11-0 a.m. 27th. to 11-0 a.m 28th. |

Report No. 12 (continued)

**[Stamp: 253rd (NORTHUMBRIAN) BRIGADE, R.F.A.]**

10-15 a.m.   B.M.            Advised that one section of B/250 and one section of A/253 had moved to new positions, and were busy registering.

11-40 a.m.   Liaison Officer  Advises our Infantry now established at strong posts at M 28 a 6 6 and M 28 b 3 8.

             O.C.            Informed O.R.A. by wire.

11-55 a.m.   O.R.A.          Ordered as weather conditions are likely to be unfavourable, present instructions re ammunition at battery positions are cancelled.

             O.R.A.          Batteries are ~~informed~~ now to get a good supply of ammunition before roads get into a bad condition

             O.C.            Batteries and wagon lines informed.

Report No. 13.        Daily Diary of Information.
                From 12 noon 27/9/16 to 12 noon 28/9/16.

> 253rd (NORTHUMBRIAN) BRIGADE, R.F.A.

| Time | Information from: | |
|---|---|---|
| 12-15 p.m. | F.O.O. | Reports road N 1 a & c is still being used by small parties of enemy in a southerly direction. |
| 12-45 p.m. | Liaison Officer | Reports position of Division on our left. |
| 1-15 p.m. | O.C. | Instructions given to D/250 and C/253 for afternoon bombardment to assist Division on our right. |
| 2-0 p.m. | Liaison Officer | Reports our Infantry have obtained their objective. |
| 2-30 p.m. | F.O.O. | Reports our Infantry are in the quarry 22 d. Various other reports from F.O.O. confirming this. Also that Division on our right got Infantry into EAUCOURT l'ABBAYE. |
| 2-55 p.m. | Wireless | At 2-47 p.m. Huns seen on road N 7 a 9 0. |
| 2-55 p.m. | C.R.A. | Instructed to lift fire to FLERS LINE. |
|  | O.C. | Batteries informed. |
| 3-20 p.m. | O.P. | Reports light enemy barrage in neighbourhood. |
| 3-20 p.m. | M.N. | Reports Infantry on the right seen to get clear of their barrage. |
| 3-35 p.m. | O.C. | Discussed question of "Intense Fire" with C.R.A., who laid down definitely that 3 rounds per gun per minute was to be the maximum. |
| 5-5 p.m. | Liaison Officer | Reports Division on our right entered EAUCOURT l'ABBAYE, bombing up FLERS LINE. Our Infantry transport have orders to be prepared to move at short notice. |
| 6-15 p.m. | F.O.O. | Vary Lights and Green Rockets seen in front of EAUCOURT l'ABBAYE. |
|  | F.O.O. | Reports dense volumes of smoke in EAUCOURT l'ABBAYE. |
| 6-30 p.m. | O.C. | Reported to B.M. that move forward to new positions by B/250 and A/253 complete. |
| 6-45 p.m. | O.C. | New S.O.S. barrage handed to batteries. |
| 7-40 p.m. | C.R.A. | Altered barrage. |
|  | O.C. | Batteries advised. |
| 7-50 p.m. | Liaison Officer | Reports our Infantry in FLERS LINE and supposed to be joined up on right and left. |
| 10-5 p.m. | O.C. | Batteries informed that in event of S.O.S. to lift. |

Report No. 13. (continued)

| | | |
|---|---|---|
| 10-15 p.m. | C.R.A. | Arranged with O.C. to look out for new positions in the EAUCOURT L'ABBAYE valley, and that B.M. would go with him at 6-30 a.m. |
| 11-30 p.m. | Liaison Officer | Reported a rumour that the Cavalry had been through near BAUPAUME, but he could not get it confirmed. |

28/9/16.

| | | |
|---|---|---|
| 8-0 a.m. | C.R.A. | Instructed that C/253 relieve B/250, personnel only. The relief to be completed by 12 noon. |
| | O.C. | Advised both batteries. |
| 9-50 a.m. | C.R.A. | Instructed M.N. to bombard FLERS LINE about S.O.S. barrage line, 400 rounds per day, slow rate of fire. |
| | O.C. | Advised M.N. |
| 10-10 a.m. | O.C. | Authorised C/253 to remove new range slip to forward battery (C/253) thus making four new slips on forward guns and four old slips on rear guns at BAZENTIN. |
| 10-30 a.m. | O.C. | Asked Capt. Hollorns to make a full report on wire in front of FLERS Line or on any part of it he could see; as per request of 3rd. Corps. |
| 11-0 a.m. | C.R.A. | Reports short shooting at M 21 d 9 7, 4-30 to 5-0 a.m. in bursts. |
| 11-20 a.m. | O.C. | Informed C.R.A. none of our batteries shooting. |

Report No. 14.    Daily Diary of Information
                  from 12 noon 27/9/16 to 12 noon 29/9/16.

| Time | Information from: | |
|---|---|---|
| 12-0 p.m. | O.C. | Wired S.C. to try and make some arrangements to keep watering orders off main road. |
| | O.C. | Wired C.R.A. full particulars as to ~~whether~~ wire on FLERS LINE. |
| 12-10 p.m. | O.C. | Advised C.R.A. of relief of B/250 by C/253. |
| 12-30 p.m. | Balloon | Informed us 276 Bde. had a direct line to them, and would not need to use ours. |
| 12-40 p.m. | C.R.A. | Ordered cease fire with How. battery. |
| | O.C. | Battery advised. |
| 3-0 p.m. | | A rumour that our Infantry were back in FLERS LINE. Cannot get confirmation. |
| 5-35 p.m. | O.C. | Informed C.R.A. that III Corps, R.E. arranging to commence a chalk pit at this Headqtrs. and demolish some of the dugouts. |
| 5-40 p.m. | O.C. | Telegraphed C.R.A. further particulars of wire on FLERS LINE. |
| 6-15 p.m. | O.C. | Reported to C.R.A. motor transport at M 23 3 a 2 2. |
| 7-20 p.m. | | A report that enemy Infantry are massing at M 29 a 2 1. |
| | C.R.A. | C.R.A. enquired if these could be observed from our O.P.. |
| | O.C. | Reported, No; but that a battery was laid on ready to fire. |
| 8-30 p.m. | O.C. | New S.O.S. barrage given to all batteries. |
| 9-30 p.m. | O.C. | Instructions issued to batteries for night firing. |
| 29/9/16. | | |
| 7-0 a.m. | O.C. | O.C. at C.R.A. in consultation re gun positions. |
| 8-45 a.m. | B.M. | Ordered no shooting on FLERS LINE until further orders. |
| 9-25 a.m. | O.C. | O.C. rang up to say that B/251 had to commence work on position allotted to B/253; ~~alternativ~~ alternative position suggested. |
| 9-30 a.m. | B.M. | Said we must stick to orders and occupy position at B 6 1. |
| 10-10 a.m. | S.C.R.A. | Said that ammunition at D.E. position would have to be taken over by our own batteries. |
| | O.C. B/250 | Arranged for A/253 to take it over. B/250 telephoned approximately 990 A and 930 A X. |
| 10-30 a.m. | Balloon | Asked for targets requiring registering. |
| | C.R.A. | Advised to ask O.C. 276 the time 39 Bde. were expected to relieve him. |

Report No. 14 (continued)

| | | |
|---|---|---|
| 10-35 a.m. | Liaison Officer | Reported L B are said to have occupied farm 21 a. |
| | O.C. | Informed C.R.A. |
| 11-0 a.m. | B.M. | Telephoned not depending on How. battery to-day, to enable them to get on with new position. |
| 11-25 a.m. | B.M. | Said B/250 would be required to shoot as per programme to-day and would not be able to move their guns till about 5-55 p.m. |

253rd (NORTHUMBRIAN) BRIGADE, R.F.A.

Report No. 15.          Daily Diary of Information
                        from 12 noon 29/9/16 to 30/9/16. (noon)

253rd (NORTHUMBRIAN) BRIGADE, R.F.A.

| Time | Information From: | |
|---|---|---|
| 12-30 p.m. | Liaison Officer | Reports a statement from prisoner that the main enemy line is three miles further back. |
| 1-10 p.m. | Liaison Officer | Canadians are holding M 14 and are linking up with M 21 a. |
| 4-45 p.m. | O.C. | Spoke to Major Chapman re getting in guns to new position; said he needed a bridge and permission to go along trench tramway. |
|  | O.C. | Informed B.M. who said bridge might be got from 39 Bde, but permission could not be given to go along trench tramway. |
| 5-15 p.m. | B/253 | Reported unable to register forward guns. |
| 5-25 p.m. | D/250 | Informed that bridge issued in the first instance could not be taken up as it was broken. |
| 6-10 p.m. | C.R.A. | Reported short shooting. |
|  | O.C. | Batteries spoken to on the matter. |
| 6-20 p.m. | C.R.A. | Informed battery lines carefully checked and did not consider short shooting could be from batteries of this Brigade. |
| 6-35 p.m. | O.C. | A/253, C/253 and B/250 ordered to lift fire of left section 100 yards. |
| 7-20 p.m. | C.R.A. | Reduced rate of fire to one round per gun per six minutes. |
| 7-30 p.m. | O.C. | Informed B.M. by wire, MARTINPUICH being shelled |
| 8-0 p.m. | B.M. | Cease fire on barrage and come to normal work. |
|  | O.C. | Batteries advised. |
| 8-30 p.m. | C.R.A. | Orders re open barrage. |
| 9-10 p.m. | C.R.A. | Orders cease barrage. |
| 9-35 p.m. | O.C. | Batteries given night work. |
| 9-45 p.m. | C.R.A. | Asks for bursts of fire during night on M 22 a 4 1 to M 16 c 7 4. |
|  | O.C. | Batteries advised. |
| 12-0 midnight | O.C. | Spoke to Adjutant, 251 Bde. and told him we could not return bridge handed over by 251 Bde. same was broken. |

Report No. 15 (continued)

253rd (NORTHUMBRIAN) BRIGADE, R.F.A.

No............
Date...........

30/9/16

| | | |
|---|---|---|
| 2-0 a.m. | I.O.M. | Wired that gun was ready. |
| | O.C. | Handed to B.S.M. Chappell. |
| 5-0 a.m. | O.C. | Spoke to MN re forward position. |
| 10-30 a.m. | O.C. | Spoke to C.R.A. re leaving section of D/250 in old position to-night: also mentioned that Lieut. Darling and two men had been wounded last night up at the guns. |
| 10-30 a.m. | Liaison Officer | Reports small parties of enemy Infantry at M 16 b 9 9, N. of BUTTE-de-WARLENCOURT. |

Roving Battery had fired on them.

Report No. 15.    Daily Diary of Information
from 12 noon 30/9/16 to 12 noon 1/10/16

253rd (NORTHUMBRIAN) BRIGADE, R.F.A.

| Time | Information from: | |
|---|---|---|
| 5-10 p.m. | | 18-prs. reported falling short at M.22 c 7 7. All lines checked, and Battery Commanders being at O.P's observed every round. |
| | O.C. | Advised B.M. that he was satisfied not his Brigade. |
| 6-10 p.m. | O.C. | Conversation with S.C. re Officer casualties |
| 6-45 a.m. | B/253 | Received a message for DG dropped by a pigeon. |
| | O.C. | Informed DG and B.M. |
| 9-0 p.m. | O.C. | Informed B.M. D/250 have registered forward section: B/253 have registered battery in forward position. Wire cutting carried out well in accordance with programme. Barrage has been thoroughly and satisfactorily, viewed from O.P. |
| 11-35 p.m. | B.M. | Addendum to Operation Orders received. |
| | | Winter Time came into operation at 12 o'clock midnight. |

1/10/16.

| | | |
|---|---|---|
| 8-15 a.m. | B.M. | Ordered after 9-0 a.m., if you consider it necessary to do a little extra wire cutting, to make certain that your Bde. front is thoroughly done in. Infantry are not satisfied with Divisional front as a whole. |
| 10-10 a.m. | Lieut. Hitchinson, | Reported about 25 yards might have extra attention. |
| | O.C. | Instructed A/253 to see to this. |
| 10-55 a.m. | B.M. | Addendum to Operation Order No. 2 acknowledged. |

15TH SEPTEMBER, 1916.

| Time | Information or orders recd. from | |
|---|---|---|
| Zero Time 6.20 a.m. | | |
| 6.0 a.m. | R.A. 3rd Cps. | Bdes. to carry their Wireless masts with them in case of an advance. |
| 7.0 a.m. | 50 Div. | Orders for Artillery action three hours after Zero. |
| 7.12 a.m. | 252 Bde. | First objective achieved. Fwd. to G Office. |
| 7.21 a.m. | 253 " | Two hundred prisoners brought in. |
| 7.37 a.m. | 251 " | Very large explosion reported in direction of H.27.c. at 7.29 a.m. Fwd. G Office. |
| 7.50 a.m. | 15 D.A. | Message that 15 Div. have gained last objective. Fwd. G Office. |
| 7.55 a.m. | 50 Div. | Orders sent to 253 and 276 to lift Barrage and fire to be intense three hours after Zero. Liaison/reports second objective Gained. officer |
| 7.58 a.m. | 253 Bde. | CLARKES TRENCH and IVE TRENCH being shelled by 5.9. Hostile balloon over LE SARS WOOD. Fwd. G and C.B. Offices. |
| 8.0 a.m. | 252 Bde. | Bde. on right held up at HIGH WOOD. |
| 8.22 a.m. | 252 Bde. | Heavy hostile barrage on area N.E. of HIGH WOOD. Repeated C.B.Office. |
| 8.30 a.m. | 253 Bde. | Third objective reported achieved. Not confirmed. |
| 8.40 a.m. | 252 Bde. | |
| 8.57 a.m. | 15 D.A. | Verbal from 15 D.A. that Germans reported advancing in K.27.d. Repeated G Office. |
| 9.7 a.m. | 15 D.A. | Enemy reported massing in K.33.a. and K.33.b. Rates of barrage of 253 and 276 Bdes. increased. |
| 9.8 a.m. | 252 Bde. | Heavy enemy barrage CLARKS & SHARKEA TRENCHES. C.B.Office informed. Hostile balloon came down in flames. Another being pulled down. |
| 9.09 a.m. | 253 Bde. | Heavy barrages on our old front line and captured ground. |
| 11.0 a.m. | 251 Bde. | Enemy transport seen on POZIERES - LE SARS ROAD moving N.E. 3rd Corps H.A. informed. |

(2)

| Time | Unit | Message |
|---|---|---|
| 11.50 a.m. | 253 Bde. | Second objective reported consolidated. |
| 1.35 p.m. | 251 Bde. | Had one gun put out of action owing to burst in bore. |
| 1.45 p.m. | - | O.C. 253 ordered to move A and B batteries forward and come into action in square S.8.b. |
| 2.5 p.m. | 47 D.A. | Enemy reported massing in N.29.b and N.35.a. |
| 2.34 p.m. | 253 Bde. | Hostile infantry advancing about N.31.d. One battery turned on to search and sweep. |
| 2.45 p.m. | 50 Div. | Use of Code letters as designations of Units to cease. |
| 2.45 p.m. | 253 Bde. | Definitely reported that the whole of HIGH WOOD is now in our hands. |
| 3.30 p.m. | 50 Div. | Bombardment to take place from 4.15 to 4.45 p.m. Second objective to be consolidated. Instructions sent to 4 Bdes. |
| 4.17 p.m. | 253 Bde. | Has put two 18 pdrs batteries at 2 rds. per min. on N.33.b.5.3. to 3.6. How. Bty. 1 round per min. on Junction CRESCENT ALLEY STARFISH LINE. |
| 4.45 p.m. | 253 Bde. | Reports impossible to get batteries forward tonight. |
| 5.45 p.m. | 50 Div. | Infantry to attack from N.34.b. 8.8 to CRESCENT ALLEY at 7.30 p.m. Particulars of barrages to be forwarded to four Bdes. |
| 6.0 p.m. | 15 D.A. | Morbal from 15 D.A. Infantry moving south in N.27.d. |
| 6.20 p.m. | 251 Bde. | Hostile barrage put up immediately behind INTERMEDIATE TRENCH. Apparently a counter attack on 150 Bde. Commander asked for fire to lift 400 yards towards BAPAUME to enable South Camerons to take Ridge N.E. of MARTINPUICH. |
| 6.50 p.m. | 253 Bde. | MARTINPUICH SECTOR. |
| 7.0 p.m. | 50 Div. | Attack tonight is 8.0 p.m. instead of 7.0 p.m. |
| 7.40 p.m. | 50 Div. | " " "8.30 p.m. " " 8.0 p.m. |
| 7.45 p.m. | R.A.3rd Cps. | Forwarding barrages for night 15/16. |
| 8.40 p.m. | 50 Div. | 151 have had to postpone attack till 9.40 p.m. Intense barrage will be be from 9.35 to 9.40 p.m. Necessary orders forwarded Bdes. |

15th September, 1916.

| TIME. | Information or orders recd. from. | |
|---|---|---|
| A.M. | | |
| 5.50 | 50th Div. | Fourth Army will renew the attack today. 50th Division to seize and occupy PRUE TRENCH. Assault will take place at 9.25 preceded by 15 minutes bombardment beginning at 9.10 a.m. Orders given verbally by phone. |
| 8.50 | 252 Bde. | 149th Infantry Bde. ask for Artillery fire on GORE about M.34.b.2.8. with heavies. Bombardment carried out with our D&A. Considered too close for Heavy Artillery. |
| 9.0 | - | 252 Bde. ordered to turn their hows on to STARFISH ROAD. Barrage replaced by spare battery. |
| 9.15 | 50 Div. | 15th division have located left post of 50th Div. on PRUE TRENCH and are intouch. |
| 9.20 | - | All batteries ordered to lower rate to 1 Rd. per gun per minute. Hows. to 1 Rd. per 2 minutes. |
| 9.40 | R.A.3rd Corps | Artillery Instructions No. 72 received. |
| 10.30 | 252 Bde. | Reporting heavy bombardment of HIGH WOOD and heavy M.G. fire on Western portion of HOOK TRENCH. |
| 10.56 | 252 Bde. | 151 Inf.Bde. ask for Artillery to destroy CRESCENT ALLEY as far south as M.27.d. Two 4.5 Hows. batteries turned on. |
| 11.4 | 251 Bde. | Hows shortened range of all 18 pdrs. by 100 yards and increased fire to intense at 10.20 a.m. Slackened at 10.23 a.m. rate of two right batteries and lifted 100 yards. Two left batteries still firing at intense rate. Hows. firing on C.T. targets at intense rate and searching 50 yards short of target. |
| 11.4 | 251 Bde. | At 10.20 F.O.O. reported Germans with fixed bayonets in front of their trenches and inside our barrage. Barrers dropped and Germans dispersed. |
| 11.45 a. | Arty.3rd Corps | Positions to which batteries have moved forward to be reported. |
| 11.30 | 251 Bde. | Have reduced rate of fire of two left batteries to 1 Rd. per gun per minute and lifted them back to original barrage. |
| P.M. | | |
| 12.10 | 251 Bde. | Orders given for C257 to diverge and come into action at about S.9.b.8.5. Registration to be carried out this afternoon. |

(2)

| Time | Unit | Notes |
|---|---|---|
| P.M. | | |
| 1.13 | 251 Bde. | R.A.3rd Corps informed that A253 and B253 have moved forward. D250 now moving and C251 has been ordered to move. |
| 1.23 | 251 Bde. | F.O.O.reports enemy put up a slow barrage between first and second objectives. |
| 1.40 | R.A.3rd Corps | 4.5" How. fire to be put on CRESCENT ALLEY. Orders given to 251 and 276 Bdes. |
| 1.50 | 251 Bde. | Reports barrage is about 100 yards beyond German front line where Germans can be seen. Ordered to drop fire on to Germans at once. |
| 2.50 | 252 Bde. | Infantry Brigadier considers 18 pdr. barrages may be stopped but wishes How. fire to be continued on CRESCENT ALLEY AND PRUE TRENCH. |
| 4.50 | 50 Div. | Heavies have been ordered to shell PRUE TRENCH and PRUE COPSE. |
| 5.6 | 252 Bde. | 252. Asking permission to move H.L. wagon lines forward to A.1.b.1.3. Permission given. |
| 5.32 | 253 Bde. | Large amount of transport and troops reported on Road. Forwarded to G office. |
| 8.33 | R.A.3rd Corps | Night lines to be as last night. Tasks as usual 50% AX to be used. |
| 9.5 | 251 Bde. | Reporting C Battery in action in new position and partially registered. |
| 10.11 | 251 Bde. | Enemy putting heavy barrage of gas shells in hollows NORTH of BAZENTIN-LE-GRAND and BAZENTIN-LE-PETIT. |
| 10.55 | 50th Div. | 3rd Corps will continue to reorganise and consolidate its position. 50th Division to establish strong points in PRUE TRENCH. |
| 11.15 | 50th Div. | German prisoners reported to have stated that enemy intend to make a counter attack at 3.0 in the morning. All concerned to take precautions accordingly. |
| 11.40 | 50th Div. | Copy of warning order no.131 Fourth Army will renew the attack of 18th September. 3rd Corps will attack FLERS LINE up to EAUCOURT L'ABBAYE inclusive and other enemy's trenches. |

17th September, 1916.

| TIME | Information or orders recd. from | |
|---|---|---|
| A.M. | | |
| 8.17 | 252 Bde. | Reports quiet night. A few gas shells near batteries. |
| 8.25 | 253 Bde. | Tear shells and 10.5 near road in S.14.B.9.9. 11.0 p.m. to 3.0 a.m. |
| 9.32 | 251 Bde. | Reports quiet night. Enemy's heavies shelled S end of MARTINPUICH. Enemy artillery now less active. |
| 10.20 | — | Moves of batteries forward complete. C/252 now in action. Another 18 pdr. battery is moving forward to Square S.3.c. C/276, B/276 and D/276 to move forwd to about square S.8.d. A/251, B/251 D/251 and A/250 ordered to move to square S.9.b., batteries ordered to move by sections. |
| 10.37 | 253 Bde. | Enemy bombing down STARFISH. Has put on a barrage with 3 18 pdr. batteries and 1 How. Bty. at rate of one round per gun per minute. |
| 11.5 | — | Counter battery office informed that two enemy howitzers can be seen firing from the neighbourhood of G.34. |
| 11.24 | 252 Bde. | Heavy shelling continues on our support trenches from HIGH WOOD to MARTINPUICH. |
| 11.42 | 252 Bde. | F.O.O's. Report PRUE TRENCH up to junction CRESCENT ALLEY strongly held. Infantry brigadier asks for heavy bombardment on TRENCHs PRUE GORSE. Arranged for this B.A. to bombard. |
| P.M. | | |
| 12.12 | 251 Bde. | F.O.O. reports all quiet on their brigade front. |
| 12 noon | 252 Bde. | Orders sent 252 Bde. to move another 18 pdr. battery forward to come into action close to C/252's position. |
| 1.52 | 253 Bde. | Have turned on one battery 18 pdrs. to barrage N.33ȼ 5.5.-2.6. Rate 1 round per gun per minute. At request of Infantry Brigadier. |
| 1.50 | 50th Div. | During afternoon and evening operations will be taken with a view to occupying PRUE TRENCH and giving times of artillery bombardments. Programme sent to brigades. |
| 3.30 | 50th Div. | Time of bombardment of the CRESCENT TRIANGLE. |

(2)

| P.M. | | |
|---|---|---|
| 5.15 | 252 Bde. | Heavy hostile barrage now on area between BETHELL SAP & CLARKES TRENCH. |
| 5.40 | 252 Bde. | A high velocity gun from direction of SAUCOURT L'ABBAYE reported to be doing considerable damage in CATERPILLAR VALLEY. C.B.Office informed. |
| 5.46 | 252 Bde. | Enemy barrage on 50th front almost ceased. |
| 6.0 | 252 Bde. | Enemy are heavily shelling MARTINPUICH. |
| 6.5 | 50th Div. | 50th Div. is to capture PRUE TRENCH on 18th. Zero time to be 5.50. Further orders to be issued after tonight's operations. |
| 6.10 | 50th Div. | Aeroplane reconnaissance report. |
| 7.20 | 50th Div. | Two letter code calls allotted to Units will be used in all messages from 7.30 p.m. R.A. |
| 7.30 | — | Evening report forwarded/3rd Corps. |
| 7.39 | 276 Bde. | At 7.0 p.m. enemy bombarded our front line very heavily. |
| 8.22 | 252 Bde. | Reports a direct hit was obtained by our havies on a hostile battery and a large sheet of flame was seen. |
| 8.15 | 50th Div. | Our bombing attack was held up by heavy hostile barrage. Enemy was driven back on an attack on SUNKEN ROAD. |
| 9.22 | 253 Bde. | Report on progess of Registration of batteries. |
| 10.10 | 251 Bde. | F.O.O. reports that all is now quiet on Divisional front. Enemy artillery now slackened down. |
| 11.55 | 50th Div. | 150 Bde. will consolidate on 18th, having gained their objective. 151st Bde. to make good STARFISH LINE. Giving times of Artillery bombardments. |

18th September, 1916.

| Time | Information or orders recd. from | |
|---|---|---|
| A.m. 7.30 | 252 Bde. | Hostile infantry reported to be in extended order in his trenches opposite the BOW. Batteries warned. |
| 12 noon | R.A.3rd Corps | D.A. to arrange to engage with concentrated fire any active hostile batteries in area and be prepared to take on batteries reported by Counter Battery Office. |
| P.m. 12.10 | 252 Bde. | 151 Inf.Bde. will consolidate present position before any more operations are attempted. |
| 3.38 | 252 Bde. | Reports hostile artillery quiet. |
| 3.45 | R.A.3rd Corps. | Artillery Programme No. 7. received. |
| 4.10 | 50th Div. | 69th Bde. to take over a portion of front now held by 50th Division on morning of 19th. Artillery to cover same zones as at present. |
| 4.30 | 50th Div. | 4th Army will cease the attack on the 21st inst. in conjunction with the French. A steady bombardment of the hostile positions to commence at 7.0 a.m. on 20th and will continue till 6.30 p.m. To recommence at 6.30 a.m. on 21st. Fire of the artillery to be intense when the Infantry advance to the assault, at Zero, which will probably be in the afternoon. 151 Inf.Bde. to attack the CRUCIFIX on 19th. Heavy Artillery to bombard in conjunction with Field Artillery. Artillery Instructions and Warning order forwarded to Brigades. |
| 6.10 | 252 Bde. | Reports usual forward areas shelled also CATERPILLAR VALLEY, but not as heavy as last few days. |
| 6.45 | 276 Bde. | Situation report. All 18 pdr. batteries have moved forward and are registered. Two howitzers are forward but not yet registered. |
| 7.34 | 253 Bde. | Conditions of platforms and light have made it impossible to register STARFISH LINE. Will endeavour to register tomorrow morning. |
| 11.41 | R.A.3rd Corps. | Heavy Artillery will bombard PRUE COPSE, PRUE TRENCH and STARFISH LINE from 9.0 a.m. to 10.0 a.m. 19/9/16. 50th D.A. will arrange to co-operate by enfilade fire by hows. and 18 pdrs. |

19th September, 1916.

| TIME. | Information or orders recd. from | |
|---|---|---|
| A.M. | | |
| 1.0 | 50th Div. | Heavy Artillery will bombard PRUE TRENCH, PRUE COPSE, and STARFISH LINE from 9.a.m.to 10.0 a.m. |
| 8.0. | 50th Div. | All Brigades ordered to register with 18 pdrs. and 4.5 Hows. on STARFISH LINE. Act to start before 10.0 a.m. |
| 10.45 | 252 Bde. | Reports that night has been quiet. |
| 11.15 | 252 Bde. | Reporting reconnaissance made to obtain place to view PRUE TRENCH and STARFISH. |
| P.M. | | By was |
| 1.0 | 3rd Corps H.A. | Heavy Artillery will bombard PRUE TRENCH and STARFISH LINE between 4.0 and 5.0 p.m.today. |
| 2.45 | 251 Bde. | Reporting movement of Germans seen whilst registering PRUE TRENCH. |
| 3.50 | 253 Bde. | At request of Inf. Bde. on 50th Div.left have turned a battery on to CRESCENT ALLEY. Apparently Germans have been bombing down it. |
| 6.55 | 50th D.A. | Intelligence Wire. Sent R.A. 3rd Corps. |
| 7.22 | T,M's. | For permission to send six 2" T.M's. to I.O.M. for modification of Temple Silencers. Permission given for them to be sent two at a time. |
| 7.54 | 251 Bde. | Enemy shelling Divisional front trenches with 10 cm How. and 7.7 cm gun. |
| 8.20 | 252 Bde. | At 4.0 p.m. enemy made a bombing attack on the CRESCENT. This was beaten back. 252 Bde.fired in support of our bombers until attack finished. |
| 9.20 | 253 Bde. | Very lights in pairs sent up in several places between MARTINPUICH,HIGH WOOD. O.C. has stopped D253 firing,except one gun on programme. D350 also firing on programme. Other batteries firing on programme at increased rate of fire, one round per gun per minute. |
| 10.30 | 50 Div. | 4th Army attack fixed for 21st now postponed to 22nd or 23rd. Brigades informed. |

30th September, 1916.

| TIME | Information or orders recd. from | |
|---|---|---|
| A.M. | | |
| 3.20 | 251 Bde. | F.O.O. reports enemy are shelling our front line very heavily. |
| 4.45 | 251 Bde. | F.O.O. reports all quiet on Divisional front. |
| 8.14 | 251 Bde. | F.O.O. reports all quiet on Divisional front. |
| 11.0 | 253 Bde. | Applying for road control on main road through X.20. Passed to H.Q.Division. |
| 11.17 | 251 Bde. | 10 cm how. shelled battery positions for half an hour commencing 10.30 a.m. |
| 11.30 | 50th Div. | Orders received from Corps that defensive attitude is to be maintained for the present and energy devoted to strengthening positions already gained. |
| 11.35 | 50th Div. | Reporting to Corps that a large amount of ammunition was expended last night owing to German RED LIGHTS being mistaken for ours. Recommending former light signal be used if supply can be maintained. |
| P.M. | | |
| 12.10 | Arty.Trl Corps. | Instructions that ammunition must only be used in proportion to the rate of getting it up to gun positions, and fire stopped altogether if necessary. |
| P.M. | | |
| 5.25 | 253 Bde. | Orders are lying S.A.D.O.4. for registering PRUE TRENCH & STARFISH LINE. |
| 7.45 | D.A.C. | Reporting arrival in forward area H.Q. in X.27.A. |
| 8.30 | 251 Bde. | B251 reports that it evident that enemy is firing by observation from balloons or aeroplane. It is noticed that he shelled road from BAZENTIN to HIGH WOOD only on occasions when transport was on it. |

21st September, 1916.

| Time | Information or orders recd. from. | |
|---|---|---|
| 3.50 | 251 Bde. | S.9.b. fairly heavily shelled with tear shells. |
| 4.20 | 251 Bde. | Reports all quiet on Division front. |
| 11.56 P.M. | 251 Bde. | S.9.b. again heavily shelled by 5.9 Bty. from direction W of LE SARS. |
| 2.30 | 251 Bde. | Our Infantry Patrols being out tonight digging and to ascertain situation in STARFISH LINE. |
| 5.20 | 23rd D.A. | Report having fired 700 rounds into CRESCENT ALLEY and 250 rounds HOW. on STARFISH LINE. They have received report that 1st Division have entered STARFISH LINE and have established strong point at H.34.b.4.1. |
| 6.0 | 50th Div. | S.O.S. signal from 6.0 p.m. to day will be THREE RED Rockets instead of TWO. |
| 6.15 | 3rd Corps R.A. | Artillery Instruction No. 75 received. 4th Army to renew the attack on date to be notified later. Instructions forwarded to Brigades. |
| 6.15 | - do - | By night 22nd as much ammunition as possible is to be with the guns. |
| 7.15 | | Situation Report forwarded R.A.Corps. |
| 9.15 | 252 Bde. | Liaison Officer reports brigade on left and right have entered STARFISH LINE. 149 have also entered. Whole propose to enter PRUE TRENCH. |
| 10.30 | 50th Div. | Giving corrector for Secret Code A from midnight 22/23rd. |
| 10.30 | - do - | On night 22/23rd 150th Infantry Bde. will relieve 149th Infantry Bde. On completion 150th will be in trenches, 151 in Support and 149th in Reserve. |
| 10.40 | 251 Bde. | From 10.30 p.m. area S.9.b. has been shelled by gas or tear shells. Shelling continues but not intense. |
| 11.57 | 252 Bde. | Liaison Officer reports Infantry have occupied STARFISH LINE without opposition. Patrols have pushed out to PRUE TRENCH. |

22nd September, 1916.

| TIME | Information or orders recd. from | |
|---|---|---|
| A.M. | | |
| 12.40 | 253 Bde. | Enemy has sent up very few VERY lights in spite of our continuous bombardment. |
| 12.45 | 253 Bde. | Our Infantry have occupied CRESCENT ALLEY. |
| 5.10 | 252 Bde. | 149 Bde. now have some troops in PRUE TRENCH. |
| 5.45 | 252 Bde. | Our Infantry have joined up on both flanks in STARFISH LINE. Have not met with any opposition. |
| 9.30 | 253 Bde. | Report that patrols have pushed forward from line of second objective and report no enemy in sight between them and EAUCOURT L'ABBAYE. |
| 9.55 | - | All batteries ordered to cease fire but to be on the alert. |
| 10.10 | | Brigades informed of Corrector for Secret Code A. |
| 10.20 | | Informing Brigades of Infantry Reliefs night 23/24 Sept. |
| 10.20 | - | 18 pdr. ammunition is to be used sparingly except for fleeting opportunities. Any parties seen digging to be immediately engaged. |
| 10.50 | 253 Bde. | Report that hostile aeroplanes have been flying unmolested over Battery positions for last two hours. |
| 11.30 | R.A.3rd Corps | To cancel Artillery Instructions No.75 (Received 22.9.16). |
| 11.55 | 276 Bde. | At 11.30 a.m. our Infantry were holding PRUE TRENCH. Patrols were then out on MARTINPUICH - EAUCOURT L'ABBAYE Road and proceeding to second objective. |
| P.M. | | |
| 2.20 | 252 Bde. | 149th Inf. Bde. are consolidating on line M.27.d. and M.28.c. |
| 1.30 | 251 Bde. | Large party of Germans working from M.5.b.2.9. to 500 yards to E of that point. Out of range of D.A. Heavy Artillery informed. |

(2)

| P.M. | | |
|---|---|---|
| 2.45 | 251 Bde. | Long line of Germans seen digging in square NORTH of N.1.a. Apparently working very hard. Heavy Artillery informed. |
| 3.15 | 251 Bde. | F.O.O. reports cannot see any of enemy working in trench S of EAUCOURT L'ABBAYE. Slight shelling of PRUE TRENCH & BAZENTIN-LE-GRAND. |
| 5.30 | 251 Bde. | Cannot see any enemy movement in Bde. area. No working parties or transport. Enemy aeroplanes very active over Battery positions. |
| 5.33 | 251 Bde. | Enemy balloon seen on ground at X roads G.33.b. Heavy artillery informed. |
| 6.50 | 251 Bde. | F.O.O. reports large fire has broken out West of LE SARS. |
| 7.30 | 50 D.A. | Situation report sent 3rd Corps. |
| 7.40 | 251 Bde. | Battery engaged column of Infantry marching SW on road at M.18.c.5.6. Shells fell well amongst Infantry who dispersed. |
| 7.47 | 251 Bde. | Reports gas cloud seen coming from German lines M.21b.3.8. |
| 8.35 | 252 Bde. | Liaison Officer reports Infantry do not wish any artillery fire S. of line M.27 Central to M.29.a.2.0. |
| 8.55 | 252 Bde. | There appears to be a German bombing attack N.E. of MARTINPUICH. Germans have put up a heavy barrage on N. side of MARTINPUICH. |

23rd September, 1916.

| TIME | Information or orders recd. from | |
|---|---|---|
| A.M. | | |
| 6.25 | 251 Bde. | F.O.O. Reports very quiet night, and no movement of enemy observed. |
| 7.5 | 251 Bde. | F.O.O. Reports too misty to observe anything closely up to present. |
| 7.36 | 253 Bde. | F.O.O. reports entire absence of enemy VERY lights on Divisional front. Rather points to retirement of enemy to EAUCOURT -L'ABBAYE. |
| 9.26 | 252 Bde. | Reports quiet night, PRUE and HOOK trenches shelled during the night and M.G.fire at long range. |
| 9.55 | R.A. | Pole has been erected at S.3.b.1.9. Bdes to report whether visible (Pole is where CRESCENT ALLEY leaves HOOK TRENCH). |
| 10.7 | 251 Bde. | Reports all quiet on Divl. front. We have established strong point at M.27.c.8.3. Low mist making visibility poor. |
| 11.0 | C.R.A. | Programme for previous 24 hours to be repeated. |
| P.M. | | |
| 12.17 | 253 Bde. | May a flag be put on identification pole. |
| 4.25 | 253 Bde. | O.P. reports large fire in enemy lines 10 degs. Right from THILLOY CHURCH from S.3.a.9.9. |
| 6.12 | 253 Bde. | Reports heavy hostile barrage on front line N.E. of MARTINPUICH. |
| 6.18 | 251 Bde. | Has fired on party of Germans walking about at M.18.c.3.2. and dispersed them. |
| 6.30 | C.R.A. | Instructing R.O. to arrange for one gun to enfilade road running M.22.c.9.0. to M.16.d.8.8. |
| 6.30 | C.R.A. | Instructing bdes that no artillery fire is to be brought to bear on area South of a line M.27 Central to M.29.a.2.0. |
| 7.5 | 253 Bde. | At 6.0 p.m. enemy shelled our trenches heavily for ten minutes. |

| | | |
|---|---|---|
| P.M. | | |
| 7.5 | C.R.A. | Situation report forwarded R.A. 3rd Corps. |
| 7.52 | 251 Bde. | No movement observed in hostile area. |
| 7.50 | 253 Bde. | Front line trenches being heavily bombarded by 4.2" |
| 7.52 | 253 Bde. | M.G.fire bothering working party at SUNKEN ROAD. 253 Bde. ordered to deal with |
| 7.52 | C.R.A. | A/252, C/250 & D/250 to move forward to about S.3.d.3.1. & S.10.a.1.1.. Moves to be made by Sections. Leading section to be registered before 2nd section moves up. |
| 8.5 | 252 Bde. | All batteries are registered and in communication with Bde H.Q. |
| 8.28 | 251 Bde. | Large number of Germans seen digging line South of LE BARQUE. |
| 10.10 | 252 Bde. | Liaison Officers report on enemy's trenches and our O.P's. |
| 10.40 | R.A.3rd Corps. | Artillery Instructions No. 75 received. 4th Army are to renew attack on 25th and Reserve Army on 26th. Artillery Instructions forwarded brigades with Programme. |

24th September, 1916.

| TIME | Information or orders recd. from | |
|---|---|---|
| A.M. | | |
| 3.21 | 251 Bde. | F.O.O. reports all quiet on front except for intermittent shelling by 10.5 cm on our Div.front. |
| 7.23 | 251 Bde. | F.O.O. reports all quiet. No enemy activity seen but observation difficult owing to mist. |
| 10.0 | C.R.A. | Confirmation of orders given re move forward of A/252, C/250 and D/252. |
| 10.10 | 50 Div. | 150 Inf. Bde. is to reconnoitre enemy line M.29.a.2.3. -M.28.b.8.7. -M.28.a.3.6. No artillery to fire South of an E & W line through the cutting from 3.30 a.m. to 5.0 a.m. on 25th instant. Instructions fwd. to Bdes 3.30 p.m. |
| 2.35 | 50th Div | 1st Div. will seize and hold the FLERS front and support line as far as the C.T. at M.29.d.4.9. Zero hour 8.30 p.m. 24th. |
| 3.20 | 276 Bde. | Road through N.1.a.7.7. reported to be used by enemy transport. |
| 3.29 | 47th D.A. | Asking us to take on part of new enemy trench in our area running from M.28.b.6.7. to M.29.B.2.1½. |
| 4.6 | 253 Bde. | Bde. on left have taken trench running through 27 A & D. They are going for trench running thro. 26 B & C. StAR QUARRY in 22D very strongly fortified. |
| 6.35 | 252 Bde. | Reporting quiet day. Fired on and dispersed transport. |
| 7.35 | C.R.A. | Situation report forwarded 3rd Corps. |
| 8.30 | 251 Bde. | Report on day's work, points shelled etc. |
| 8.48 | 252 Bde. | PRUE TRENCH, STARFISH LINE & SUNKEN ROAD in JACKSON STREET being steadily shelled by a 4.2 Bty. from direction of LE SARS. Forwarded C.B.Office. |
| 8.52 | 251 Bde. | F.O.O. reports situation normal. |
| 9.0 | C.R.A. | Reporting to R.A. 3rd Corps move of A/252, D252 & C250 to S.3.d.3.1., S.9.b.7.4. & S.3.d.2.2. respectively and all batteries registered. |

25th September, 1916.

| TIME | Information or orders recd. from | |
|---|---|---|
| A.M. | | |
| 5.20 | 251 Bde. | Reports all quiet on Divisional front. Hostile artillery very quiet during night. |
| 8.2 | 253 Bde. | Reporting premature in D250. Five men wounded. |
| 12.35 | - | Zero hour for attack. 50 D.A. carrying out 3 minutes intense bombardment. |
| 12.40 | 50 Div. | C.E.reports small parties of Germans seen about 12.20 p.m. retiring N.E. from EAUCOURT L'ABBAYE, up road through M.23.b. |
| 1.1pm | 252 Bde. | F.O.O. reports hostile barrage along whole front line. Infantry of Right Division appear to have reached first objective. |
| P.M. | | |
| 1.15 | 252 Bde. | 4th E.Y. report Germans collecting on FLERS LINE S of EAUCOURT L'ABBAYE. A and D/252 turned on to them. |
| 1.40 | 252 Bde. | Reporting heavy barrage on MARTINPUICH. |
| 1.46 | 252 Bde. | Movement on Right appears to have been entirely successful and our men consolidating both positions |
| 2.15 | 50 D.A. | Verbal. Div. on right have gained objective and are in touch with our Infantry. 50th Div. are going to gain further enemy trenches by bombing. |
| 2.34 | 252 Bde. | Hostile shelling of MARTINPUICH has practically ceased. |
| 4.7 | C.R.A. | 252 Bde. ordered to fire with 4.5" Hows. on trench M.23.c.0.7. where movement has been observed, by G.O.C. 150th Inf. Bde. |
| 4.18 | 276 Bde. | Our Infantry believed to be in trench about M.29.a.0.5. Heavy enemy shelling about junction of PRUE TRENCH & CRESCENT ALLEY. |
| 4.58 | 253 Bde. | Large fire reported in EAUCOURT L'ABBAYE. Said to have been caused by our Heavy Artillery. |
| 5.0 | 50th Div. | 3rd Corps report verbally that British havecaptured LES BOEUFS, the Northern half of MORVAL |

25th September, 1916.

| TIME | Information or orders recd. from | |
|---|---|---|
| A.M. | | |
| 5.20 | 251 Bde. | Reports all quiet on Divisional front. Hostile artillery very quiet during night. |
| 8.2 | 253 Bde. | Reporting premature in D250. Five men wounded. |
| 12.35 | - | Zero hour for attack. 50 D.A. carrying out 3 minutes intense bombardment. |
| 12.45 | 50 Div. | C.E. reports small parties of Germans seen about 12.20 p.m. retiring N.E. from EAUCOURT L'ABBAYE, up road through M.23.b. |
| P.M. | | |
| 1.1pm | 252 Bde. | F.O.O. reports hostile barrage along whole front line. Infantry of Right Division appear to have reached first objective. |
| 1.15 | 252 Bde. | 4th E.Y. report Germans collecting on FLERS LINE S of EAUCOURT L'ABBAYE. A and D/252 turned on to them. |
| 1.40 | 252 Bde. | Reporting heavy barrage on MARTINPUICH. |
| 1.46 | 252 Bde. | Movement on Right appears to have been entirely successful and our men consolidating both positions |
| 2.15 | 50 D.A. | Verbal. Div. on right have gained objective and are in touch with our Infantry. 50th Div. are going to gain further enemy trenches by bombing. |
| 2.34 | 252 Bde. | Hostile shelling of PARTINPUICH has practically ceased. |
| 4.7 | C.R.A. | 252 Bde. ordered to fire with 4.5" Hows. on trench M.23.c.0.7. where movement has been observed, by G.O.C. 150th Inf. Bde. |
| 4.18 | 276 Bde. | Our Infantry believed to be in trench about M.29.a.0.5. Heavy enemy shelling about junction of PRUE TRENCH & CRESCENT ALLEY. |
| 4.58 | 253 Bde. | Large fire reported in EAUCOURT L'ABBAYE. Said to have been caused by our Heavy Artillery. |
| 5.0 | 50th Div. | 3rd Corps report verbally that British have captured LES BOEUFS, the Northern half of MORVAL |

(2)

| | | |
|---|---|---|
| P.M. | | and we are in GUEUDECOURT. |
| 5.1 | 252 Bde. | 3rd Inf. Bde. is now 100 yards in front of second objective. At present held up in FLERS support line by counter attack. |
| 5.57 | 252 Bde. | F.O.O. reports road from EAUCOURT L'ABBAYE to LE BARQUE much used by German Infantry. They are firing on it with 18 Pdrs. |
| 6.12 | 251 Bde. | Party of 20 Germans seen on road M.17.d.7.2. and shelled. Casualties caused. Visibility now poor owing to ground mist. |
| 6.27 | 251 Bde. | At 3.30, 4.0 and 5.30 p.m. small parties engaged by 18 Pdrs on road EAUCOURT L'ABBAYE -LE BARQUE. |
| 6.48 | 253 Bde. | Divisional barrage put up at 12.30 p.m. exceedingly good. Very evenly distributed over whole Zone. No gaps at all and Bursts good. |
| 7.10 | C.R.A. | Situation Report forwarded R.A. 3rd Corps. |
| 7.39 | 253 Bde. | Small enemy party engaged and scattered at M.23.d.5.8. Another party engaged at M.18 Central. Result not observed owing to poor light. |
| 9.49 | 252 Bde. | PRUE TRENCH & STARFISH LINE being heavily shelled by 5.9 from direction of LE SARS. Counter Battery office informed. |
| 11.20 | 251 Bde. | F.O.O. reports all normal on this Divisional Zone. |

(2)

P.M.

and we are in GUEUDECOURT.

5.1 252 Bde. 3rd Inf. Bde. is now 100 yards in front of second objective. At present held up in FLERS support line by counter attack.

5.57 252 Bde. F.O.O. reports road from EAUCOURT L'ABBAYE to LE BARQUE much used by German Infantry. They are firing on it with 18 Pdrs.

6.12 251 Bde. Party of 20 Germans seen on road M.17.d.7.2. and shelled. Casualties caused. Visibility now poor owing to ground mist.

6.27 251 Bde. At 3.30, 4.0 and 5.30 p.m. small parties engaged by 18 Pdrs on road EAUCOURT L'ABBAYE - LE BARQUE. Very evenly distributed over whole

6.48 253 Bde. Divisional barrage put up at 12.30 p.m. exceedingly good. Very evenly distributed over whole Zone. No gaps at all and Bursts good.

7.10 C.R.A. Situation Report forwarded R.A. 3rd Corps.

7.39 253 Bde. Small enemy party engaged and scattered at M.23.d.5.8. Another party engaged at M.18 Central. Result not observed owing to poor light.

9.49 252 Bde. PRUE TRENCH & STARFISH LINE being heavily shelled by 5.9 from direction of LE SARS. Counter Battery office informed.

11.20 251 Bde. F.O.O. reports all normal on this Divisional Zone.

26th September, 1916.

| TIME | Information or orders recd. from | |
|---|---|---|
| A.M. | | |
| 12.35 | 251 Bde. | S.O.S.Signal observed on left at 11.18 Opened out on S.O.S.Barrages. Right Bn R.O.O.was not aware of necessity for S.O.S. Fire slackened down and stopped except for programme tasks by 11.45 p.m. |
| 1.0 | 50th Div. | Giving details of points which are to be gained prior to assault at Zero on 27th. |
| 9.30 | 251 Bde. | Situation on our front normal. Enemy appear to be bombarding heavily in and around GUEUDECOURT. |
| 10.11 | 252 Bde. | Reports quiet night. Hostile artillery fired intermittently on our front during the night. |
| 10.40 | 251 Bde. | Party of Infantry seen on LE BARQUE - EAUCOURT L'ABBAYE Road were engaged and casualties inflicted. |
| 12noon | C.R.A. | Orders to Bdes. to engage hostile Batteries by their Roving Battery. |
| P.M. | | |
| 12.18 | 251 Bde. | Horse and motor transport seen on BAPAUME Road and large working party on trench in M.4. & M.5. and M.6. Heavy artillery informed. |
| 12.30 | 50th Div. | Third Corps wires that 21st Div. have taken the whole of GIRD trench and are in touch with the Guards on their Right. 14th Corps. have patrols in COMBLES in touch with the French |
| 1.40 | 50th Div. | Corps reports verbally that the French have taken COMBLES. |
| 2.55 | do. | 150 Inf. Bde. to carry out attack at 11.0 p.m. Div. Arty to co-operate by putting up a light barrage and 4.5" to bombard trenches in vicinity. |
| 3.0 | 252 Bde. | Reports M.G. emplacement very strongly built commands ground on our front from BUTTE-DE-WARLENCOURT. Few hostile guns in action against our front. |
| 4.30 | 50th Div. | Corps reports that 2nd Corps have captured THIEPVAL. Unofficial report says 1500 prisoners and 40 machine guns. 15th Corps got 360 prisoners in Gird trench. Canadian Corps have captured high ground N.W. of COURCELETTE. |

26th September, 1916.

| TIME | Information or orders recd. from | |
|---|---|---|
| A.M. | | |
| 12.35 | 251 Bde. | S.O.S.Signal observed on left at 11.18 Opened out on S.O.S.barrages. Right Bn F.O.O.was not aware of necessity for S.O.S. Fire slackened down and stopped except for programme tasks by 11.45 p.m. |
| 1.0 | 50th Div. | Giving details of points which are to be gained prior to assault at zero on 27th. |
| 9.30 | 251 Bde. | Situation on our front normal. Enemy appear to be bombarding heavily in and around GUEUDECOURT. |
| 10.11 | 252 Bde. | Reports quiet night. Hostile artillery fired intermittently on our front during the night. |
| 10.40 | 251 Bde. | Party of Infantry seen on LE BARQUE - EAUCOURT L'ABBAYE Road were engaged and casualties inflicted. |
| 12noon | C.R.A. | Orders to Bdes. to engage hostile batteries by their Roving Battery. |
| P.M. | | |
| 12.15 | 251 Bde. | Horse and motor transport seen on BAPAUME Road and large working party on trench in M.4. & M.5. and M.6. Heavy artillery informed. |
| 12.30 | 50th Div. | Third Corps wires that 21st Div. have taken the whole of GIRD trench and are in touch with the Guards on their Right. 14th Corps. have patrols in COMBLES in touch with the French |
| 1.40 | 50th Div. | Corps reports verbally that the French have taken COMBLES. |
| 2.55 | do. | 150 Inf. Bde. to carry out attack at 11.0 p.m. Div. Arty to co-operate by putting up a light barrage and 4.5" to bombard trenches in vicinity. |
| 3.0 | 252 Bde. | Reports M.G. emplacement very strongly built commands ground on our front from BUTTE-DE-WARLENCOURT. Few hostile guns in action against our front. |
| 4.30 | 50th Div. | Corps reports that 2nd Corps have captured THIEPVAL. Unofficial report says 1500 prisoners and 40 machine guns. 15th Corps got 360 prisoners in Gird trench. Canadian Corps have captured high ground N.W. of COURCELETTE. |

(2)

| P.M. | | |
|---|---|---|
| 4.33 | 251 Bde. | Germans seen massing for counter attack about M.19 Central. Barrage was put up and attack subsided. |
| 6.0 | 50th Div. | Attack tonight will be at 11.5 p.m. Artillery tasks to be altered to five minutes later. |
| 7.10 | C.R.A. | Evening situation report forwarded R.A. 3rd Corps. |
| 8.25 | 50th Div. | 15th Corps report that 21st Division have taken whole of GUEUDECOURT and hold a line thence to the Guards Division at LES BOEUFS. Strong hostile counter attack at 1.0 p.m. repulsed by artillery fire. |
| 9.28 | C.R.A. | Four Brigades informed that if P.S. is required and S.K. is available, S.K. will be issued and used in lieu of P.S. |
| 10.0 | 50 Div. | 47th Division (less Artillery) will relieve 1st Division on night 28/29th Sept. |
| 10.5 | C.R.A. | F.U. and R.O. ordered to move A/276 and B/276 and A/253 and B/250 forward. First sections to move at dawn and second sections when first have completed registration in new positions. |
| 10.48 | 276 Bde. | Very little movement observed on their front today. |

(2)

P.M.
4.33  251 Bde.     Germans seen massing for counter attack about M.19 Central. Barrage was put up and attack subsided.

6.0   50th Div.    Attack tonight will be at 11.5 p.m. Artillery tasks to be altered to five minutes later.

7.10  C.R.A.       Evening situation report forwarded R.A. 3rd Corps.

8.25  50th Div.    15th Corps report that 21st Division have taken whole of GUEUDECOURT and hold a line thence to the Guards Division at LES BOEUFS. Strong hostile counter attack at 1.0 p.m. repulsed by artillery fire.

9.28  O.R.A.       Four Brigades informed that if P.S. is required and S.K. is available, S.K. will be issued and used in lieu of P.S.

10.0  50 Div.      47th Division (less Artillery) will relieve 1st Division on night 28/29th Sept.

10.5  C.R.A.       F.U. and R.O. ordered to move A/276 and B/276 and A/253 and B/253 and B/250 forward. First sections to move at dawn and second sections when first have completed registration in new positions.

10.48 276 Bde.     Very little movement observed on their front today.

27th September, 1916.

| TIME | Information or orders recd. from | |
|---|---|---|
| A.M. | | |
| 1.25 | 50 D.A. | Warning Order. Corps on right is continuing the attack today. Divisions to arrange their own Field Artillery Barrages on enemy's front line. |
| 1.27 | 251 Bde. | Situation practically unchanged since 11.0 p.m. last night. |
| 2.10 | 50th Div. | Two Battalions 150th Inf.Bde. assaulted at 11.0 p.m. 26.9.16 and though enemy trench was strongly held they effected a lodgement. Right Bn. driven out by German counter attack but left Bn. is consolidating in German trench. |
| 2.20 | R.A.3rd Corps. | Artillery Instructions No. 78 received and acknowledged. |
| 3.15 | 50th Div. | Notifying Zero hour today viz:- 2.15 p.m. |
| 3.30 | 50th Div. | Situation report on front. |
| 4.15 | do. | As soon as it is light enough 18 pdrs. and 4.5" hows. are to bombard enemy trenches |
| 9.5 | C.R.A. | Programme for night 27/28 to be as required by situation. No P.S. or Thermit shell will be fired. |
| 9.30 | 50th Div. | C.E. is to take remainder of objective this afternoon. Intense bombardment to open at Zero and continue for 20 minutes when it will lift 200 yards and slacken. Infantry to enter enemy trenches at Zero plus 20 minutes. Operation order No. 36 issued with Artillery Programme. |
| 10.21 | 253 Bde. | First Sections A/253 and B/250 came into action in new position at 8.0 a.m. and are registered. |
| 11.5 | 251 Bde. | C/251 Reports railway along main road in H.31.d. appears to be used. Out of range for Field Artillery. Heavy Artillery informed. |
| 11.20 | 252 Bde. | Liaison Officer reports that Infantry think enemy have vacated their front line. Infantry are investigating. |
| P.M. | | |
| 12.30 | C.R.A. | 50th Division will in conjunction with 1st Division intend to take remainder of objective at 2.15 this afternoon. Operation Order No. 36 issued with Programme of Bombardment for 50th D.A. assisted by 23rd D.A. |

27th September, 1916.

| TIME | Information or orders recd. from | |
|---|---|---|
| A.M. | | |
| 1.25 | 50 D.A. | Warning Order. Corps on right is continuing the attack today. Divisions to arrange their own Field Artillery Barrages on enemy's front line. |
| 1.27 | 251 Bde. | Situation practically unchanged since 11.0 p.m. last night. |
| 2.10 | 50th Div. | Two Battalions 150th Inf.Bde. assaulted at 11.0 p.m. 26.9.16 and though enemy trench was strongly held they effected a lodgement. Right Bn. driven out by German counter attack but left Bn. is consolidating in German trench. |
| 2.20 | R.A.3rd Corps. | Artillery Instructions No. 78 received and acknowledged. |
| 3.15 | 50th Div. | Notifying Zero hour today viz:- 2.15 p.m. |
| 3.30 | 50th Div. | Situation report on front. |
| 4.15 | do. | As soon as it is light enough 18 pdrs. and 4.5" hows. are to bombard enemy trenches |
| 9.5 | C.R.A. | Programme for night 27/28 to be as required by situation. No P.S. or Thermit shell will be fired. |
| 9.30 | 50th Div. | C.R.A. is to take remainder of objective this afternoon. Intense bombardment to open at Zero and continue for 20 minutes when it will lift 200 yards and slacken. Infantry to enter enemy trenches at Zero plus 20 minutes. Operation order No. 36 issued with Artillery Programme. |
| 10.21 | 253 Bde. | First Sections A/253 and B/250 came into action in new position at 8.0 a.m. and are registered. |
| 11.5 | 251 Bde. | C/251 Reports railway along main road in H.31.d. appears to be used. Out of range for Field Artillery. Heavy Artillery informed. |
| 11.20 | 252 Bde. | Liaison Officer reports that Infantry think enemy have vacated their front line. Infantry are investigating. |
| P.M. | | |
| 12.30 | C.R.A. | 50th Division in conjunction with 1st Division intend to take remainder of objective at 2.15 this afternoon. Operation Order No. 36 issued with Programme of Bombardment for 50th D.A. assisted by 23rd D.A. |

(2)

| TIME | Information or orders recd. from | |
|---|---|---|
| P.M. | | |
| 1.50 | 252 Bde. | Infantry are now bombing up CRESCENT ALLEY from M.28.a.6.5. |
| 1.1 | 276 Bde. | Forward Sections of A and B/276 have now completed registration and rear sections are moving up. |
| 1.40 | 50th Div. | 150 Bde. have gained ground by bombing and have established blocks at about M.28.b.1.7. and 1.8. Further bombing to be carried out when barrage lifts. |
| 2.35 | 50 Div. | At 3.0 p.m. all artillery will lift to FLERS line to enable Infantry to push patrols forward. Brigades informed. |
| 3.36 | 252 Bde. | F.O.O. report states all objectives up to CRESCENT ALLEY in M.22.d. appear to have been gained. Hostile barrage missed our men. |
| 5.35 | 253 Bde. | Liaison Officer reports Division on our Right entered EAUCOURT L'ABBAYE and were bombing up FLERS LINE. |
| 6.50 | 50th Div. | 23rd Division situation report. |
| 8.6 | Arty.3rd Corps | Giving night tasks for 27/28th. |
| 8.10 | 50th Div. | Operation to be undertaken by 150th Inf.Bde. tonight. |
| 9.50 | C.R.A. | Instructions re operations by Infantry night 27/28th. |
| 10.15 | 50th Div. | Giving situation report on Divisional front and on 1st and 23rd Divisions' front. |

(2)

| Time | Information or orders recd. from | |
|---|---|---|
| P.M. | | |
| 1.50 | 252 Bde. | Infantry are now bombing up CRESCENT ALLEY from M.28.a.6.5. |
| 1.1 | 276 Bde. | Forward Sections of A and B/276 have now completed registration and rear sections are moving up. |
| 1.40 | 50th Div. | 150 Bde. have gained ground by bombing and have established blocks at about M.28.b.1.7. and 1.8. Further bombing to be carried out when barrage lifts. |
| 2.35 | 50 Div. | At 3.0 p.m. all artillery will lift to FLERS line to enable Infantry to push patrols forward. Brigades informed. |
| 3.36 | 252 Bde. | F.O.O. report states all objectives up to CRESCENT ALLEY in M.22.d. appear to have been gained. Hostile barrage missed our men. |
| 5.35 | 253 Bde. | Liaison Officer reports Division on our Right entered EAUCOURT L'ABBAYE and were bombing up FLERS LINE. |
| 6.50 | 50th Div. | 23rd Division situation report. |
| 8.6 | Arty.3rd Corps | Giving night tasks for 27/28th. |
| 8.10 | 50th Div. | Operation to be undertaken by 150th Inf.Bde. tonight. |
| 9.50 | C.R.A. | Instructions re operations by Infantry night 27/28th. |
| 10.15 | 50th Div. | Giving situation report on Divisional front and on 1st and 23rd Divisions' front. |

28th September, 1916.

| TIME | Information or orders recd. from | |
|---|---|---|
| A.M. | | |
| 9.15 | R.A.3rd Corps | For report on wire in front of FLERS LINE. |
| 9.50 | 151 Inf.Bde. | Asking for our Artillery to fire on West corner of EAUCOURT L'ABBAYE where German machine guns have been located. One how. of 252 bde. put on and 47th D.A. asked to co-operate. |
| 10.0 | C.R.A. | 50th D.A. Operation Order No. 37 issued. 276 Bde. to be relieved on 28/29 Sept. by 39th Bde. of 1st Div. Arty.(6 gun Batteries). Batteries relieving C/276 and D/276 to move to more forward positions as soon as possible after relief. A,B and C Batteries 250 Bde. to come out of action on afternoon of 29th and proceed to Wagon Lines. |
| 10.0 | C.R.A. | Orders issued for personnel of B/250 to be relieved by personnel of C/253. Relief to be completed by 12 noon. |
| P.M. | | |
| 1.40 | 253 Bde. | Reporting completion of relief of B/250 by C/253 personnel. Timed 12.10 p.m. |
| 1.25 | 251 Bde. | D/251 fired at small party of enemy moving about behind FLERS LINE. |
| 2.10 | 251 Bde. | F.O.O. B/251 reports several hundreds of Huns working on trench in G36. Repeated G 50th Div. and H.A. 3rd Corps. |
| 4.35 | 276 Bde. | F.O.O. reports that 5th Yorks report that Infantry are now at M.22.a.7.0. |
| 5.8 | 251 Bde. | D/251 F.O.O. Reports that two lines of Germans are advancing to South through M.5.c. and d. D/251 are engaging them. |
| 8.0 | 251 Bde. | Reporting movement of transport on BAPAUME Road towards the RAVINE. Repeated to Heavy Artillery. |

28th September, 1916.

| TIME | Information or orders recd. from | |
|---|---|---|
| A.M. | | |
| 9.15 | R.A. 3rd Corps | For report on wire in front of FLERS LINE. |
| 9.50 | 151 Inf.Bde. | Asking for our Artillery to fire on West corner of EAUCOURT L'ABBAYE where German machine guns have been located. One how. of 252 Bde. put on and 47th D.A. asked to co-operate. |
| 10.0 | C.R.A. | 50th D.A. Operation Order No. 37 issued. 276 Bde. to be relieved on 28/29 Sept. by 39th Bde. of 1st Div. Arty.(6 gun Batteries). Batteries relieving C/276 and D/276 to move to more forward positions as soon as possible after relief. A B and C Batteries 250 Bde. to come out of action on afternoon of 29th and proceed to Wagon Lines. |
| 10.0 | C.R.A. | Orders issued for personnel of B/250 to be relieved by personnel of C/253. relief to be completed by 12 noon. |
| P.M. | | |
| 1.40 | 253 Bde. | Reporting completion of relief of B/250 by C/253 personnel. Timed 12.10 p.m. |
| 1.25 | 251 Bde. | D/251 fired at small party of enemy moving about behind FLERS LINE. |
| 2.10 | 251 Bde. | F.O.O. B/251 reports several hundreds of Huns working on trench in G36. Repeated G 50th Div. and H.A. 3rd Corps. |
| 4.35 | 276 Bde. | F.O.O. reports that 5th Yorks report that Infantry are now at M.22.a.7.0. |
| 5.8 | 251 Bde. | D/251 F.O.O. Reports that two lines of Germans are advancing to South through M.5.c. and d. D/251 are engaging them. |
| 8.0 | 251 Bde. | Reporting movement of transport on BAPAUME Road towards the RAVINE. Repeated to Heavy Artillery. |

29th September, 1916.

| TIME | Information or orders recd. from | |
|---|---|---|
| A.M. | | |
| 8.0 | 50th Div. | L.B. report that they have made good FARM in M.21.a. |
| 10.50 | do. | Giving Code correction for from 12 midnight 29/30 Sept. |
| 10.55 | 252 Bde. | 151 Inf. Bde. have Stokes gun in position to co-operate with Artillery. |
| 11.50 | 50th Div. | From 1/10/16 Infantry will use Yellow flares. Forwarded Bdes. |
| P.M. | | |
| 5.15 | 252 Bde. | Personnel of C/250 now out of action and guns and ammunition handed over. |
| 7.30 | 253 Bde. | MARTINPUICH being heavily shelled. |

29th September, 1916.

| TIME | Information or orders recd. from | |
|---|---|---|
| A.M. | | |
| 8.0 | 50th Div. | L.B. report that they have made good FARM in M.21.a. |
| 10.50 | do. | Giving Code correction for from 12 midnight 29/30 Sept. |
| 10.55 | 252 Bde. | 151 Inf. Bde. have Stokes gun in position to co-operate with Artillery. |
| 11.50 | 50th Div. | From 1/10/16 Infantry will use Yellow flares. Forwarded Bdes. |
| P.M. | | |
| 5.15 | 252 Bde. | Personnel of C/250 now out of action and guns and ammunition handed over. |
| 7.30 | 253 Bde. | MARTINPUICH being heavily shelled. |

30th September, 1916.

| TIME | Information or orders recd. from | |
|---|---|---|
| A.M. | | |
| 12.20 | 251 Bde. | Report on occupation of dugouts in S.15.c. |
| 9.0 | 50th D.A. | Warning Order. 50th Div. to continue the attack on 1st October. Batteries to cut wire on their own zones commencing at 11.0 am. |
| 9.35 | 151 Inf.Bde. | Report on wire cutting 29.9.16. |
| P.M. | | |
| 5.0 | 50th D.A. | Operation Order No. 38 issued with Bombardment Programme for Artillery on 1st October. |
| 5.35 | 50 Div. | Report on air reconnaissance. |
| 6.45 | 251 Bde. | Information from Infantry re wire cutting. |
| 7.25 | 50 D.A. | Situation report forwarded R.A. 3rd Corps. |
| - | 251 Bde. | Report on position for Brigade H.Q. at S.20.b.8.8. |
| 8.0 | 50 Div. | Third Corps wire that economy is to be exercised in expenditure of 18 Pdr. shrapnel. 18 Pdr. H.E. to be used in preference to shrapnel on all occasions when the use of the latter is not essential to the object in view. Brigades informed accordingly. |
| 9.0 | 253 Bde. | D/250 and B/253 have moved to forward positions and have registered. Wire cutting has been carried out in accordance with programme and barrage has been practised and found satisfactory. |
| 11.22 | 251 Bde. | H.Q. Wagon Lines had bomb dropped on them. 12 horses killed and 2 O.R. wounded. |

30th September, 1916.

| TIME | Information or orders recd. from | |
|---|---|---|
| A.M. 12.26 | 251 Bde. | Report on occupation of dugouts in S.15.c. |
| 8.0 | 50th D.A. | Warning Order. 50th Div. to continue the attack on 1st October. Batteries to cut wire on their own zones commencing at 11.0 am. |
| 9.35 | 151 Inf.Bde. | Report on wire cutting 29.9.16. |
| P.M. 5.0 | 50th D.A. | Operation Order No. 38 issued with Bombardment Programme for Artillery on 1st October. |
| 5.35 | 50 Div. | Report on air reconnaissance. |
| 6.45 | 251 Bde. | Information from Infantry re wire cutting. |
| 7.25 | 50 D.A. | Situation report forwarded R.A. 3rd Corps. |
| - | 251 Bde. | Report on position for Brigade H.Q. at S.20.b.8.8. |
| 8.0 | 50 Div. | Third Corps wire that economy is to be exercised in expenditure of 18 Pdr. shrapnel. 18 Pdr. H.E. to be used in preference to shrapnel on all occasions when the use of the latter is not essential to the object in view. Brigades informed accordingly. |
| 9.0 | 253 Bde. | D/250 and B/253 have moved to forward positions and have registered. Wire cutting has been carried out in accordance with programme and barrage has been practised and found satisfactory. |
| 11.22 | 251 Bde. | H.Q. Wagon Lines had bomb dropped on them. 12 horses killed and 2 O.R. wounded. |

## 50th Divisional Artillery.

Daily Intelligence Summary, 9.0am 29/9:16 to 9.0am 30/9:16.

---

1. Operations (Other than those included in Daily Programme):-

   Commencing at 5.35p.m. we carried out our bombardment programme on and around the FLERS LINE in M.22.

   During the night we kept enemy C.T.'s and roads in M.16. and M.22. under fire.

---

2. Information about work done etc., on our own trenches:-

---

3. Information about enemy's trenches, work, wire, M.G. and T.M. emplacements, O.P's, Strong points, etc:-

   A hostile trench mortar fired from the S.W. end of LE SARS at about 4.0p.m.

4. Artillery activity:-

S.3. and S.9. were shelled intermittently during the morning with 7.7cm's.

During our attack in the afternoon a heavy hostile barrage was put up from M.21.Central to M.22.d.Central back to PRUE TRENCH., and at night MARTINPUICH was heavily shelled.

Observers report that the enemy appears to be shelling the road between MARTINPUICH and EAUCOURT L'ABBAYE with the object of damaging the surface and rendering it unfit for traffic.

------------------------------------------------------------------------

5. Miscellaneous, including any other items of intelligence:-

The visibility being very poor, little movement was seen behind the enemy's lines.

Major R.A.,
B.M. 50th D.A.

## 50TH DIVISIONAL ARTILLERY.

Daily Intelligence Summary, 9.0 am 28:9:16 to 9.0am 29:9:16.

1. Operations (Other than those included in Daily Programme):-

In view of prisoners statement that a relief was taking place opposite our front we paid special attention to all C.T.'s roads and tracks during the night.

Our 18 pdrs. dispersed working parties on roads in M.18 and at M.22 Central.

2. Information about work done etc., on our own trenches:-


3. Information about enemy's trenches, work, wire, M.G. and T.M.emplacements, O.P's, Strong points, etc:-

An engineer dump was seen at M.6.d.5.8.

Several hundreds of enemy were seen working on roads in G.36, during the afternoon.


4. Artillery activity:-

There was very little hostile fire during the day.

S.8.b. & d. were shelled intermittently throughout the night by 7.7.cms.


5. Miscellaneous, including any other items of intelligence:-

During the day a great deal of movement was seen behind the enemy's lines.

Several small parties were seen in the neighbourhood of the BUTTE DE WARLENCOURT, during the morning.

There appear to be troops in reserve stationed at H.31.d., and digging parties were seen.

The roads in N.1.a. were in constant use

(1) 11.20 a.m. wagons and troops were seen in H.36 Central
(2) 3.30 p.m. Company marching E on road in M.11.a.3.3.
(3) 3.35 p.m. about 250 enemy infantry seen at M.6.c.5.2. moving S.W.
(4) 4.45 p.m. large party of enemy seen advancing South in M.5.c. and b.

29th September, 1916.

Major, R.A.
B.M. 50 D.A.

50TH     DIVISIONAL:     ARTILLERY.

Daily Intelligence Summary, 9.0.a.m 27 : 9 :16 to 9.0 a.m 28: 9 :16.

1. Operations (Other than those included in Daily Programme):-

During operations in the afternoon we bombarded enemy front line in M.28 and lifted to C.T's., roads and FLERS LINE in rear whilst infantry advanced.

At night we kept enemy C.T's and roads opposite our Divisional front under fire.

One of our Batteries engaged a party of enemy infantry at X roads M.5.c.5.0 at 2.55 p.m.

2. Information about work done etc., on our own trenches:-

3. Information about enemy's trenches, work, wire, M.G. and T.M. emplacements, O.P.'s, Strong points, etc :-

At 11.0 p.m. and enemy working party was seen on trench in M.5.d.

4. Artillery activity :-

S.3 was shelled intermittently throughout the day by 7.7 cm and 5.9 and during the afternoon a 15 cm gun fired on road crossing in S.16.a.

At 12.53 p.m. and 1.10 p.m. S.4.b. was shelled with 5.9" and a few incendiary shells fell in S.3. at 5.0 p.m.

F.O.O's report that the enemy did not put up a heavy barrage until the first wave of our infantry had gained their objective.

A very quiet night is reported in our front area.

5. Miscellaneous, including any other items of intelligence :-

At 12.0 p.m. the road in N.1.a. & c. was in constant use by small parties of men moving south.

At 2.55 p.m. a company of infantry was seen advancing in a southerly direction in the road at M.5.b.1.5.

5.50 p.m. a large fire broke out in EAUCOURT L'ABBAYE.

7.45 p.m. signalling lamps were observed in use on a mag. bearing of 17 degs. from S.3.a.9.9.

During the day the Railway in H.31.d. appeared to be in use, and 8 trucks were seen standing on it and parties of the enemy moving round them.

5 enemy balloons were observed on the afternoon of the 27th inst. in mag. bearings of 51°, 53°, 63°, 65°, and 69°, from S.3.a.9.9. and at 5.30 p.m. a hostile balloon broke loose on a true bearing of 16° from S.9.b.9.4.

At 8.35 a.m. this morning 14 hostile balloons were up.

28th September, 1916.

Major, R.A.
B.M. 50 D.A.

## 50TH DIVISIONAL ARTILLERY.

Daily Intelligence Summary, 9.0 a.m : 26/9/16 to 9.0 a.m : 27/9/16.

---

1. Operations (Other than those included in Daily Programme):-

    At 12.30 p.m. we barraged in M.27. & M.28. to assist the attack on our right and left and during the afternoon engaged hostile batteries at M.15.c.3.4., M.15.b.4.3. M.18.d.1.5. M.23.c.5.9. M.15.b.4.9. and M.21.b.2.3. also one of our F.O.O's registered the heavy artillery on a hostile battery at M.18.b. Central.

    Small parties of the enemy in roads at M.17.d.7.0 and M.22.d.6.2. were dispersed by our 18 pdrs. and transport at M.16.a.7.3.

    At 8.0 p.m. our howitzers bombarded EAUCOURT L'ABBAYE with gas and inflammable shells

    At 11.10 p.m. we put up light barrage behind enemy front line in M.28.a. & b. to assist our infantry and bombarded junctions of C.T's. and X roads in rear.

---

2. Information about work done etc., on our own trenches:-

---

3. Information about enemy's trenches, work, wire, M.G. and T.M. emplacements, O.P.'s, Strong points, etc :-

    There is a strong M.G. emplacement in the BUTTE-DE-WARLENCOURT.

    At various times throughout the day large enemy working parties were seen digging trenches in G.35 Central and M.4, M.5, and M.6.

4. Artillery activity :-

During the morning our front line and supports were intermittently shelled with 10 cm Howitzers.

At 12.50 p.m. a H.V. gun shelled battery position in S.9.b.

7.45 p.m. to 8.45 p.m. our trenches in M.27.d. & M.28.c. were heavily bombarded

From 10.0 p.m. to 4.0 am BAZENTIN-LE-PETIT road and village were shelled with 7.7cm 4.2" and 5.9".

5. Miscellaneous, including any other items of intelligence :-

A great deal of movement was seen behind the enemy's lines. At 12.15 p.m. a convoy of about 6 vehicles was seen and again at 3.35 p.m. 2 convoys of about 20 motor lorries were observed at N.1.a.5.8. 5 Railway wagons were seen standing at the R.E. dump N.1.a.0.2. During the last few days there has only been one wagon there.

The roads running thro. M.3.a. & b. & M.4.a.& b. were in constant use in both directions.

Several parties of men were seen in N.19.a.& b. where there appears to be a new trench.

At 4.15 p.m. about two companies of infantry in single file were observed advancing in an easterly direction along track running through M.8. Central.

An F.O.O. reported that at 4 p.m. he saw enemy preparing to counter attack about N.19. Central and that it was dispersed by our barrage which was put up at once.

27th September, 1916.

Major, R.A.
B.M. 50 D.A.

Daily Intelligence Summary, 9.0 a.m 25: 9:16 to 9.0 a.m 26: 9:16.

1. Operations (Other than those included in Daily Programme):-

Throughout the day we kept all new enemy work under continuous fire and at night bombarded the FLERS LINE in M.23.c with gas shells.

During the attack in the afternoon we dispersed groups of the enemy on roads at M.18.c.0.3. & M.23.d.5.8., a large party collecting in the FLERS LINE in M.23.c. and engaged hostile batteries at M.17.c.2.4. and M.23.a.8.9.

2. Information about work done etc., on our own trenches:-

3. Information about enemy's trenches, work, wire, M.G. and T.M. emplacements, O.P.'s, Strong points, etc :-

The roads M.23.a.9.2½ to M.24.c.1.3. and M.28.a.9.2½ to M.18.a.0.3. were in constant use by small parties of the enemy during the afternoon

4. Artillery activity :-

From 12.35 p.m. to 3.30 p.m. whilst operations were in progress on our right and left the enemy put up a heavy barrage in front of our new trench running through M.27, he also shelled CRESCENT ALLEY, PRUE TRENCH and STARFISH LINE with 5.9 and 4.2., and at 3.30 p.m. the road from M.28.d.1.7. to M.28.d.8.0 was shelled.

During the night our front area was comparatively quiet, bur S.8.a. and b. were heavily shelled with 5.9" and 4.2" and lacrymatory shells.

5. Miscellaneous, including any other items of intelligence :-

At 4 p.m. a company of infantry were seen in M.6.b. marching towards LE SARS and a great deal of movement was seen on the roads in N.1.a.

At 4.0 p.m. a fire was ignited in a wood behind EAUCOURT L'ABBAYE and at 4.10 p.m. a large fire broke out in LE BARQUE.

26/9/16.

Major, R.A.
B.M. 50 D.A.

Daily Intelligence Summary, 9.0 am 24 : 9 :16 to 9.0 am 25 : 9 :16.

1. Operations (Other than those included in Daily Programme):-

During the day our Howitzers kept under fire all new enemy work in M.21.22.27.& 28., doing considerable damage to new trench running from M.28.b.8.8. - M.29.a.2.3. -M.29.b.1.2. and bombarded LE SARS and EAUCOURT L'ABBAYE, our 18 pdrs dispersed enemy working parties, small groups of men in road at M.18.c.4.6½, and transport at M.17.c.2.5. and during the night sprinkled the roads and C.T's opposite our Divisional front with shrapnel paying particular attention to the sunken road junction at M.22.c.9.0. whilst the Howitzers bombarded the valley running through M.16.d. and M.22.b. & d. with gas shells.

2. Information about work done etc., on our own trenches:-

3. Information about enemy's trenches, work, wire, M.G. and T.M. emplacements, O.P.'s, Strong points, etc :-

The quarry at M.22.d.3.1. appears to be strongly held.

There is a large quantity of material in the dump at

M.24.c.1.3.

4. Artillery activity :-

Between 3.0 p.m. and 4.0 p.m. a large party of infantry walked over the crest in HIGH WOOD and drew heavy enemy fire.

AT 9.45 p.m. PRUE TRENCH & STARFISH line were heavily bombarded with 5.9 and 4.2 from the direction of LE SARS. The remainder of the night was quiet and at dawn hostile activity was very slight.

Constant reports are received that the hostile artillery is firing from a long way off and in many cases the reports of the guns are not heard.

5. Miscellaneous, including any other items of intelligence :-

A great deal of transport was seen moving both N.E. and S.W. in the roads in N.1.a.

25/9/16.

Major, R.A.
B.M. 50 D.A.

## 50th Divisional Artillery.

Daily Intelligence Summary, 9.0am : 16 to 9.0 am : 16.
23 9          24 9

---

1. Operations (Other than those included in Daily Programme):-

Our 18-pdrs. dispersed working parties at M.18.c.3.2. also a battalion of infantry 600 strong marching on road M.17.c.6.0. - M.17.b.7.0. They also enngaged two large lorries travelling South on road about M.18.d. which, when fired at, halted and appeared to be abandoned.
During the past 24 hours we kept the new enemy trenches, C.T.'s and roads opposite our Divisional front under continuous fire.

---

2. Information about work done etc., on our own trenches:-

---

3. Information about enemy's trenches, work, wire, M.G. and T.M. emplacements, O.P.'s, Strong points, etc :-

From 5.0 to 6.0pm a large fire was seen burning in THILLOY, about N.8.a.8.9.
Enemy were seen moving along the road M.18.c. - M.18.d. - M.23.b.7.6., and entered a deep open trench which appeared to lead to a sunken road running from EAUCOURT L'ABBAYE to M.24.c. They were also seen in road running through M.18.c. to M.23.a. thence going across country to a deep open trench about M.23.b.7.4.
Activity was also noticed in a quarry about M.23.a.9.4. worked on
The BUTTE de WARLENCOURT appears to have been covered in; a great deal of fresh turned chalk can be seen on the Southern slope.
Enemy dug-outs have been located at M.22.d.4.2. and M.22.d.6.2.
The road from M.22.d.6.2. to EAUCOURT L'ABBAYE is used during the day by men on foot.

4. Artillery activity :-

   3.15am.    Intermittent shelling on our front line trenches.

  4.0 to 5.0pm. Enemy shelled MARTINPUICH - EAUCOURT L'ABBAYE road
          in M.27.b. and M.28.a.

   6.22pm.   HIGH WOOD shelled with 7.7cm.

         An anti-aircraft gun was observed shooting from
      G.34.c.9.5.

5. Miscellaneous, including any other items of intelligence :-

Between 1.45am and 3.15am there was a considerable amount of machine gun fire and sounds of bombing N.E. of MARTINPUICH, also a large number of coloured lights was seen, but there was no artillery fire.

   From M.34.a.3.6. the road M.22.d.0.3. - M.16.d.7.8. can be seen and a good view is obtained of NO MANS LAND and the FLERS LINE opposite our front from M.27.d.7.6.

                                               Major R.A.,
24. 9. 16.                                     B.M. 50th D.A.

50th Divisional Artillery.

Daily Intelligence Summary, 9.0am 21:9:16 to 9.0am 22:9:16.

1. Operations (Other than those included in Daily Programme):-

Our batteries took full advantage of the clear visibility and during the day carefully re-registered PRUE TRENCH and STARFISH LINE, the latter trench being kept under continuous bombardment all day.
Following on a wireless call one of our batteries engaged a hostile battery in action at M.23.a.5.4. We opened fire at 5.20pm and at 5.40pm the hostile battery was reported to have stopped firing.
During the night our batteries barraged in front of PRUE TRENCH whilst our infantry advanced.

2. Information about work done etc., on our own trenches:-


3. Information about enemy's trenches, work, wire, M.G. and T.M. emplacements, O.P.'s, Strong points, etc :-

PRUE TRENCH is reported by F.O.O.'s to be not much more than a mud hole and that it appears to have been evacuated in good order as no wounded were left behind.
An enemy party was observed digging at trench at M.14.b.5.5.
At 5.15pm a big explosion was caused, probably an ammunition dump, in the enemy's lines behind COURCELETTE; a quarter of an hour afterwards the enemy bombarded our line North of COURCELETTE heavily.
Enemy aircraft were active during the day. One 'plane reconnoitred HIGH WOOD area from 10.30am to 11.30am and at 6.20pm two hostile machines flew over BAZENTIN-LE-GRAND. They were fired at by A.A.guns One is supposed to be hit as it swerved left and dropped a big red and white paper, probably a message.
At 2.15pm two convoys, each consisting of three wagons were seen proceeding towards WARLENCOURT from the S.W.

4. Artillery activity :-

Following the reconnaissance of a hostile 'plane at 10.30am, at various times throughout the day our battery positions in S.9.b. were shelled with 5.9", 7.7cm and 8" and at 10.20pm bombarded with tear shell.

There was a heavy bombardment of HIGH WOOD back to CATERPILLAR VALLEY during the afternoon.

At 6.45pm enemy shelled N.W. edge of BAZENTIN-LE-PETIT, bursts being very high in air.

Enemy shelled S.2.a. and b. with 5.9 and 4.2's continuously throughout the day.

5. Miscellaneous, including any other items of intelligence :-

At 12.40a.m. F.O.O. reported that in spite of continuous bombardment of our artillery the enemy have sent up very few VERY lights and no coloured lights or rockets, which is very unusual.

Twenty hostile balloons observed up during the afternoon.

F.O.O. reported early this morning that there were no signs of the enemy between EAUCOURT L'ABBAYE and Cross roads in M.28.d.

22. 9. 16.

Major R.A.,
B.M. 50th D.A.

## 50th Divisional Artillery.

|  | 22.9 | 23.9 |
|---|---|---|
| Daily Intelligence Summary, 9.0am | :16 to 9.0am | :16. |

---

1. Operations (those other than those included in Daily Programme).
During the whole of the day and night we kept the new enemy trenches in M.23.c., 28 a. and b., and 21.d. under continuous bombardment, enfiladed the road M.22.c.9.0. to M.16.d.8.8. with shrapnel and between 9.0p.m. and dawn fired a number of gas shells into LE SARS, EAUCOURT L'ABBAYE and the FLERS line.

Our 18-pdrs. effectively dealt with a working party in the FLERS line in M.23.c., transport on a road at M.22.b.2.0. and a column of infantry about 100 strong marching S.W. on a road at M.18.c.5.6.

---

2. Information about work done etc., on our own trenches:-

---

3. Information about enemy's trenches, work, wire, O.C. and T.M. emplacements, strong points, etc.-
An R.E. Officer who reconnoitred to M.27.b.8.2. reported that there are no Germans in CRESCENT ALLEY and that the enemy are now holding a line running approximately from M.23.c.6.1. to M.28.b.7.8. to M.28.a.5.7. to M.21.d.2.1.

A great deal of movement was seen behind the enemy's lines at various times during the day. Railway trucks, and digging parties of Germans nearly a mile long were seen on the high ground between BAPAUME and WARLENCOURT in H.31. and M.5.b., both targets the heavy artillery were asked to engage. Working parties were seen in the FLERS line and new trenches in M.23.c. and at M.21.d.8500, and movement of transport and men was seen in the neighbourhood of the BUTTE de WARLENCOURT and on roads at M.18.c.5.6., M.21.b.6.8., M.6.b.5530 and M.11.b.7045.

From our O.P.'s wire in front of the FLERS line in M.22 and 23 can be seen but no wire in front of new trenches in M.23.c., 28 a. and b. and 21.d.

There is a high wooden erection with a platform at top at M.28.b.1.2. which the enemy may use as an O.P.

4. Artillery activity :-

   3.10p.m. PRUE TRENCH was shelled with 10cm.

   BAZENTIN-LE-GRAND heavily bombarded during the afternoon.

   9.30p.m. MARTINPUICH heavily shelled.

   10.0p.m. S.9.b. shelled with 8"

   HOOK and PRUE trenches were bombarded during the night.

5. Miscellaneous, including any other items of intelligence :-

   Hostile 'planes were very active, reconnoitring in flights of four at a low altitude over the HIGH WOOD - MARTINPUICH area.

   A hostile balloon was observed on the ground in G.33.b. The Heavy Artillery were informed.

   At 6.42p.m. a fire was seen to have broken out W. of LE SARS; it was probably the result of our ballon 'strafe'.

   During the shelling of MARTINPUICH at 9.30p.m. the enemy used a searchlight and an electric signalling lamp on true bearings of 48°, and 46° respectively, both from S.3.a.9.9.

   F.O.O.'s report there was a very marked absence of VERY lights during the night in front of our new line.

   From PRUE TRENCH at M.33.b.0.7. good observation can be obtained of the area M.28, M.22, M.23, M.21.b. and d. and LE SARS. THE MILL is a good O.P. for country W. of LE SARS.

23.9.16.

Major R.A.,
B.M. 50th D.A.

50th ~~Divisional~~ Artillery.

Daily Intelligence Summary, 9.0 a.m : :16 to 9.0 a.m : :16.
                                  20  9               21  9

---

1. Operations (Other than those included in Daily Programme):-

    An enemy working party carrying planks along the road from M.22.d.1.2. to M.28.b.9.6. was dispersed by our 18-pdrs.

---

2. Information about work done etc., on our own trenches:-

---

3. Information about enemy's trenches, work, wire, M.G. and T.M. emplacements, O.P.'s, Strong points, etc :-

4. Artillery activity :-

Hostile 'planes over our lines at 10.20a.m. and shortly afterwards our Bty. positions in S.9.b. shelled with 10cm. How.

MARLBORO COPSE shelled with 5.9 at 9.30.a.m.

During the day A.2.a and b. were heavily shelled with 5.9's.

At 1.0a.m. tear gas was felt in S.2.b. and d. and at 2.10a.m. S.9.b. was shelled with tear shell.

Hostile fire on our front area reported normal during the night.

5. Miscellaneous, including any other items of intelligence :-

F.O.O. reports no transport could be seen in the afternoon of the 20th inst: in rear of enemy's lines.
Road from LE BARQUE to EAYCOURT L'ABBAYE appears to be very much used, being very muddy and no grass at sides. Small parties of the enemy were constantly seen passing along it in both directions.
Also small parties seen on roads in N.1.a. and b.
The main roads from LE SARS to BAPAUME and BEAULENCOURT to BAPAUME were not used at all during the day.
He is of the opinion that all enemy ammunition and supplies come up after dark.
It is reported that the enemy is doing a lot of his firing by balloon or aeroplane observation as it was noticed on the 20th that he shelled the BAZENTIN-LE-PETIT - HIGH WOOD road only when transport was on it.

Major R.A.,
B.M. 50th D.A.

21. 9. 16.

## 50th Divisional Artillery.

Daily Intelligence Summary, 9.0am 19/9/16 to 9.0am 20/9/16.

1. Operations (Other than those included in Daily Programme):-

   From 8.0pm to 9.0pm in response to S.O.S. Signal and message from F.O.O. that enemy were bombing along PRUE TRENCH our two Left Brigades fired on S.O.S. lines.

2. Information about work done etc., on our own trenches:-

3. Information about enemy's trenches, work, wire, M.G. and T.M. emplacements, O.P.'s, Strong points, etc :-

   Wire on screw posts has been seen in front of the STARFISH LINE at M.34.b.1.0. and further East. It does not appear to be a serious obstacle.

4. Artillery activity :-

   Enemy put up heavy barrages at various times during the day from MARTINPUICH to HIGH WOOD.

   7.30pm to 7.33pm our new front trenches were shelled with 10cm How. and 7.7cm guns.

   At 3.45am enemy shelled our front line very heavily.

5. Miscellaneous, including any other items of intelligence :-

   Whilst one of our How. batteries was registering PRUE TRENCH a small party of the enemy was seen to leave it and disappear in the valley in M.28.d. They appeared to be carrying machine guns or light trench mortars.

   The following bearings were taken to enemy balloons at 2.20 p.m. 12°, 25¾°, 41°, 70½°, 85½°, 91¼°, 96°, and 101°, all magnetic bearings from S.9.b.2½, 5½.

20. 9. 16.

Major R.A.,
B.M. 50th D.A.

## 50th DIVISIONAL ARTILLERY.

Daily Intelligence Summary, 9.0 a.m 18/9/16 to 9.0 a.m 19/9/16.

---

1. Operations (Other than those included in Daily Programme):-

    Our howitzers fired a number of gas shells into EAUCOURT L'ABBAYE, during the night.

---

2. Information about work done etc., on our own trenches:-

---

3. Information about enemy's trenches, work, wire, M.G. and T.M. emplacements, O.P.'s, Strong points, etc :-

    U.O.O. reports new enemy trench opposite PRUE TRENCH, viewed from MARTIN ALLEY, appears to run from M.33.b.4.9. for 50 yards parallel to PRUE TRENCH then runs off in a Northerly direction to the MARTINPUICH - EAUCOURT L'ABBAYE road.

    There is a shostile strong point with several machine guns reported at M.34.b.4.1.

    Hostile machine guns are also reported to fire from PRUE COPSE in M.34.b. and CRESCENT ALLEY.

4. Artillery activity :-

   Hostile artillery much less active than usual.
   HIGH WOOD, HOOK TRENCH, MARTIN TRENCH and MARTINPUICH
   areas barraged at various times on the 18th.

   From 12.30pm to 8.0pm S.15.d. and d. and S.21. a and b.
was shelled with a 15cm gun and from 5.30pm to 11.0pm the
samebgun fired a few rounds into CATERPILLAR VALLEY.

   F.O.O.'s report a particularly quiet night in our
sector.

5. Miscellaneous, including any other items of intelligence :-

   On the 18th at various times small parties of the enemy
were sen going in a Northerly direction from shell hole to
shell hole across country from PRUE TRENCH and THE CRESCENT.

   F.O.O.'d report that from O.P. S.3.a.8.8. they can obtain a view
of PRUE TRENCH west of THE CRESCENT also a good view of the banks of
EAUCOURT L'ABBAYE - MARTINPUICH road and a good deal of the
intermediate ground between it and PRUE TRENCH in M.27.d. and M.33.b.

   Hostile Infantry were seen in trenches opposite THE BOW.

19. 9. 16.

Major R.A.,
B.M. 50th D.A.

## 50th DIVISIONAL ARTILLERY.

Daily Intelligence Summary, 9.0 am 17/9/16 to 9.0 am 18/9/16.

---

1. Operations (Other than those included in Daily Programme):-

---

2. Information about work done etc., on our own trenches:-

---

3. Information about enemy's trenches, work, wire, M.G. and T.M. emplacements, O.P.'s, Strong points, etc :-

   THE CRESCENT, TRIANGLE, and PRUE TRENCH in M.34.a. and b. were reported in the morning by F.O.O.'s to be strongly held by the enemy, also CRESCENT ALLEY North of PRUE TRENCH; they also reported the COPSE in M.34.b. to be strongly held with machine guns.

   During the night the enemy put up Very lights from a point about 300 yards N.E. of M.33.d.5.9.

*14 g Bde.*
*N.F.*

*M33d*

4. Artillery activity :-

  10.0am to 11.0am. Hostile artillery from LE SARS barraged in
              M.33.b. and d.
  5.0pm to 8.0pm. Heavy barrage on BETHELLS SAP - CLARKES TRENCH
              towards MARTINPUICH which was preceded by white and green
              rockets; it was probably put up to counter our attack.
  5.30pm. Transport in CATERPILLAR VALLEY shelled with a high
              velocity gun.

           A F.O.O. observed a direct hit by our heavy
artillery on a hostile battery ay M.23.d.4.7. and a large
sheet of flame was seen to go up.

5. Miscellaneous, including any other items of intelligence :-

At 9.45am two hostile planes passed over our lines between
HIGH WOOD and MARTINPUICH.

F.O.O. of 47th D.A reported that he had seen men in M.28.a.
getting out of trench and running to MARTINPUICH - LE SARS
road; this happened during our bombing attack on the
CRESCENT between 5.0 and 6.0p.m.

A new signal light used by Germans consisted of from 8 to 12
brilliant white lights on one tail. It ascended very rapidly
and appeared to go as high as the clouds which were very low.

Enemy can still bring heavy machine gun fire over most of the
area recently taken by the Division.

One or two enemy snipers reported in shell holes in our lines.

                                                Major R.A.,
18. 9. 16.                                B.M. 50th D.A.

50th Divisional Artillery.

Daily Intelligence Summary, 9.0am 13/9/16 to 9.0am 14/9/16.

1. Operations (Other than those included in Daily Programme.):-

   NIL.

2. Information about work done etc., on our own trenches.

   NIL.

3. Information about enemy's trenches, work, wire, M.G. and T.M. emplacements, O.P.'s, Strong points, etc :-

   New work going on in enemy trench running from M.33.b.2.6. to M.34.a.2.2.

   Machine guns were located firing at aeroplanes from S.4.a.6.7., S.2.b.4.7, and M.33.c.2.1.

   Enemy sniper was active from S.3.b.8.3.

   Magnetic bearings of enemy balloons from S.3.b.7.2. were $19° 5'$, $54° 2'$, $56° 5'$, $67° 4'$.

4. Artillery activity :-

   12.15pm. S.8.b.5.3. and 5.8.a. shelled with 4.2" and 7.7cm. From 10.0am to 2.0pm hostile artillery from the direction of FLERS was very active on our front areas, CAMERON, CLARKES, and SANDERSON trenches, and the rear of DELVILLE WOOD were heavily shelled.

   During the night WELCH ALLEY and SWANSEA TRENCH were heavily shelled with 5.9" and 7.7cm.

   At 12.20am enemy put up 3 red rockets 200 yds. right of BETHELL. This was followed by heavy rifle fire and shelling all over the front area. The situation became normal about 1.30a.m.

   1.0am to 2.0am. CLARKES TRENCH heavily shelled.

5. Miscellaneous, including any other items of intelligence :-

   The following hostile battery positions were located by flash and bearings :-
   7.7cm at M.28.d.6.4. (Approx.)
   10 cm. at M.21.a.7.4.

14.9.16

Major R.A.,
B.M.50th D.A.

Vol. 18.

Headquarters,
50th Div. Artillery.

October 1916.

Army Form A. 2007.

# CENTRAL REGISTRY.

Central Registry No. and Date.

Attached Files.

## SUBJECT, AND OFFICE OF ORIGIN.

OPERATION ORDERS FROM

50th DIVISION.

NOVEMBER, 1916.

DECEMBER, 1916

| Referred to | Date | Referred to | Date | Referred to | Date |
|---|---|---|---|---|---|
| | | | | | |

| P. A. | Date |
|---|---|
| | |

Schedule of Correspondence.

Army Form C. 2118.

CONFIDENTIAL

# WAR DIARY
or
# INTELLIGENCE SUMMARY

*(Erase heading not required.)*

50th DIVISIONAL ARTILLERY HEADQUARTERS.

WAR DIARY
FOR
MONTH OF

OCTOBER 1916.

VOLUME XIX.

Army Form C. 2118.

## WAR DIARY or INTELLIGENCE SUMMARY

(Erase heading not required.)

**VOL XIX**

**PAGE 1.**

Instructions regarding War Diaries and Intelligence Summaries are contained in F.S. Regs., Part II. and the Staff Manual respectively. Title Pages will be prepared in manuscript.

H.Q., 50th Divisional Artillery.

October 1916.

| Place | Date | Hour | Summary of Events and Information | Remarks and references to Appendices |
|---|---|---|---|---|
| RAILWAY COPSE. | 1 | 1.0am | Summer time altered to Greenwich mean time and clocks put back one hour. | |
| | | 7.0am | Div. Arty. commenced a deliberate bombardment of two lines of German trenches between M.22.b.3.4. and M.21.b.8.5. (rILERS LINE & SUPPORT LINE). Programme of bombardment and Operation Order No. 38 attached (Appendix 19/1) | 19/1. |
| | | 3.15 pm. | Artillery barrage commenced and 50th Division attacked, with 23rd Div. on left. and 47th Div. on Right. Infantry gained objective without difficulty on left and centre. On the Right Infantry gained the German first line but were driven out. They subsequently re-took it. Artillery barrages in these operations reported as being perfect. | |
| near MILLENCOURT. | 3 | | H.Q. 50th D.A. came out of the line for a rest and returned to Camp near MILLENCOURT. Brigades remained in, the 251, 252 and 253 Bdes. R.F.A. being placed under the tactical command of C.R.A. 23rd Division at 6.0p.m. and 39th Brigade R.F.A. under the tactical command of C.R.A. 47th Div. at the same hour. Corps front is now one of two Divisions, i.e., Right Group, 47th D.A. less 1 Bde., with two Brigades 1st D.A., commanded by C.R.A. 47th Div. Left Group, 23rd D.A., 2 Bdes. 15th D.A., plus 1 How Bty., and 3 Bdes. of 50th D.A., commanded by C.R.A. 23rd Division. Operations Order No. 39 (Appendix 19/2) attached. | 19/2 |
| | | | C.R.A. and his A.D.C. proceeded on leave to England. Duties of C.R.A. taken over by Lieut-Col. F.B.Moss-Blundell, Comdg: 251 Bde. R.F.A. | |
| | 8/9 | | 15th D.A. relieved 23rd D.A. and took over tactical command of 251, 252, 253 Bdes R.F.A. of 50th D.A. | 19/3. |
| | 10 | | 251 Bde. R.F.A. less D/251 relieved by 250 Bde. R.F.A. less D/250 (personnel only) 251 Bde. R.F.A. marched to Rest Billets at BEHENCOURT. Operation Order No. 40 (Appendix 19/3) attached | 1471 |
| | 14 | | C.R.A. and his A.D.C. returned from leave and former assumed command of D.A. | |
| | 17 | | 252 Bde. R.F.A. (less D/252) came out of action and proceeded to Rest Billets at FRECHENCOURT. Tactical command of D/252 arranged by C.R.A. 15th Division. Personnel and 2 guns of D/250 also came out of action and proceeded to wagon lines. Operation Order No. 41 (Appendix 19/4) | 19/4 |

Army Form C. 2118.

# WAR DIARY
## or
## INTELLIGENCE SUMMARY

*(Erase heading not required.)*

Instructions regarding War Diaries and Intelligence Summaries are contained in F. S. Regs., Part II. and the Staff Manual respectively. Title Pages will be prepared in manuscript.

472

| Place | Date | Hour | Summary of Events and Information | Remarks and references to Appendices |
|---|---|---|---|---|
| | 19 | | Brigade Major R.A. proceeded on leave. Duties taken over by Major C.H.Lemmon R.F.A., 251 Bde. R.F.A. | |
| | 20 | | Hows. of D/250 placed in action again and personnel proceeded from wagon lines to Rest Billets at ST. GRATIEN. | |
| | 24/25 | | 9th Division relieved by 50th Division.(less Artillery). 50th Div. Trench Mortars relieved those of 9th Division and came under tactical command of C.R.A. 9th Division at 12 noon on 25th. | |
| | 25 | | Brigade Major R.A. returned from leave and re-assumed duties. | |
| | 29 | | Staff Captain R.A. proceeded on leave. Duties taken over by Captain A.D.Currie, Adjt., 253 Bde. R.F.A. | |

[signature]
Major R.A.,
Brigade Major R.A. 50th Division.

## 50th Divisional Artillery.

Daily Intelligence Summary, 9.0am 30:9:16 to 9.0am 1:10:16.

1. Operations (Other than those included in Daily Programme):-

During the day we cut the wire in front of the FLERS line in M.22. and at night kept the enemy trenches, roads, etc., opposite our front under fire.

Our 18-pdrs. dispersed a hostile working party at M.16.b.9.6.

2. Information about work done etc., on our own trenches:-

3. Information about enemy's trenches, work, wire, M.G. and T.M. emplacements, O.P's, Strong points, etc:-

A great deal of work is going on on the ALBERT - BAPAUME road in M.6.c. and M.12.d.

The railway at M.6.d.5.9. was in use during the day and the dump previously reported at M.6.d.5.8. has increased in size.

F.O.O.'s report the FLERS line appears to be strongly held.

4. Artillery activity:-

S.3.b. was shelled at irregular intervals during the afternoon with a high velocity gun, 4.2" How's, and 7.7cm., and at night HIGH WOOD, S.3., S.4., and our front line trenches in M.28. were shelled intermittently.

-------------------------------------------------------------------

5. Miscellaneous, including any other items of intelligence:-

A great deal of movement was seen at various times on the ALBERT - BAPAUME road.

At 9.0p.m. a hostile aeroplane dropped bombs in Square F.6.

1/10/16.

Major R.A,
B.M. 50th D.A.

50TH    DIVISIONAL    ARTILLLERY.

Daily Intelligence Summary, 9.0am 1:10:16 to 9.0am 2:10:16.

1. Operations (Other than those included in Daily Programme):-

During the morning and up to 3.15 p.m. we continued the wire cutting and bombardment of the FLERS LINE, then carried out one barrage programme whilst the infantry advanced, our final barrage being placed across M.16.a. and b.  We also kept the BUTTE de WARLENCOURT under fire, engaged hostile M.G's. at the Mill M.22.b.9.5. and in front line at M.22.a.2.0. and dispersed enemy supports advancing from M.5 towards LE SARS and parties retiring from M.22.a.2.0. to support line.

During the night we kept the valleys and sunken road in M.16.d. under fire.

2. Information about work done etc., on our own trenches:-

3. Information about enemy's trenches, work, wire, M.G. and T.M. emplacements, O.P's, Strong points, etc:-

During the operations M.G. fire came from the BUTTE de WARLENCOURT, work at M.22.a.8.8., and mill at M.22.b.9.5., also from LE SARS.

The work at M.22.a.8.8. is visible from O.P's in HIGH WOOD and appears to be strongly wired and held.

4. Artillery activity:-

   From 10.0 a.m. to noon the enemy barraged our front trenches in M.21.d. and M.22.c. with 4.2" and 7.7 cms.

   During our attack the hostile barrage was almost entirely confined to our front trench area. It appeared to be late and offered little opposition to the infantry.

   At 4.22 p.m. enemy barrage shortened to N of EAUCOURT L'ABBAYE and at 5.35 p.m. it considerably decreased.

   HIGH WOOD and BAZENTIN-LE-PETIT were shelled by 5.9 and 8" during the afternoon.

   At 6.15 p.m. the enemy shelled LE SARS heavily.

   F.O.O's report a fairly quiet night.

------------------------------------------------------------

5. Miscellaneous, including any other items of intelligence:-

   The following movement was seen behind the enemy lines:-

   1.15 p.m. Working parties in M.17.a. and b.
   2.0 p.m. Enemy moving front line at M.22.a.2.0. to support line in small groups.
   2.30 p.m. Many Germans in trenches M.4.b. and M.5.a.
   2.50 p.m. A strong enemy force advancing from M.5.a. and b. towards LE SARS; the Heavy Artillery were informed.
   2.55 p.m. A group of infantry in main road in M.1.b. and M.6.a.

   The enemy sent up numerous red lights at the commencement of our attack.

   At 5.45 p.m. a fire was seen behind the enemy lines in the direction of the BUTTE de WARLENCOURT and two were seen in the direction of FLERS at 5.50 p.m.

2nd October, 1916.

Major, R.A.
B.M. 50 D.A.

50th Divisional Artillery.

Daily Intelligence Summary, 9.0am 2/10/16 to 9.0am 3/10/16

1. Operations. (Other than those included in Daily Programme) :-

   At 5.50pm on receipt of a message from 151 Inf. Bde. that enemy were concentrating for an attack at M.22.b.5.8., we turned out 18-pdrs. on to this point and searched South down the Valley in M.22.b., and quickened the rate of fire of our How's. on the portion of the FLERS line held by the enemy in M.22.b. and d. which we had been bombarding all day. Our T.M.'s also assisted in dispersing the enemy who eventually attempted to bomb along the FLERS line.

   At night we put up a light barrage on THE TANGLE in M.22.a. and SUNKEN ROAD running through M.22.b. and d.

2. Information about work done etc., on our own trenches.

3. Information about enemy's trenches, work, wire, M.G. and T.M. emplacements, O.P.'s, Strong points, etc :-

4. Artillery activity :-

   There was comparatively little hostile fire during the day.

   From 11.0a.m. to 1.0p.m. our front area, principally in M.22.c. was heavily shelled.

5. Miscellaneous, including any other items of intelligence :-

   The visibility was very poor during the day and very little movement could be seen behind the enemy's lines.

3/10/16.

Major R.A.,
B.M. 50th D.A.

SECRET.

Copy No 12

19/1

## 50th DIVISIONAL ARTILLERY OPERATION ORDER NO. 38.

30.9.16.

1. On October 1st, the 50th Division will capture and hold the two lines of German trenches between M.22.b.3.4. and M.21.b.8.4.
The 47th Division will attack on the right and the 23rd Division on the left.
Objectives are shewn on attached map.

2. 151st Inf. Bde. with one Battalion of 149th Inf. Bde. will carry out the attack. The 149th Bde., less one Battalion will be in support. 150th Bde. will be in reserve.

3. At Zero the supporting brigade will be in PRUE TRENCH - JACKSON STREET and BOAST TRENCH (both inclusive).
The Reserve Brigade between HOOK TRENCH and INTERMEDIATE LINE (both inclusive).

4. A Contact Patrol will fly over the objective from Zero onwards. YELLOW Flares will be shewn when called for at 4.0p.m., 5.0p.m., and 6.0p.m. on 1st October.

5. All ground gained will be consolidated at once, the main line of resistance being from M.23.Central and trenches in vicinity of M.23.a.2½.5. - round THE MILL - thence to FLERS LINE.

6. C.R.E. will arrange to continue the repair of the road between the North-west corner of HIGH WOOD and MARTINPUICH.

7. A.D.M.S. will arrange for an advanced dressing station about M.27.b.7.2., evacuating through MARTINPUICH and BAZENTIN-LE-PETIT.

8. The Artillery will begin a deliberate bombardment of the objectives at 7.0a.m. on 1st October. The Infantry will advance to the attack at Zero, at which hour the artillery barrage will begin. The various lifts of artillery barrages are shown in the attached bombardment programme.

9. At plus thirty minutes the 50th Division will push forward to the work in M.22.a.2.8., and the 23rd Division will push forward strong patrols into LE SARS and to THE QUARRY in M.15.d.7.8.

10. At plus one hour and thirty minutes, 50th and 23rd Divisions will push patrols due North and form an outpost line on the line M.23.a.2.8. - M.16.a.9.1. - round the village of LE SARS - QUARRY in M.15.d.7.8.

11. Correct clock time will be distributed to representatives of Infantry and Artillery Brigades at 47th Division Advanced H.Q. at FRICOURT FARM at 10.0a.m. on 1st October by a Staff Officer, IIIrd Corps. This will be Greenwich mean time and not Summer time. The change from Summer time to normal Greenwich time will take place at 1.0a.m. on 1st October at which hour clocks will be put back one hour, i.e., to 12 mid-night.

12. Acknowledge.

Issued at 6.0p.m.

Major R.A.,
B.M. 50th D.A.

Copies to - No. 1 - 39 Bde. R.F.A.
2 - 251 Bde. R.F.A.
3 - 252 Bde. R.F.A.
4 - 253 Bde. R.F.A.
5 - Left D.A. Group.
6 - Right D.A. Group.
7 - 10, H.Q. 50th Div.
11 - R.A., IIIrd Corps.
12 - War Diary.
13, 14, 15, Spare.

PROGRAMME OF BOMBARDMENT, 1st OCTOBER, 1916.

| Serial No. | Unit bombarding. | Time. | Objective. | Rate of fire. | Remarks. |
|---|---|---|---|---|---|
| 1. | 2 Bde. 251 18-pdrs. | 0.00 | 50 yards short of German front line. | Intense, viz :- Three rounds per gun per minute till 0.04 | This should be a deep barrage, guns being laid to give a depth of 50 yards. |
| | | 0.03 | Rake back on to German front line H.22.b.3.1. to H.22.a.9.0. | | |
| 2. | -do- | 0.04 | Lift to H.22.b.5.8. to H.22.b.1.8. | Decrease to one round per gun per minute. | Lift at rate of 50 yards a minute. |
| 3. | -do- | 0.30 | Lift to M.16.d.7.1. to M.16.d.3.3. | One round per gun per minute till 1.30. | Lift at rate of 50 yards a minute. |
| 4. | -do- | 1.30 | Lift to M.17.a.4.8. to M.11.c.2.1. and remain. | Decrease to one round per gun per three minutes. | Lift at rate of 50 yards a minute. |

PROGRAMME OF BOMBARDMENT.   1st OCTOBER 1916.

SHEET 2.

| Serial No. | Unit bombarding. | Time. | Objective | Rate of fire. | Remarks. |
|---|---|---|---|---|---|
| 5. | 251 Bde., 18-pdrs. | 0.00 | 50 yards short of German front line. | Intense, viz :- Three rounds per gun per minute till 0.04. | This should be a deep barrage, guns being laid to give a depth of 50 yards. |
|  |  | 0.02 | Rake back to German front line M.22.a.9.0. to M.22.a.6.0. |  |  |
| 6. | -do- | 0.04 | Lift to M.22.b.1.8. to M.22.a.7.8. | Decrease to one round per gun per minute. | Lift at rate of 50 yards a minute. |
| 7. | -do- | 0.30 | Lift to M.16.d.3.3. to M.16.c.8.5. | One round per gun per minute till 1.30 | -do- |
| 8. | -do- | 1.30 | Lift to M.1.c.2.1. M.10.d.7.3. | Decrease to one round per gun per 3 minutes. | -do- |

PROGRAMME OF BOMBARDMENT.    1st OCTOBER, 1918.                SHEET 3.

| Serial No. | Unit bombarding. | Time. | Objective. | Rate of fire. | Remarks. |
|---|---|---|---|---|---|
| 9. | 253 Bde. 18-pdrs. | 0.00 | 50 yards short of German front line. | Intense, viz :- Three rounds per gun per minute till 0.04 | This should be a deep barrage, guns being laid to give a depth of 50 yards. |
|  |  | 0.02 | Rake back to German front line, M.22.a.6.0. to M.22.a.2.1. |  |  |
| 10. | -do- | 0.04 | Lift to M.22.a.7.8. to M.22.a.3.8. | Decrease to one round per gun per minute. | Lift at rate of 50 yards per minute. |
| 11. | -do- | 0.30 | Lift to M.16.c.8.5. to M.16.c.4.7. | One round per gun per minute till 1.30 | -do- |
| 12. | -do- | 1.30 | Lift to M.10.d.7.3. to M.10.d.3.4. | Decrease to one round per gun per three minutes. | -do- |

SHEET 4.

PROGRAMME OF BOMBARDMENT, 1st OCTOBER, 1916.

| Serial No. | Unit bombarding. | Time. | Objective. | Rate of fire. | Remarks. |
|---|---|---|---|---|---|
| 13. | 39 Bde., 18-pdrs. | 0.00 | 50 yards short of German front line. | Intense, viz :- Three rounds per gun per minute till 0.04 | This should be a deep barrage, guns being laid to give a depth of 50 yards. |
|  |  | 0.02 | Rake back to German front line, M.22.a.2.1. to M.31.b.7.4. |  |  |
| 14. | -do- | 0.04 | Lift to M.22.a.3.8. to M.31.b.8.8. | Decrease to one round per gun per minute. | Lift at rate of 50 yards per minute. |
| 15. | -do- | 0.30 | Lift to M.16.c.4.7. to M.16.a.0.1. | 1 round per gun per minute till 1.30 | -do- |
| 16. | -do- | 1.30 | Lift to M.10.d.3.4. to M.10.c.8.6. | Decrease to one round per gun per three mins. | -do- |

# PROGRAMME OF BOMBARDMENT FOR 4.5" HOWITZERS.

**1st OCTOBER, 1916.**
**SHEET 5.**

| Serial No. | Unit bombarding. | Time. | Objective. | Rate of fire. | No. of Rounds. | Remarks. |
|---|---|---|---|---|---|---|
| A. | 4.5" HOWITZERS. | 7.0a.m. to 2.0p.m. | C.T.'s on own Zone and work at M.22.a.8.8. | Slow bombardment | 100 bX 100 bX 50 bX 50 bX | 251 Bde. 252 Bde. 253 Bde. 39 Bde. |
| B. | | 2.0p.m. to 0.02 | Front line, own zone. | One round per gun per 1½ minutes. | | |
| C. | | 0.02 to 0.04 | Support line, own zone. | One round per gun per two minutes. | | |
| D. | | 0.04 to 0.30 | Lift along roads and C.T.'s to a line M. 22.b.5.8. to M.16.c.1.4. | One round per gun per two minutes. | | Lift 50 yards a minute. |
| E. | ALL | 0.30 | Jump to N.E. end of LE SARS about M.16.Central and Road Junction M.16.b.9.0. | Slow bombardment till 1.30 | 80 bX 30 bX 40 bX 40 bX | 251 Bde. 252 Bde. 253 Bde. 39 Bde. |

**"C" Form (Original).**
**MESSAGES AND SIGNALS.** No. of Message..........

| Prefix......... Code......... Words......... | Received From.......... By.......... | Sent, or sent out At.........m. To......... By......... | Office Stamp. |
|---|---|---|---|
| £ s. d. Charges to collect Service Instructions. | | | |

Handed in at.......... Office..........m. Received..........m.

TO

| *Sender's Number | Day of Month | In reply to Number | AAA |
|---|---|---|---|
| | | | |
| | | two | |
| | | | M 23 A 3½ . 0 |
| M.22.B 3½ . | rear | M 23 A 3½ 0 | |
| M.23.B 8½.5 | | | |

aaa ...... 

..... B.M. 69

FROM
PLACE & TIME

* This line should be erased if not required.
Wt. 432—M437  500,000 Pads.  H W V  5 16  Forms C.2123.

ADDENDUM NO. 2 to

50th DIVISIONAL ARTILLERY OPERATION ORDER NO. 38.

1. Para. 8.
   Arrangements will be made so that the 18-pdr barrage rests for one minute on the FLERS Support line during the lift in Serial Nos. 2, 6, 10, and 14.

2. ACKNOWLEDGE.

1. 10. 16.
10.20a.m.

Major R.A.,
B.M. 50th D.A.

Copies to -   39th Bde. R.F.A.
              251st Bde. R.F.A.
              252nd Bde. R.F.A.
              253rd Bde. R.F.A.

*Ordered barrage to slacken 5-45 p.m.*

ADDENDUM NO 1 to

50th DIVISIONAL ARTILLERY OPERATION ORDER NO. 38.

30. 9. 16.

1. From 10.0a.m. to 10.10a.m., 4.5" Howitzers will fire at rapid rate on their objectives.

    10.10a.m. to 10.14a.m. - Pause.

    10.14a.m., re-commence normal rate of fire with a salvo from all batteries.

2. All 18-pdr Batteries, 10.7a.m. to 10.10a.m. bursts of fire on front trenches.

    10.10a.m. to 10.14a.m., Lift 300 yards.

    10.14a.m., 2 rounds gun fire on front line trenches.

3. Acknowledge.

Issued at 11.50p.m.

Major R.A.,
B.M. 50th D.A.

    39th Bde. R.F.A.
    251st Bde. R.F.A.
    252nd Bde. R.F.A.
    253rd Bde. R.F.A.

B.M. 1631/9.

## 50th Divisional Artillery.

### S.O.S. BARRAGES.

The following S.O.S. Barrages will come into operation forthwith :-

#### 18-POUNDERS.

252 Bde. :-   M.22.b.9.6.
              to
              M.22.b.2.9.

251 Bde :-    M.22.b.2.9.
              to
              M.16.c.7.1.          *M.16.d.7.0*

253 Bde. :-   M.16.c.7.1.
              to
              M.16.c.4.2.

39 Bde. :-    M.16.c.4.2.
              to
              M.15.d.8.6.

#### 4.5" HOWITZERS.

D/250         C.T. from M.22.a.5.6.
              to
              M.16.c.7.1.

30th Bty.     1 Sect.on M.16.c.3.2.

              1 Sect.on M.22.b.5.8.

\* \* \* \* \* \*

D/252 and D/251 Batteries will fire at a slow rate throughout the night on the following :-

D/252         M.22.d.9.8.
              to
              M.22.b.5.1.

D/251         M.22.b.9.1.
              to
              M.22.b.5.4.

\* \* \* \* \* \*

ACKNOWLEDGE.

2.10.16.

F. Brunson
Major R.A.,
B.M. 50th D.A.

SECRET.

Copy No 15

19/2

## 50th DIVISIONAL ARTILLERY OPERATION ORDER NO. 39.

2.10.16.

479-

1. The 23rd Division will relieve 50th Division on Tuesday, 3rd October, and latter will then be in Corps Reserve.

2. Two bns. 68th Infantry Brigade of 23rd Division will relieve 1st Infantry Brigade of 50th Division as Support Brigade, beginning at 8.0a.m. to-morrow (3rd).

3. To-morrow, (3rd) afternoon and evening 68th Infantry Brigade will relieve 149th Infantry Brigade, and latter will move back to MAMETZ WOOD.

4. 70th Infantry Brigade of 23rd Division is moving up to the area SWANSEA TRENCH - O.G. LINE both inclusive, with Headquarters in O.G. LINE, on 3rd October.

5. Command of the Divisional front will pass to G.O.C., 23rd Division at 2.0p.m. 3rd October, from which time 149th Infantry Brigade will be under the orders of G.O.C. 23rd Division until relieved.

6. 50th Division Headquarters will close at RAILWAY COPSE at 2.0pm 3rd October, and will re-open at D.6.b.Central, near MILLENCOURT at the same hour.

7. On account of the re-distribution of the Corps front into one of two Divisions the following redistribution of the Divl. Artillery will take place:-
   (a) From Centre Group to Right Group, 39th F.A.Bde, 1st Division.
   (b) From Centre Group to Left Group, 251, 252, and 253 Bdes., 50th Divisional Arty.

   Redistribution to be complete by 6.0a.m., 4th inst.

8. When redistribution is complete there will only be two Divl. Arty. Groups, as follows :-
   Right Group:-     Commander, Brig-Gen. E.W.Spedding, C.M.G.
                     47th Div. Arty. less 1 Brigade.
                     2 Bdes. 1st Div. Arty.

   Left Group :-     Commander, Brig-Gen. D.J.M.Fasson, C.B.
                     23rd Div. Arty.
                     2 Bdes, 15th Div. Arty., plus 1 How. Bty.
                     3 Bdes, 50th Div. Arty.

9. The tactical command of 39th Bde. will pass to C.R.A. 47th Div. and tactical command of 251, 252, and 253 Bdes will pass to C.R.A., 23rd Division at 6.0p.m., 3rd October, at which hour H.Q., 50 Div. will close at RAILWAY COPSE and will re-open at D.6.b. Central, near MILLENCOURT at the same hour.

10. ACKNOWLEDGE.

Major R.A.,
B.M. 50th D.A.

Issued at 11.50p.m.
Copies to :-   1 - 39th Bde. R.F.A.        10 - Left Group D.A.
               2 - 251 Bde. R.F.A.         11 - Right Group D.A.
               3 - 252 Bde. R.F.A.         12 - R.A. IIIrd Corps.
               4 - 253 Bde. R.F.A.         13 - 50th Div. Train.
               5 - 250 Bde. R.F.A.         14 - A.D.M.S. 50th Divn.
               6 - 50th D.A.C.             15 - War Diary.
               7 - 50th D.T.M.O.           16, 17, 18 - Spare.
               8 & 9 - H.Q. 50th Div.

BM1578

50th Division.
G.X.2541/10.

C.R.A.
C.R.E.
7th D.L.I. Pioneers.
"Q".

Third Corps Telegrams G.352 and G.352/1 dated 4th October are repeated for information.

G.352:-
"The 47th Division will take over maintain and extend the tramway constructed by the 50th Division from BETHELL SAP to EAUCOURT L'ABBAYE and will have the use of the road through BAZENTIN-LE-PETIT to N.W. Corner of HIGH WOOD AAA Transfer to take place at once AAA 23rd Division will also give facilities to 47th Division to utilise the main road CONTALMAISON - MARTINPUICH - EAUCOURT L'ABBAYE for a limited number of Carts AAA"

G.352/1 :-
"Reference G.352 of to-day Field Company R.E. employed on the tramway will remain so employed for the present under 47th Division AAA".

4th October 1916.

Major.
General Staff.
50th. Division.

19/3

SECRET. 480.

Copy No. 12

## 50th DIVISIONAL ARTILLERY OPERATION ORDER NO. 40.

8.10.16.

1. 250 F.A.Bde., less D/250, will relieve 251 F.A.Bde., less D/251, (personnel only) on the morning of 10th October. Relief to be complete by 12 noon, at which hour D/251 will come under the tactical command of O.C. 250 F.A.Bde.

2. On relief on 10th October, 251 F.A.Bde., less D/251 will proceed to Rest billets at BEHENCOURT, marching via MILLENCOURT - HENENCOURT - BAIZIEUX.

3. Details of relief will be arranged by O.C. bdes. concerned.

4. Completion of relief will be reported to Left D.A. Group and to C.R.A., 50th Div.

5. Acknowledge.

Issued at 10.0p.m.

Copies to -   1 - 250 Bde. R.F.A.
     2 - 251 Bde. R.F.A.
     3 - 252 Bde. R.F.A.
     4 - 253 Bde. R.F.A.
     5 - 50th D.A.C.
     6 and 7 - H.Q. 50th Div.
     8 - R.A., IIIrd Corps.
     9 - C.R.A. 15th Div.
     10 - A.D.M.S., 50th Div.
     11 - 50th Div. Train.
     12 and 13 - War Diary.
     14 and 15 - Spare.

Major R.A.,
B.M. 50th D.A.

## ATTACK OF 1ST OCTOBER.

50th Div. in centre; 23 on their left; 47 on their right.  Very successful attack delivered at 3.15 p.m. remarkable for most excellent artillery barrages, Infantry particularly of 50 Div. who kept very close to it suffered very few casualties.

Analyse causes of 50 Div. Barrages.  Front attacked 750 yards; direct observation possible on most of the commencing lines. No. of 18 Pdrs. available for barrages.

| | |
|---|---|
| 39th Bde. | 18 |
| 251 Bde. | 12 |
| 252 Bde. | 12 |
| 253 Bde. | 12 |

total 54.  18 Pdr. guns each gun a frontage of 13.7 yards; the rate of fire of first barrage was 3 rounds a gun per min. The average range was 3200 yards.

Nobatteries being less than 2800 nor more than 3500, the majority 3100.

Slow bombardment began at 7.0 a.m. and continued to Zero which was at 3.15 p.m. when an intense barrage was placed 50 yards in front of German line for two minutes, when it began to move forward at 50 yards a min. till it reached the next objective where it remained for thirty mins. when the Infantry advanced to this attack when it again moved forward at 50 yards a min. till it reached the third objective.

Chief causes of success of barrage in my opinion, were

(a) good observation and careful previous registration.

(b) very careful checking of all sights.

(c) Good gun platforms, weather was fine and dry.

(d) Fire entirely frontal no enfliade, whatever range of barrage 3200 yards is about the most satisfactory range for an 18 Pdr. shrapnel barrage.

(e) The feeling of confidence existing between the Infantry and Artillery and the great keenness and splendid discipline of the forces enabled them to keep close up to their artillery barrage and gain their objective with very slight casualties.

CRA MKB
18th DB
LC
GDC

BM 1590

III Corps.
G.O.553.

50th DIVISION.
——————————

      Forwarded for your information.

      The attached report was sent in at request of G.O.C.3rd Corps, and is of special value as being that of an entirely independent observer who went up mainly to observe flying conditions generally, and not with any intention of reporting specially on the attack.

      Particular attention is drawn to the para. marked in blue.

                    (Sgd) C.F.ROMER.
                      Brigadier-General,
7th October 1916.          General Staff III Corps.

——————————

                (2).           50th Division.
                                     G.X.2737.

C. R. A.
C. R. E.
149th Inf. Brigade.
150th  "    "
151st  "    "
7th B.L.I.Pioneers.
A. D. M. S.
——————————

      For information.

      The G.O.C. considers that the greatest credit is due to the Company Officers and N.C.Os. for the way in which they got their men into line from most difficult positions on this occasion.

                            H. Karslake
                              Lt-Col.
                        General Staff.
8th October 1916.          50th. Division.

50th Division.
G.X.2767.

## REPORT ON OPERATIONS ON THE 1st INST. AS SEEN FROM THE AIR.

At 3.15 p.m. the steady bombardment changed into a most magnificent barrage. The timing of this was extremely good. Guns opened simultaneously and the effect was that of many Machine Guns opening fire on the same order. As seen from the air the barrage appeared to be a most perfect wall of fire in which it was inconceivable that anything could live. The first troops to extend from the forming up places appeared to be the 50th Division who were seen to spread out from the sap heads and forming up trenches and advance close up under the barrage, apparently some 50 yards away from it. They appeared to capture their objective very rapidly and with practically no losses while crossing the open.

The 23rd Division I did not see so much of owing to their being at the moment of Zero at the tail end of the Machine.

The 47th Division took more looking for than the 50th. and it was my impression at the time that they were having some difficulty in getting into formation for attack from their forming up places, with the result that they appeared to be very late and to be some distance behind the barrage when it lifted off the German front line at EAUCOURT L'ABBAYE, and immediately to the west of it. It was plain that here there was a good chance of failure and this actually came about, for the men had hardly advanced a couple of hundred yards apparently, when they were seen to fall and take cover among shell holes, being presumably held up by machine-gun and rifle fire. It was not possible to verify this owing to the extraordinary noise of the bursting shells of our barrage.

The tanks were obviously too far behind, owing to lack of covered approaches, to be able to take part in the original attack, but they were soon seen advancing on either side of the EAUCOURT L'ABBAYE - FLERS Line, continuously in action and doing splendid work. They did not seem to be a target of much enemy shell fire.

The enemy barrage appeared to open late, quite 5 minutes after the commencement of our own barrage, and when it came it bore no resemblance to the wall of fire which we were putting up. I should have described it as a heavy shelling of an area some 3 to 400 yards in depth from our original jumping off places.

Some large shells were falling in DESTREMONT FARM but these again were too late to catch the first line of the attack, although they must have caused some losses to the supports.

30 minutes after Zero the first English patrols were seen entering LE SARS. They appeared to be meeting with little or no opposition, and at this time no German shells were falling in the Village. Our own shells were falling in the Northern half.

To sum up: the most startling feature of the operations as viewed from the air was the extraordinary volume of fire of our barrage and the straight line kept by it.
(2). The apparent ease with which the attack succeeded where troops were enabled to go forward close under it.
(3). The promiscuous character and comparative lack of volume of enemy's counter-barrage.

(Sgd) J.CHAMIER. Major.
Commanding 34th Sqn.,
R. F. C.

8th October 1916.

SECRET.

Copy No 11

## 50th DIVISIONAL ARTILLERY OPERATION ORDER NO. 41.

1. 252 F.A.Bde., Less D252 will come out of action and move to billets at FRECHENCOURT on the 17th Oct.

2. Route will be BECOURT - ALBERT, AMIENS main road as far as LAHOUSSOYE. Rear of column to be clear of ALBERT by 10 a.m. on 17th.

3. Batteries will move with limbers and wagons full. B. and C/252 will hand over any surplus ammunition to 250 F.A. Bde., and A/252 to 253 F.A.Bde. Amounts thus handed over to be reported to this office by wire.

4. The transfer of tactical command of D/252 will be arranged by Left D.A. Group.

5. D/250 will arrange to cover up their guns, and, leaving a guard on the gun positions and sufficient telephonists to care-take wires will proceed to rest in their wagon lines, on 17th.

6. Details will be arranged by O.C. Brigades concerned.

7. Completion of moves to be reported to Left D.A. Group and to R.A. 50th Div.

8. Acknowledge.

F. Brown

Major R.A.,
B.M. 50th D.A.

Issued at 3.0p.m.

Copies to - 1 - 250 Bde. R.F.A.
           2 - 252 Bde. R.F.A.
           3 - 253 Bde. R.F.A.
           4 - 50th D.A.C.
           5 and 6 - H.Q. 50th Div.
           7 - R.A., IIIrd Corps.
           8 - Left D.A. Group.
           9 - A.D.M.S. 50th Div.
          10 - 50th Div. Train.
          11 and 12 - War Diary.
          13 and 14 - Spare.

1st October, 1916.

| TIME. | Information or orders recd. from | |
|---|---|---|
| A.M. | | |
| 8.0 | C.R.A. | Ordering all lights and fires to be extinguished after dark. |
| P.M. | | |
| 2.10 | 39 Bde. | Enemy seen retiring in four parties to support line from front line. |
| 2.20 | 253 Bde. | Report on shoot at M.G. emplacement at M.22.a.0.2. |
| 2.50 | 253 Bde. | Reports strong enemy force seen advancing from M.5.a. and b. towards WARLENCOURT. Orders given for 2 18 pdrs. Batteries to watch and Corps H.A. informed. |
| 3.39 | 252 Bde. | Our infantry are well across German front line. very heavy M.G. fire across right flank. |
| 3.45 | 252 Bde. | A/252 turned on to counteract M.G. fire referred to in previous message. |
| 3.53 | 252 Bde. | 151 Infantry Brigade state 23rd and 50th Divisions have taken first objective. |
| 5.5 | 251 Bde. | F.O.O. of I.M. reports three Red lights sent up N.E. of EAUCOURT L'ABBAYE. |
| 6.11 | 252 Bde. | F.O.O. reports our patrols are in cutting in M.16.c. which they found unoccupied. |
| 6.20 | 252 Bde. | Liaison officer report LE SARS being heavily shelled. Otherwise quiet. |
| 6.32 | 252 Bde. | 23rd Division have gained their 3rd Objective. |
| 6.49 | 3rd Corps. | Night tasks for night 1st/2nd. |
| 8.30 | 50th Div. | Situation report. |

NOTE.

Owing to the network of trenches at M.22.a.8.8. not being secured, patrols were not able to go as far forward as had been intended and a night barrage was therefore placed from North end of LE SARS to MILL in M.22.b.9.5.

1.10.16.

NOTE.

2/10/16.

At 5.50p.m. on receipt of a message from 151 Inf. Bde. that enemy were concentrating for an attack at M.22.b.5.8., we turned our 18-pdrs. on to this point and searched South down the Valley in M.22.b. and quickened the rate of fire of our How's. on the portion of the FLERS line held by the enemy in M.22.b. and d., which we had been bombarding all day. Our T.M.'s also assisted in dispersing the enemy who eventually attempted to bomb along the FLERS line.

2nd October, 1916.

| TIME | Information or orders recd. from | |
|---|---|---|
| A.M. | | |
| 6.30 | 50th Div. | Patrols report TANGLE protected by wire and held by Germans. Further reconnaissance *ordered* |
| 6.40 | do. | D.G. are to gain touch with enemy along whole front by means of patrols and work down communication trench to the TANGLE. |
| 9.30 | do. | 149 Inf. Bde. to relieve 151. On completion 149th will be in front system 151 in Support, 150 in Divisional Reserve. Brigades informed. |
| 10.55 | do. | 4.5" hows to be turned on to FLERS front and support line through MILL M.22.b.9.5. to Bank parallel with MARTINPUICH - WARLENCOURT road. Heavy Artillery will fire on TANGLE. |
| P.M. | | |
| 7.10 | R.A.3rd Corps | Night tasks for night 2nd and 3rd. |
| 7.56 | do. | Special attention to be paid to expenditure of AX in preference to A. Bdes. informed. |
| 8.35 | D.G. | Enemy launched heavy bombing attack at 5.30 p.m. Was entirely repulsed assisted by artillery fire and light and medium trench mortars. |
| 8.35 | D.G. | Enemy bombing attack has been driven off. Normal conditions now prevail. |
| 11.50 | C.R.A. | 50th Division Operation Order issued giving redistribution of Artillery. 251,252 and 253 Bdes. to come under orders of C.R.A. 23rd Division, and 39 Bde. to come under C.R.A. 47th Div. |

During the night of 2nd. and 3rd. October, 1916, and during the day of the 3rd., and 18-pdr. barrage was kept along the line M.15.d.8.6. to M.22.b.9.6.

During the night of the 2nd. and 3rd., the FLERS front line was bombarded with Howrs., from M.22.b.4.1. to M.22.d.9.8., and the FLERS support line from M.22.b.9.1. to M.22.b.5.4., until 9 A.M., on the 3rd.

At 12 A.M., on the 3rd., 4.5" Howrs., were ordered to fire on points M.22.b.4.1. and M.22.b.5.4., and an 18-pdr. barrage was placed along the line M.22.b.5.4. - M.22.b.6.7.

An 18-pdr. barrage was also placed along the line M.22.b.6.7. - M.22.b.1.9.

On receipt of information from 47th. D. A., that their Infantry were working their way along the FLERS line from the south of EAUCOURT L'ABBAYE the fire of howrs., on M.22.b.4.1. and M.22.b.5.4., was stopped and the 18-pdr. barrage lifted from M.22.b.5.4. - M.22.b.6.7., to M.22.b.6.7. - M.16.d.8.0.

On handing over the tactical command of 251., 252., and 253 Brigades, RFA., to C.R.A., 23rd. Division this 18-pdr. barrage was still continuing.

3rd October, 1916.

| TIME | Information or orders recd. from. | |
|---|---|---|
| A.M. 10.17 | R.A. 3rd Corps | Giving Heavy Artillery dispositions in case of enemy counter attack. |
| P.M. 2.18 | 252 Bde. | Infantry report that they are now investigating part of FLERS LINE not occupied by us and which they think has been evacuated by enemy. |
| 6.0 | — | Tactical command of 251, 252 and 253 Bdes passed to C.R.A. 23rd Div. and tactical command of 39th Bde. passed to C.R.A. 47th D.A. Arty. H.Q. returned to Camp in D.6.b. near MILLENCOURT. |

Report No. 17.    Daily Diary of Information
from 12 noon 1/10/16 to 12 noon 2/10/16 excluding the
hours of 3-15 p.m. to 6-0 p.m. which were sent you
separately.

> 25rd
> (NORTHUMBRIAN)
> BRIGADE, R.F.A.

| Time | Information from: | |
|---|---|---|
| 11-25 a.m. | C.R.A. | Reported machine gun giving trouble at M 22 a 2 0-2 1. |
| | O.C. | Instructed B/253 to engage it with H.E. |
| 2-20 p.m. | O.C. | Reported to B.M. result of shooting on machine gun emplacement. |
| 3-5 p.m. | C.R.A. | Reported strong enemy force on road running through M 5 a & b. |
| | O.C. | Warned roving battery and O.P. O.P. unable to spot the party before programme started, when smoke hid all possibilities of doing so. |
| 6-30 p.m. | Wireless | Reported several messages had been received during the day, all to the effect that aeroplanes had been unable to observe anything owing to smoke. |
| 6-55 p.m. | C.R.A. | Reduce rate of fire to one round per gun per ~~four minutes~~ ten minutes covering the whole zone by sweeping. |
| | O.C. | Instructed batteries accordingly. |
| 9-20 p.m. | Liaison Officer | Reports Sunken road not occupied by Germans. They hold strong point in nest of trenches South. Yellow flares seen in last house in LE SARS. |
| 10-45 p.m. | C.R.A. | Instructions to ~~lift~~ continue barrage during the night. |
| | O.C. | Batteries instructed. |
| 11-0 p.m. | O.C. | B/253 instructed to fire at irregular intervals on sunken road running north of present barrage line from M 16 b 3 5 - M 10 d 5 6, and on path from M 16 a 7 5 - M 10 d 4 8 up till 3 o'clock. A/253 to take over these duties from 3 to 6-30. |

2/10/16.

| | | |
|---|---|---|
| 2-20 a.m. | B.M. | Instructed to drop barrage 300 yds. bringing centre of zone to approximately M 16 c 7¾ 8½, continuing the same rate of fire. |
| | O.C. | Instructed batteries accordingly. |
| 6-0 a.m. | B.M. | Instructed to stop firing. The barrage for S.O.S. was to be along the Sunken road from M 16 c 8 0 - 3½ 2½. |
| | O.C. | Instructed batteries accordingly. |

Report No. 17 (continued)

9-0 a.m.

During the evening and night different reports as to position varying to some extent. The position this morning seems to be as follows: We have joined up with the Division on our left and hold the whole of first FLER Line and supports with the exception of a section about 300 yds. of the support south of LE SARS village across the BAUPAUME road.
We have bombing parties up communication trench running through 29 a through towards nest of trenches which is strongly held by Germans. There is a gap of 500 yds. between ourselves and the Division on our right, apparently to the north-west of EAUCOURT l'ABBAYE where there is a net-work of trenches behind the Bosche support line. It is doubtful whether the line is occupied by Germans or British.
We captured and hold EAUCOURT l'ABBAYE, the trenches being dug on the north-western edge.

10-5 a.m.   O.R.A.   Altered barrage to M 16a 1 0 - a 7 4, no shooting south of road, one round per gun per four minutes. Hows. not to shoot. Search 200 yds. in rear of barrage line.

O.C.   Instructed batteries verbally, and confirmed by telephone.

1/10/16

### 253rd ( Northumbrian ) Brigade R.F.A.

The following observed from HIGH WOOD O!P!

| Time | Observation |
|---|---|
| 3.15. | Our infantry went over.  Barrage started. |
| 3.16 | Our infantry going over in hundreds. |
| 3.17. | Our infantry are approaching first line. |
| 3.19. | Smoke getting very intense. |
| 3.20 | Our infantry have entered front line. Difficulty in observing owing to smoke. |
| 3.23 | Our barrage observed to be less intense. |
| 3.25 | Enemy shells falling near O.P. Also on our old front line. |
| 3.26 | No sign of our men, who have disappeared in the smoke of our barrage. |
| 3.29 | Slight enemy barrage on CRESCENT ALLEY |
| 3.32 | Smoke so intense that Roads are invisible. behind Flers |
| 3.38 | 5.9" shells falling over FLERS first line. |
| 3.40 | Enemy barrage HIGH WOOD and to the right of S, 4, b. |
| 3.44 | Supports seen to go over bags towards FLERS line. |

Lt Col R.F.A
Comdg 253rd ( Northumbrian )Brigade R.F.A.

251st Brigade R.F.A.

Daily Intelligence Summary, 9.0 a.m. 2;10;16 to 9.0 a.m. 3;10;16.

1. Operations. (Other than those included in Daily Programme) :-

Acting under orders from D.A;Hqrs received at 10.10 a.m. 2nd inst, 18-pr Batteries put light barrage of one round per gun per four minutes on line M.16.d.5.8. to M.16.b.1.0 and searching back 200 yards from that line. No firing SOUTH of line SUNKEN ROAD in M.16.c., 22.d, - MILL M.22.b.9.5. ~~Any movement seen NORTH of that line to be dealt with at once.~~

At 1.57 p.m. rate of fire on this barrage was reduced by one half.

At 8.40 a.m. 3rd inst orders were received for 18-pr Batteries to stop firing on barrage, and fire occasional bursts.

At 10.30 a.m. 2nd inst D.Battery was ordered to fire very carefully observed shoot on FLERS SUPPORT LINE M.22.b.9.1. to M.22.b.5.4. Slow bombardment until further orders. At 6.30 p.m. orders were received to quicken up rate of fire to one round per how. per two minutes. per how.

At 7.0 p.m. orders were received to reduce rate of fire to one round per five minutes.

This rate was continued until 9.0 a.m. 3rd inst when orders were received to cease firing.

2. Information about work done etc., on our own trenches.

3. Information about enemy's trenches, work, wire, M.G. and T.M. emplacements, O.P.'s Strong points, etc.:-

Visibility too poor to get intelligence

4. Artillery activity.

Between 11 AM and 1 PM on 2nd considerable hostile artillery activity about the forward area principally M.22.c. Very little hostile fire all day on the back area.

5. Miscellaneous, including any other items of intelligence.

At 10.30 a.m. F.O.O. reported he had met an Infantry Brigadier in M.22.c. who informed him main line held by us was FLERS SUPPORT line. TANGLE probably held by enemy as sniping appeared to come from there. He also thought we had parties in LE SARS.

At 11.35 a.m. F.O.O. reported no movement could be seen in enemy lines. Visibility was poor.

At 9.20 p.m. F.O.O. reported all quiet on this Divisional front. There had been some bombardment on left.

At 12.20 a.m. 3rd inst. F.O.O. reported all quiet on this Divisional Front.

At 5.35 a.m. -ditto-

3 : 10 : 1916. Comdg: 251st bde. R.F.A.

253rd (NM) Bde. R.F.A.

Daily Intelligence Summary, 9.0am 2/10 :16 to 9.0am 3/10 :16.

------------------------------------------------------------

1. Operations (Other than those included in Daily Programme):-

   Nil

   Rising Battery unable to shot targets during day on account of mist. During night continual fire at irregular intervals along road M16 b 3.3. to M10 d 5.7 and on pathway M16 a 7.4 through M10 c 9.0 to M10 d 4.8

------------------------------------------------------------

2. Information about work done etc., on our own trenches:-

   Consolidating O P's

------------------------------------------------------------

3. Information about enemy's trenches, work, wire, M.G. and T.M. emplacements, O.P's, Strong points, etc:-

   Nil

4. Artillery activity:-

Very little hostile shelling round (K.D) position.

During the heavy strafe on left about 8 P.M all quiet on our front

A fair amount of shelling by 4.2 guns on wagon lines & back country

---

5. Miscellaneous, including any other items of intelligence:-

Nothing to add to intelligence wires sent in during the day.

Howitzer fuse shell of premature which fell in B/253 for inspection

A.D. Lewis
Capt. for Lieut Col
Commdg. 253 Bde R.F.A

252 Brigade R.F.A.

Daily Intelligence Summary, 9.0 a.m. 2:10:16 to 9.0 a.m. 3:10:16.

1. Operations. (Other than those included in Daily Programme) :-

Germans reported messing in valley about M22 B 5 8 Brigade put up a barrage from Mill at M22 b 9 5 South to FLERS LINE. A hostile bombing attack was developed was satisfactorily dealt with by Infantry at about 7.30 pm Attack was on a point West of EAUCOURT L'ABBAYE

2. Information about work done etc., on our own trenches.

3. Information about enemy's trenches, work, wire, M.G. and T.M. emplacements, O.P.'s Strong points, etc.:-

4. Artillery activity.

Hostile artillery was active during the night and our infantry during relief had some casualties otherwise quiet.

A few 5.9 on BAZENTIN LE PETIT Road during the day.

On the whole a quiet day.

5. Miscellaneous, including any other items of intelligence.

A dull day on which observation was difficult.

3·10· 1916.  Comdg: 252 bde. R.F.A.

Frank H. Pickersgill

The 50th Divisional Artillery with the 276th Brigade R.F.A. attached was mainly disposed in CATTERPILLAR VALLEY and in the valley west of BAZENTIN LE GRAND WOOD.

As such they formed the "Centre Group" of the III Corps Divisional Artillery. The batteries of the 250th Brigade R.F.A. were severally attached to the other three F.A.Brigades of the 50th Divisional Artillery. The sub-groups were commanded as follows:-

```
252 F.A.Bde.   Lieut.Colonel   F.L.Pickersgill.
251    "            "    "     F.B.Moss-Blundell.
253    "            "    "     H.E.Hanson, D.S.O.
276    "            "    "     T.E.Toppin, D.S.O.
```

The front occupied by the 50th Division was divided into four equal sections, each being covered by one of the above sub-groups, the 252 F.A. Brigade covering the right section.

Liaison Officers were sent to each of the Infantry Brigades and some of the Battalions.

The enemy trenches were prepared by a preliminary bombardment lasting three days by all natures of Heavy Howitzer assisted by 4.5" Hows. of Divisional Artillery.

The 18 Pdr. barrages had to be registered by aeroplane and balloon as only the enemy front line was visible from O.P's.

On the morning of attack at Zero 18 Pdrs. opened a barrage 150 yards from our front line, this advanced 50 yards a minute till a line 200 yards from 1st objective was reached. It dwelt there for an hour and then again lifted at same rate till a similar line was reached beyond 2nd objective, and a similar procedure was adopted with the final objective.

The attack of this Division was assisted by one Tank which worked on the left flank of the Division moving up between our flank and the village of MARTINPUICH.

(4497) W. 4884/M680  250,000  8/16  McA. & W., Ltd.  (Est. 279)  Forms/W 3091/3.    Army Form W. 3091.

## Cover for Documents.

Vol 19

Nature of Enclosures.

WAR    DIARY    VOLUME  XX,

NOVEMBER  1916

50th    DIVISIONAL    ARTILLERY.

---

Notes, or Letters written.

Army Form C. 2118

# WAR DIARY

## INTELLIGENCE SUMMARY

VOLUME XX.

(Erase heading not required.)    H.Q. 50th DIVISIONAL ARTILLERY.

Page 1.

Instructions regarding War Diaries and Intelligence Summaries are contained in F. S. Regs., Part II. and the Staff Manual respectively. Title Pages will be prepared in manuscript.

| Place | Date | Hour | Summary of Events and Information | Remarks and references to Appendices |
|---|---|---|---|---|
| Near MILLENCOURT | 1 | – | Lieut W.A.Denham, 253rd Bde R.F.A appointed A.D.C to C.R.A, 50th Division in succession to Lieut E.H.Johnson, returned to Regimental duty with 252 Bde R.F.A. | |
| do. | 4 | – | Staff Captain returned from leave and re-assumed duty. Capt A.D.Currie returned to 253 Bde. | |
| do. | 4 | – | Lieut W.A. Denham, A.D.C to C.R.A proceeded on leave. Duties being performed by Lieut. E.H. Johnson. | |
| X.27.B.98 | 6 | – | H.Q. 50th D.A relieved 15th D.A at X.27.b.88 (LOZENGE WOOD ) and took over command of Left D.A.Group, consisting of 70, 71, 73 Bdes of 15th D.A., 102 and 103 bdes of 23rd D.A, and 250 and 253 bdes of 50th D.A. Operation order No 42 ( Appendix 20/1 attached ) | 20/1. |
| do | 8 | – | Personnel of 73rd Bde R.F.A relieved personnel of 72nd Bde R.F.A (15th D.A ). | |
| do | 9 | 3.15 p.m. | Chinese attack took place. Artillery of Left Group carried out bombardment as per programme Appendix 20/2 attached ). | 20/2 |
| do | 10 | 9.10 a.m. | Chinese attack. All guns and howitzers bombarded GALLWITZ LINE for three minutes. (Appendix 20/3 attached ). | 20/3 |
| do | 10 | – | Re-adjustment of Left D.A Group commenced with a view to 50th D.A being relieved to re-organise. Operation order No 43 (Appendix 20/4 attached ). | 20/4 |
| do. | 10 | midnt 12 | Two bdes carried out a 15 minutes bombardment of GALLWITZ LINE from 12 mid-night to 12.15 a.m. in support of 4th Canadian Div's operations. (Appendix 20/5 attached ) | 20/5 |
| do | 11 | p.m 12.5 to 12.15 | Withdrawal of Bdes of 50th D.A and re-adjustment of Left D.A Group proceeding. 12.5 to 12.15 p.m Left D.A Group carried out a bombardment on GALLWITZ LINE in connection with Chinese attack. Programme of bombardment (Appendix 20/6 attached ) | 20/6. |
| do. | 11 | | Withdrawal of Bdes. of 50th D.A from the line completed. Bdes now in wagon lines. | |
| do | 12 | | A.D.C to C.R.A returned from leave, and Lieut E.H.Johnson returned to Regimental duty with 252 Bde R.F.A. | |

Army Form C. 2118

# WAR DIARY
or
## INTELLIGENCE SUMMARY
(Erase heading not required.)

Page 2

| Place | Date | Hour | Summary of Events and Information | Remarks and references to Appendices |
|---|---|---|---|---|
| LOZENGE WOOD. | 12 | 8.15 a.m | Artillery programme same as for preceeding day. Zero hour 8.15 a.m. | |
| do | 13 | 5.45 a.m | Artillery of IIIrd Corps carried out Chinese attacks in support of Fifth Army operations. Left D.A group carried out a bombardment as per programme attached. Appendix 20/7. | 20/7 |
| do | 13 | - | 250 Bde ( less 'D' Bty ) with D/251 attached, and 253 bde with D/252 attached marched from their wagon lines to BAVLINCOURT - BEHENCOURT - FRECHENCOURT area to re-organise. Operation order I.O 44 ( Appendix 20/8 attached ) | 20/8 |
| do | 14 | 6.45 a.m | Left D.A Group carried out a bombardment to assist attack of Right Division (50th). Operation order No 45 issued. ( Cancelled by No 46 ) Appendix 20/9 attached ). | 20/9 |
| do | 14 | 10.0 a.m | Command of Left D.A Group handed over by C.R.A 50th Div, to C.R.A, 23rd Div. at 10.30 a.m., and H.Q 50th Div Arty. marched to BAVLINCOURT CHATEAU. ( See appendix 20/9 ) | |
| do. | 14 | - | 50th D.A.C relieved by 23rd D.A.C. H.Q and Nos 1,2 and 3 Sections of 50th D.A.C marched to BAVLINCOURT - BEHENCOURT + FRECHENCOURT area with H.Q at BEAUCOURT. No 4 Section to LAVIEVILLE. See appendix No 20/8 ). | 20/9 |
| BAVLINCOURT | 15 | - | C.R.A held conference of Brigade Commanders. | |
| do. | 16) 18) | - | Re-organisation of 50th Div.Arty proceeding, and following re-adjustment took place :- H.Q Staff, 253 Bde. broken up. A/253 Bty and 1 Section C/253 to 250 Bde R.F.A B/253 Bty and 1 Section C/253 to 251 Bde R.F.A 250 and 251 Bdes R.F.A now consist of three 18-pdr 6 gun batteries and a 4.5" How Battery. C/252 Battery divided up so as to form two 18-pdr batxxx 6 gun batteries in the brigade. | |
| do | 19 | - | do. | |
| do | 20 | - | Batteries completing re-organisation and getting cleaned up. | |

Army Form C. 2118

# WAR DIARY
## or
## INTELLIGENCE SUMMARY
(Erase heading not required.)

Instructions regarding War Diaries and Intelligence Summaries are contained in F. S. Regs., Part II. and the Staff Manual respectively. Title Pages will be prepared in manuscript.

484-

| Place | Date | Hour | Summary of Events and Information | Remarks and references to Appendices |
|---|---|---|---|---|
| BAVLINCOURT | 21 | - | First half 351 Bde R.F.A with D/250 instead of their own, relieved 51 Bde R.F.A ( 9th D.A ), and first half 252 Bde R.F.A (12th D.A ), forming part of Right Group under 1st D.A. Operation order No 47. ( Appendix 20/10 attached ) | 20/10 |
| do | 22 | - | Second half of 351 and 352 Bdes R.F.A completed relief of 51 and 62 Bdes R.F.A. Remaining batteries take up winter rest quarters in BAVLINCOURT and BERNICOURT. | |
| do | 24 | - | 50th D.A.G relieved 9th D.A.G, and came under command of 1st D.A. Operation order No 48 ( Appendix 20/11 attached ) | 20/11 |

R.C. Denman Lt.
R.D.C. & R.H. 53? Div.

Appendix 20/1

SECRET.

Copy No. 13

## 50th DIVISIONAL ARTILLERY OPERATION ORDER NO. 42.

6.11.16

1.  Headquarters 50th Divisional Artillery are relieving Headquarters 15th Divisional Artillery at 10. a.m. on 6th November, at which hour the command of Left Group Divisional Artillery passes to C.R.A. 50th Division.

    This office opens at 10. a.m. at X.27.b.8.8.

2.  Acknowledge.

F. Brunner
Major R.A.,
B.M. 50th D.A.

Issued at 8.0a.m.

Copies to - 1 - 250 Bde. R.F.A.
           2 - 251 Bde. R.F.A.
           3 - 252 Bde. R.F.A.
           4 - 253 Bde. R.F.A.
           5 - 50th D.A.C.
           6 - 50th D.T.M.O.
           7 and 8 - H.Q. 50th Div.
           9 - R.A. 3rd Corps.
          10 - A.D.M.S. 50th Div.
          11 - 50th Div. Train A.S.C.
          12 - C.R.A. 15th Division.
          13 and 14 - War Diary.
          15 and 16 - Spare.

Appendix 20/2

SECRET.

LEFT D.A. GROUP.    PROGRAMME OF BOMBARDMENT, at 3.15p.m., 9.11.16.

| Serial No. | Unit bombarding | Time. | Objective. | Rate of fire. | Remarks. |
|---|---|---|---|---|---|
| 1. | 18-pounders of all Brigades. | P.M. 3.15 to 3.20 | GALLWITZ front line on own S.O.S. front. | Two rounds per gun per minute. | 80% A.X. 20% A. |
| | | 3.20 to 3.22 | Lift 200 yards. | | |
| | | At 3.22 | Return to original objective and fire two salvoes. | | |
| 2. | 4.5" Howitzers. | 3.15 to 3.17 | GALLWITZ front line on Brigades S.O.S. front. | Two rounds per how. per minute. | B.X. |
| | | 3.17 to 3.20 | GALLWITZ Support line and LITTLE WOOD. | | |
| | | At 3.22 | Two salvoes on GALLWITZ front line. | | |
| 3. | All 18-pdrs. & 4.5" Hows. that can reach. | 3.28 | LOUPART WOOD. | Two salvoes. | A.X. and B.X. |

O.C., All Bdes R.F.A. (Y)

1. Watches will be synchronised from this Office at 12.30p.m.
2. Acknowledge by wire.

B.M./1775.

(Sgd) J Browwn
Major R.A.,
B.M. 50th D.A.

9/11/16.

Appendix 20/3

SECRET.

LEFT D.A. GROUP.    PROGRAMME OF BOMBARDMENT ON 10.11.16.

| Serial No. | Unit bombarding. | Time. | Objective. | Rate of fire. | Remarks. |
|---|---|---|---|---|---|
| 1. | 253<br>71 All guns<br>73 and Hows.<br>103 | 9.10 to 9.15a.m. | GALLWITZ LINE,<br>M.10.c.96<br>to<br>M.10.c.57. | Two rounds per piece per minute. | 1. Watches will be synchronised by telephone at 8.0a.m. from this Office.<br>2. Heavy Artillery are firing on M.10.c.57 to M.10.c.37 from 9.7 to 9.10a.m.<br>3. Acknowledge by wire. |
| 2. | 70<br>102 All guns<br>250 and Hows. | | GALLWITZ LINE,<br>M.10.c.37<br>to<br>M.9.d.9065. | | |

C.C., All bdes R.F.A.

B.M. 1775/1.

5/11/16.

(sgd) J Bronson......... Major R.A.,
B.M. 50th D.A.

Appendix 20/4

SECRET.

Copy No. 19

LEFT GROUP DIVISIONAL ARTILLERY OPERATION ORDER NO. 43.

10.11.16

In re-adjustment of Left Group D.A., the following will take place :-

1. C/253 pull out two guns on 10th, which will proceed to wagon lines.

2. D/253 and D/71 pull out on night 10/11 and proceed to wagon lines.

3. B/250 pull out three guns of B/71 on 10th which will proceed to B/250 wagon lines. B/71 takes over position and three guns of B/250 on night 10/11, when personnel of B/250 proceed to wagon lines.

4. C/250 pull out three guns of C/71 on 10th, which will proceed to C/250 wagon lines. C/71 take over position and four guns of C/250 on night 10/11 when personnel of C/250 proceed to wagon lines.

5. D/251 pull out one section on 10th, one section on 11th, and proceed to wagon lines.

6. Personnel of D/102 relieve personnel of C/104 on night 10/11. C/104 will collect pieces of D/102 and proceed to ST. GRATIEN on 11th. D/102 comes under tactical command of O.C., 103 Bde. R.F.A. at noon on 11th.

7. Personnel of A/102 relieves personnel of A/103, first section on 10th, second and third sections on 11th.

8. Personnel of A/103 will take over position and guns and relieve personnel of A/250 (four guns), C/71 (one gun) with the addition of one gun from B/250, first section on night 10/11, second and third sections on night 11/12.

9. Personnel of B/103 will take over position and guns and relieve personnel of A/253 (four guns) and C/253 (two guns), first section on afternoon of 10th, and second and third sections on afternoon of 11th. Personnel of A/253 and C/253 will proceed to wagon lines.

10. All ammunition will be handed over in occupied positions, that in positions being vacated, to the nearest battery of Left Group D.A. Amounts handed over and taken over will be reported to D.A. concerned.

11. Bde. H.Q., 250 and 253 Bdes R.F.A. will proceed to wagon lines on completion of above moves.

12. Moves ordered by night will be carried out during the hours of darkness.

13. Brigades of 50th D.A. will march to SAVLINCOURT area under orders which will be issued later.

14. On officer of each relieved battery will remain behind if required by O.C. relieving battery.

15. Command of batteries will pass on completion of reliefs.

16. Completion of each movement will be reported to this office by wire.

17. Acknowledge.

F. Brunson
Major R.A.,
B.M. 50th D.A.

Issued at 6.30a.m.

Copies to - 1 - 15th D.A.
          2 - 93rd D.A.
          3 - 48th Div.
          4 and 5 - 50th Div.
          6 - Right Group D.A.
          7 - 70 Bde. R.F.A.
          8 - 71 Bde. R.F.A.
          9 - 73 Bde. R.F.A.
          10 - 102 Bde. R.F.A.
          11 - 103 Bde. R.F.A.
          12 - 250 Bde. R.F.A.
          13 - 253 Bde. R.F.A.
          14 - 50th D.A.C.
          15 - 50th Div. Train A.S.C.
          16 - A.D.M.S., 50th Div.
          17 - A.D.V.S., 50th Div.
          18 - R.A., IIIrd Corps.
          19 and 20 - War Diary.
          21, 22 and 23, Spare.

WAR DIARY.
Appendix 20/5

LEFT D.A. GROUP.     PROGRAMME OF BOMBARDMENT, Night 10/11 at Zero hour.

| Serial No. | Unit bombarding. | Time. | Objective. | Rate of fire. | Remarks. |
|---|---|---|---|---|---|
| 1. | 250 Bde., 18-pdrs. | 0.00 to 0.15 | GALLWITZ LINE, M.9.c.75 to M.14.b.89 | One round per gun per minute. | |
| 2. | 102 Bde., 18-pdrs. | -do- | -do- | -do- | |

B.M. 1775/2.

O.C., ...... Bde. R.F.A.

1. This is to assist 4th Canadian Div.
2. Zero hour and synchronisation of watches will be communicated later.
3. Zero hour will probably be about 10 p.m. 12 midnight 10/11 Nov.
4. Acknowledge by wire.

J. Anderson
Major R.A.,
B.M. 50th D.A.

10.11.16.

Appendix 26/6

SECRET.

LEFT D.A. GROUP.         PROGRAMME FOR BOMBARDMENT, 11.11.16.

| Serial No. | Unit bombarding. | Time. P.M. | Objective. | Rate of fire. | Remarks. |
|---|---|---|---|---|---|
| 1. | All available 18-pdrs. | 12.5 to 12.10 | GALLWITZ LINE on own zone. | Two rounds per gun per minute. | 1. "Chinese" attack. |
| 2. | -do- | 12.10 to 12.13 | Lift 200 yards on to GALLWITZ SUPPORT LINE. | One round per gun per minute. | 2. 80% A.X., 20% A. |
| 3. | -do- | At 12.13 | Fire two salvoes on original objective. | | 3. Watches will be synchronised by telephone at 10 a.m. from this Office. |
| 4. | All 4.5" hows. | 12.5 to 12.7 | GALLWITZ LINE on own zone. | Two rounds per how. per minute. | 4. Acknowledge by wire. |
| 5. | -do- | 12.7 to 12.10 | Lift on to GALLWITZ SUPPORT LINE. | One round per how. per minute. | |
| 6. | -do- | At 12.13 | Fire two salvoes on original objective. | | |

7. Every available gun and howitzer 12.21 fire two salvoes at COUPE TRENCH.

C.C., Ede. R.F.A.

B.M. /1775/3.

[signature]
Major R.A.,
B.M. 50th Div.

War Diary.
Appendix 20/7

LEFT GROUP D.A.

PROGRAMME OF BOMBARDMENT. 13.11.16.

| Serial No. | Unit bombarding. | Time. | Objective. | Rate of fire. | Remarks. |
|---|---|---|---|---|---|
| 1. | All 18-pdrs.<br>All 4.5" Hows. | 0.00 to 0.06 | GALLWITZ LINE on own zone. | 3 rounds per piece per min.<br>2 rounds per piece per min. | 1(a) The Fifth Army are attacking on 13th November. |
| 2. | All 18-pdrs.<br>All 4.5" Hows. | 0.06 to 0.10 | Lift to GALLWITZ SUPPORT, DYKE ROAD, GALLWITZ SWITCH, VILLAGE ALLEY, LITTLE WOOD, WARLENCOURT FAUCOURT in own zone. | 1½ rounds per piece per min.<br>2 rounds per piece per min. | (b) At Zero on the 13th the Artillery of the IIIrd Corps will carry out Chinese attacks. |
| 3. | All 18-pdrs.<br>All 4.5" Hows. | 0.10 to 0.14 | As in 1. | 2 rounds per piece per min.<br>3 rounds per piece per min. | (c) Watches will be synchronised from this office at 12.15a.m. |
| 4. | All 18-pdrs.<br>All 4.5" Hows. | 0.14 to 0.18 | As in 2. | 1½ rounds per piece per min.<br>2 rounds per piece per min. | (d) Zero is 5.45a.m. |
| 5. | All 18-pdrs.<br>All 4.5" Hows. | 0.18 to 0.20 | As in 1. | 3 rounds per piece per min.<br>2 rounds per piece per min. | (e) Acknowledge by wire. |
| 6. | All 18-pdrs.<br>All 4.5" Hows. | 0.20 to 0.40 | As in 1. | bursts of fire, gradually dying down.<br>1 round per piece per min. | (f) 18-pdrs, 80% A.X. |

O.C.,
Bde. R.F.A.

B.M./1789.

Major R.A.,
B.M. 50th D.A.

Appendix 20/6

SECRET.

Copy 22

## 50th DIVISIONAL ARTILLERY OPERATION ORDER NO. 44.

12.11.16.

1. 250 Bde. (Less D Bty) with D/251 attached, and 253 Bde. with D/252 attached, will march on the 13th in that order from their wagon lines in forward area to billets in BAVLINCOURT - BEHENCOURT - FRECHENCOURT area, via ALBERT - Main AMIENS Road - LAHOUSBOYE.

2. Head of Column will reach ALBERT 9.0a.m.
253 Bde. will not move on to the road until 250 Bde. is clear.

3. 50th D.A.C. will be relieved by 23rd D.A.C. on 14th inst., and will hand over their lines and Ammunition Refilling Point at FRICOURT to 23rd D.A.C. and march via ALBERT - Main AMIENS road - LAHOUSSOYE to billets as under :-

   H.Q. & 1,2,3, Sections - BAVLINCOURT - BEHENCOURT - FRECHENCOURT area.
   No. 4 Section - LAVIEVILLE.

   Head of D.A.C. will be at ALBERT at 3.0p.m.

4. While at LAVIEVILLE No. 4 Section will continue the construction of the D.A.C. lines.
   14 G.S. wagons complete will be detailed to take over the work under R.E. in relief of 23rd D.A.C. 14 G.S. Wagons.

5. Command of Left D.A. Group will pass from C.R.A. 50th Div. to C.R.A. 23rd Div. at 10.0a.m. on 14th.

6. H.Q. 50th D.A. will open at 1.0p.m. on 14th at BAVLINCOURT CHATEAU.

7. Acknowledge.

F. Brown

Major R.A.,
B.M. 50th D.A.

Issued at 4.0p.m.

Copies to - 1 - R.A., lllrd Corps.
          2 - 70 Bde. R.F.A.
          3 - 71 Bde. R.F.A.
          4 - 73 Bde. R.F.A.
          5 - 102 Bde. R.F.A.
          6 - 103 Bde. R.F.A.
          7 - 250 Bde. R.F.A.
          8 - 251 Bde. R.F.A.
          9 - 252 Bde. R.F.A.
         10 - 253 Bde. R.F.A.
         11 - 50th D.A.C.
         12 - 50th D.T.M.O.
         13 - 48th Div.
         14 and 15 - 50th Div.
         16 - 15th D.A.
         17 - 23rd D.A.
         18 - Right Group D.A.
         19 - A.D.M.S. 50th Div.
         20 - A.D.V.S. 50th Div.
         21 - 50th Div. Train A.S.C.
         22 and 23 - War Diary.
         24 - lllrd Corps H.A.
         25, 26, 27 - Spare.

Appendix 20/9

SECRET.

Copy No. 9

LEFT DIVISIONAL ARTILLERY GROUP OPERATION ORDER NO. 45.

13. 11. 16.

1. The 149th Infantry Brigade will attack on the 14th instant that part of the GIRD LINE and BUTTE TRENCH included in the area M.18.a.31 - M.18.a.03 - M.17.b.33 - M.17.a.70
   The jumping off trench of the 50th Division is new trench parallel to SNAG TRENCH, and about 100 yards to the South of it.
   The Anzac Corps is attacking on the immediate right of 149th Infantry Brigade. - The jumping off trench of the Australian Division is SNAG TRENCH, which has been continued Southwards by them parallel to the GIRD TRENCH.

2. Left Group D.A. will assist as shewn in attached Table.
   Fire of Left Group D.A. will cease at Zero plus 30 minutes but will be ready to re-commence at once if enemy shew signs of movement.

3. Hour of Zero and instructions for synchronising watches will be sent later.

4. 18-pdrs. will fire 50% A. and 50% A.X.
   4.5" Hows. ammunition as shewn in Table.

5. Barrages are shewn on attached map.

6. Acknowledge by wire.

F. Brown

Major R.A.,
B.H. 50th D.A.

Issued at 3.0p.m.
            1-
Copies to   70 Bde. R.F.A.
            2 - 71 Bde. R.F.A.
            3 - 73 Bde. R.F.A.
            4 - 102 Bde. R.F.A.
            5 - 103 Bde. R.F.A.
            6 - H.Q. 50th Div.
            7 - H.Q. 48th Div.
            8 - Right Group D.A.
            9 and 10 - War Diary.
            11 and 12 - Spare.

PROGRAMME OF BOMBARDMENT.     LEFT GROUP D.A.     14.11.16.

| Serial No. | Unit Bombarding. | Time. | Objective. | Rate of fire. | Remarks. |
|---|---|---|---|---|---|
| 1. | 71 Bde. 18-pdrs. 2 batteries. | 0.00 to 0.30 | A.17.a.33 to A.17.b.18 | Two rounds per piece per minute. | This barrage will be maintained by 2 batteries, the third battery being used to reinforce or for opportunity as required. |
| 2. | 73 Bde. 18-pdrs. | 0.00 to 0.30 | GIRD LINE, BUTTE TRENCH and GIRD SUPPORT | As shewn on map. | Two rounds per piece per minute till 0.15 One round per piece per minute 0.15 to 0.30 | All three lines of trenches to be kept under fire, also search backwards and forwards between them. |
| 3. | D/72 4.5" Hows. | 0.00 to 0.30 | BUTTE DE WARLINCOURT. | | -do- | P.S. and S.K. if wind is suitable; if not, BX |
| 4. | 103 Bde. 18-pdrs. | 0.00 to 0.30 | GIRD LINE, BUTTE TRENCH and GIRD SUPPORT. | As shown on map. | -do- | All three lines of trenches to be kept under fire, also search backwards and forwards between them. |
| 5. | D/105. 4.5" Hows. | 0.00 to 0.30 | QUARRY, centre of which is A.17.a.03 | | -do- | P.S. and S.K. if wind is suitable; if not, BX |

Major R.A.,
B.M. 50th D.A.

Appendix 20/9

SECRET.

Copy No. 9 496-

LEFT DIVISIONAL ARTILLERY GROUP OPERATION ORDER NO. 46.

13. 11. 16.

1. Left Divisional Artillery Group Operation Order No. 45 dated 13.11.16 is cancelled.

2. The 149th Infantry Brigade will attack on the 14th instant that part of the GIRD LINE and LUFFE TRENCH included in the area M.18.a.31 - M.18.a.03 - M.17.b.33 - M.17.a.70
The jumping off trench of the 50th Division is new trench parallel to SHAG TRENCH and about 100 yards to the South of it.
The Anzac Corps is attacking on the immediate right of 149th Infantry Brigade - The jumping off trench of the Australian Division is SHAG TRENCH which has been continued Southwards by them parallel to the GIRD TRENCH.

3. Left Group D.A. will assist as shewn in attached table.

4. Zero hour is 6.45a.m. (six forty-five)- Watches will be synchronised by telephone.

5. 18-pdrs. will fire 50% A. and 50% AX.

6. Barrages are shewn on map attached to Left D.A. Group Operation Order No. 45.

7. Acknowledge by wire.

F. Brown

Major R.A.,
B.M. 50th D.A.

Issued at 10.30p.m.

Copies to 1 - 70th Bde. R.F.A.
2 - 71st Bde. R.F.A.
3 - 73rd Bde. R.F.A.
4 - 102nd Bde. R.F.A.
5 - 103rd Bde. R.F.A.
6 - H.Q. 50th Div.
7 - H.Q. 48th Div.
8 - Right Group D.A.
9 and 10 - War Diary.
11 and 12 Spare.

## PROGRAMME OF BOMBARDMENT.   LEFT GROUP D.A.   14.11.16.

| Serial No. | Unit bombarding | Time. | Objective | Rate of fire. | Remarks. |
|---|---|---|---|---|---|
| 1. | 71bde. 18-pdrs., Two batteries | 0.00 to 1.00<br>1.00 onwards | M.17.a.82 to M.17.b.19<br>-do- | Two rounds per piece per minute to 1.00<br>1.00 onwards, bursts of fire. | This barrage will be maintained by two batteries, the third battery being used to reinforce or for opportunity as required. |
| 2. | 73 bde. 18-pdrs. | 0.00 onwards | GIRD LINE, BUTTE TRENCH, and GIRD SUPPORT. As shewn on map. | Three rounds per piece per min. till 0.07.<br>Two rounds per piece per min. 0.07 to 0.20.<br>0.20 onwards, bursts of fire. | All three lines of trenches to be kept under fire, also search backwards and forwards between them. |
| 3. | 103 bde. 18-pdrs. | 0.00 onwards | -do- | -do- | -do- |
| 4. | All 4.5" Hows. | 0.00 onwards | All M.G. emplacements in normal zones of 73 bde, 103 bde., and 71 bde. | Deliberate rate of fire, 40 rounds per piece per hour. | |
| 5. | 70 bde. 18-pdrs. | 0.00 to 0.30 | Normal zones of 73 bde and 103 bde, enemy front line trench. | 0.00 to 0.07, 3 rds per piece per min.<br>0.07 to 0.20, 1½ rds per piece per min.<br>0.20 to 0.30, 1 rd. per piece per min | |
| 6. | 102 bde., 18-pdrs. | 0.00 to 0.30 | Own zone, and normal zone of 70 bde and 71 bde enemy front line trench | -do- | -do- |

L.W.
Major R.A.,
50th D.A.

Appendix 20/10

SECRET.

Copy No. 16

## 50th DIVISIONAL ARTILLERY OPERATION ORDER NO. 47.

19.11.16.

1. On the nights 22/23rd and 23/24th Nov., Brigades of 50th D.A. will carry out reliefs as per attached table.

2. Guns will be taken over in position.

3. 50th D.A. will take over the 9th D.A. Ammunition Refilling Point at BOTTOM WOOD on 24th instant.

4. Details will be arranged between O.C. Bdes. and D.A.C.'s concerned.

5. Completion of each stage of relief to be reported by wire to Right D.A. Group and H.Q., 50th D.A.

6. Acknowledge.

F. Bronson
Major R.A.,
B.M. 50th D.A.

Issued at 6.0p.m.

Copies to - 1 - R.A., IIIrd Corps.
          2 - 251 Bde. R.F.A.
          3 - 252 Bde. R.F.A.
          4 - 250 Bde. R.F.A.
          5 - 50th D.A.C.
          6 - Right D.A. Group.
          7 - H.Q. 1st Div.
          8 - 9th D.A.
          9 - 12th D.A.
          10 and 11 - H.Q. 50th Div.
          12 - 50th Div. Train A.S.C.
          13 - A.D.M.S. 50th Div.
          14 - A.D.V.S., 50th Div.
          15 - H.A., IIIrd Corps.
          16 and 17 - War Diary.
          18 and 19 Spare.

Reference Maps Sheets 62D and 57D, 1/40,000.

## RELIEF OF BRIGADES OF 9th and 12th D.A. BY BRIGADES OF 50th D.A.

| RELIEVING UNIT. | | UNIT TO BE RELIEVED. | | |
|---|---|---|---|---|
| UNIT. | POSITION. | UNIT. | POSITION | WAGON LINES. |
| H.Q. 251 Bde. R.F.A. (Lt-Col. F.B.Moss-Blundell) | BERTRANCOURT | H.Q., 51 Bde. R.F.A.(9th D.A.) (Lt-Col. E.W.S. Brooke) | | |
| A/251 Bty. | -do- | A/51 Bty. | S.10.a.72 | X.29.a.15 (BOTTOM WOOD). |
| B/251 Bty. | -do- | B/51 Bty. | S.5.c.43 | -do- |
| C/251 Bty. | -do- | C/51 Bty. | S.5.c.04 | -do- |
| D/250 Bty. | ST. GRATIEN. | D/51 Bty. | S.5.c.24 | -do- |
| | | | S.9.b.82 | -do- |
| H.Q. 252 Bde. R.F.A. (Lt-Col.F.L.Pickersgill) | HOLLINS AU BOIS. | H.Q. 62 Bde. R.F.A.(12th D.A.) (Lt.Col. H.S.Wynne, D.S.O.) | | |
| A/252 Bty | -do- | A/62 Bty. | S.6.a.66 | |
| B/252 Bty | -do- | B/62 Bty. | S.6.d.79 | |
| D/252 Bty. | -do- | D/62 Bty. | S.6.b.73 | |
| | | | S.6.d.57 | |

SECRET.

Copy No 18

ADDENDUM NO.1 TO 50th DIVISIONAL ARTILLERY OPERATION ORDER NO. 47.

20.11.1916.

1. Para (1) - for 22/23rd and 23/24th Nov, read 21/22nd and 22/23rd November.

2. Para (3) - for 24th read 23rd November.

3. Routes to be followed by relieving Brigades of 50th Divisional Artillery will be as follows -

    BEHENCOURT - BAZIEUX - HENENCOURT - MILLENCOURT - ALBERT - BECORDEL - FRICOURT.

4. 251st and 252nd Brigades will march at 11.0 a.m. each day; head of column to reach HENENCOURT by 2.0 p.m.

5. Batteries are not to halt to water or feed on the line of march.

6. Acknowledge.

F. Brown
Major R. A
B. H. 50th D. A.

Issued at 9.30 pm.

Copies to - 1 - R. A. IIIrd Corps
2 - 251 Bde R. F. A
3 - 252 Bde R. F. A
4 - 250 Bde R. F. A.
5 - 50th D. A. C.
6 - Right D. A. Group.
7 - H. Q. 1st Division
8 - O. 9th D. A.
9 - 19th D. A
10 and 11 H. Q 50th Div
12 50th Div Train A. S. C
13 - A.D.M.S 50th Div
14 - A. D. V. S 50th Div,
15 - A. A IIIrd Corps
16 and 17 - War Diary
18 and 19 - Spare.

Appendix 20/11

SECRET.
Copy No 17

## 50th DIVISIONAL ARTILLERY OPERATION ORDER NO 48.

21-11-16

1. 50th Div. Amm. Col. will relieve 9th Div. Amm. Col. ( at E. 6, c ), on 24th inst, moving via - BEHENCOURT - LAZIEUX - HENENCOURT - MILLENCOURT - ALBERT - , head to reach HENENCOURT 12 noon,.

2. Acknowledge.

Issued at 6.0 p.m.

Major R.A.
B. M. 50th D. A.

Copies to - 1 - R.A. IIIrd Corps
- 2 - 251 Bde R.F.A
- 3 - 252 Bde R.F.A.
- 4 - 250 Bde R.F.A
- 5 - 50 th D.A. C.
- 6 - Right D. A. Group.
- 7 - H. Q, 1st Division.
- 8 - 9th D.A.
- 9 - 12th D.A.
-10 and 11 - H.Q 50th Div.
-12 - 50th Div Train A.S.C.
-13 - A.D.M.S 50th Div
-14 - A.D.V.S 50th Div.
-15 - H.A IIIrd Corps
-16 and 17.- War Diary
-18 and 19 - Spare.

Army Form C. 2118.

# WAR DIARY
## or
## INTELLIGENCE SUMMARY
(Erase heading not required.)

H.Q. 50th Divisional Artillery.

VOLUME XXI.

DECEMBER 1916

Vol 20

| Place | Date | Hour | Summary of Events and Information | Remarks and references to Appendices |
|---|---|---|---|---|
| BAVELIN- COURT. | Dec. 1st | | Trench Mortars less one Medium Trench Mortar Bty. moved from their Camp at S.19.d.50 to rest billets at BEHENCOURT. | 21/1 |
| | 4th | | C.R.A. inspected one section from each battery of the 242 Bde. and one section of D/251 battery on the march. | |
| | 6th | | The D.A.C. moved from E.6.c. and took over the lines of the 23rd D.A.C. at FRICOURT. | 21/2 |
| | 8/9th | | D/251 battery relieved D/252 battery, personnel only by sections. | 21/3 |
| | 9/10th | | D/252 took up the billets in BAVELINCOURT vacated by D/251. | |
| | 12/13 | | A/252 and B/252 Bde. R.F.A. were relieved by A/250 and C/250 Bde. R.F.A. personnel only on the nights of 12/13, 13/14. The first section of A/252 took over the billets vacated by A/252 at BEHENCOURT. | |
| | 13/14 | | The second section went into fresh billets at BAVELINCOURT on coming out of action. B/252 took over the billets vacated by C/250 in BEHENCOURT. | |
| | 13th | | H.Q. 250 Bde. Relieved H.Q. 252 Bde. in action. H.Q. 252 Bde. took over billets vacated by H.Q. 250 Bde. in BEHENCOURT. | |
| | 14th | | Major R.M.Knowles took over temporary command of 252 Bde., Lt-Col.F.L.Pickersgill being sick in England. | |
| | 15th | | Section of A/252 in BEHENCOURT moved to BAVELINCOURT, | |
| | 16th | | C.R.A. met the Battery Commanders and Second in Command at H.Q. 252 Bde. R.F.A. to discuss training programme. | |
| | 17th | | Medium Trench Mortars were to have given a demonstration and make craters for the school at the Small Chateau MONTIGNY but were unable to do so, as the bombs supplied would not take the normal Fuze. | |

Army Form C. 2118.

# WAR DIARY
## or
## INTELLIGENCE SUMMARY

Page 2.

*(Erase heading not required.)*

| Place | Date | Hour | Summary of Events and Information | Remarks and references to Appendices |
|---|---|---|---|---|
| BAVELINCOURT | Dec. 16th | | Arrangements were made with 34th Squadron R.F.C. for R.F.A. to fire at MONTIGNY Range with two 4.5" hows., for the purpose of training observers of the R.F.C. The aeroplane sent up lost its way so no firing took place. | |
| | 20th | | Firing as arranged on 18th instant was carried out satisfactorily D/252 providing the section of hows. | |
| | 22nd | | Firing as on 20th instant. | |
| | 24th | | Capt. Venning, Devon Yeomanry reported from England for instruction as S.C.R.A. and was attached to H.Q., 50 D.A. | |
| | 27th | | Firing as on 20th instant. | |
| | 29th | | Firing could not take place owing to wet weather. Two 4.5" hows. and a battery of 18 pdrs. were to have fired under arrangements with R.F.C. 50th Div. Trench Mortars moved up to their forward Camp at S.19.d.50. Billets vacated by the Surrey Yeomanry were taken over by A/252 Bde. R.F.A. A lecture was given by C.R.A. to all Officers in rest at the school at BEHENCOURT. | |
| | 30/31 | | Section of D/250 relieved section of 116 Bty. R.F.A. (Centre Group R.F.A.) on night 30/31 remainder of B/250 completed relief 31 Dec/1st Jan. in accordance with the relief of 1st D.A. by 50 D.A. Wagon lines X.30.a. battery position S.3.c.84. | 21/4. |

Ref.Map Sheets 57D and 62D.   Copy No. 13

SECRET.

## 50TH DIVISIONAL ARTILLERY OPERATION ORDER NO. 49.

28-11-16.

1. 50th Div. Trench Mortars, less one medium Trench Mortar Battery, will move from camp at S.19.d.50 to BEHENCOURT on 1st December, 1916.

2. Completion of move will be reported to this office.

3. Acknowledge.

Major, R.A.
B.M. 50 D.A.

Issued at 6.30 p.m.

Copies to:-   1 - R.A. IIIrd Corps
              2 - 50th Div. Trench Mortars
              3 - 251 Bde. R.F.A
              4 - 252 Bde. R.F.A.
              5 - 250 Bde. R.F.A.
              6 - 50th D.A.C.
              7 - Right D.A.Group.
              8 and 9. H.Q. 50th Div.
              10 - 50th Div. Train A.S.C.
              11 - A.D.M.S. 50th Div.
              12 and 13. War Diary.
              14 and 15. Spare.

Appendix 21/2

SECRET.

Copy No. 13.

## 50TH DIVISIONAL ARTILLERY OPERATION ORDER, NO 50.

30-11-16.

1.   50th D.A.C. will take over lines of 23rd D.A.C. at FRICOURT, on 6th December.

2.   Ammunition will be taken over in position.

3.   50th D.A.C. will move from their present lines, E.6.c. at 11.0 a.m.

4.   Acknowledge.

F. Brown

Issued at 3.0 p.m.

Major, R.A.
B.M. 50 D.A.

Copies to - 1 - R.A. IIIrd Corps.
         2 - 50th D.A.C.
         3 - 251 Bde. R.F.A.
         4 - 252 Bde. R.F.A.
         5 - 250 Bde. R.F.A.
         6 - 50th Div.Trench Mortars.
         7 - Right D.A.Group.
         8 and 9 H.Q. 50th Div.
        10 - 50th Div. Train A.S.C.
        11 - A.D.M.S. 50th Div.
        12 - A.D.V.S. 50th Div.
        13 and 14 - War Diary.
        15 and 16 - Spare.

SECRET.

Copy No. 14

## 50TH DIVISIONAL ARTILLERY OPERATION ORDER, NO.51

7-12-16.

1. D/251 Bde. R.F.A. will relieve D/252 Bde. R.F.A., personnel only, by sections, on nights 8/9 and 9/10 Dec.

2. H.Q. 250 Bde. R.F.A. will relieve H.Q. 252 Bde. R.F.A. on 13th Dec.

3. A/250 and C/250 Bde. R.F.A. will relieve A/252 and B/252 Bde. R.F.A. personnel only; first sections on night 12/13 Dec., remaining sections on night 13/14 Dec.

4. Units on relief will occupy billets in BAVELINCOURT and BEHENCOURT, respectively vacated by relieving units.

5. Routes will be:-

    (a) Relieving units - BAZIEUX - HENENCOURT - MILLENCOURT - ALBERT.
    Head of Column to reach ALBERT at 2.30 p.m. on 8th and at 12 noon on 9th, 12th and 13th Dec.

    (b) Outgoing units - ALBERT - main AMIENS ROAD - LAHOUSSOYE.
    Tail of column to be clear of ALBERT at 10.0 a.m. on 9th, 10th 13th and 14th Dec.

6. Details to be arranged by Brigade Commanders.

7. Completion of each stage of relief to be reported to this office by wire.

8. Acknowledge.

F. Brown

Major, R.A.
B.M. 50 D.A.

Issued at 1.0 p.m.

Copies to - 1 - R.A. IIIrd Corps.
2 - 250 Bde. R.F.A.
3 - 251 Bde. R.F.A.
4 - 252 Bde. R.F.A.
5 - 50th D.A.C.
6 - 50th Div. Trench Mortars.
7 - Right D.A. Group.
8 and 9 - 50th Div.
10 - 50th Div. Train A.S.C.
11 - A.D.M.S., 50th Div.
12 - A.D.V.S., 50th Div.
13 and 14 - War Diary.
15 and 16 - Spare.

Appendix 21/4

SECRET.

Copy No. 15.

## 50TH DIVISIONAL ARTILLERY OPERATION ORDER, NO.52.

28-12-16.

1. The 50th Division (less Artillery) will relieve the 1st Division (less Artillery) in the Right Sector of the 3rd Corps - relief to be complete by Jan. 1st.

2. Batteries of 50 D.A. will carry out reliefs by sections as per attached table.

3. Batteries of 50 D.A. will occupy billets in BAVELINCOURT and BEHENCOURT, respectively vacated by relieving batteries.

4. Routes will be:-

    (a) Relieving units - BAZIEUX - HERRINCOURT - MILENCOURT - ALBERT.
        Head of Column to reach ALBERT at 12 noon each day.

    (b) Relieved units - ALBERT - main AMIENS ROAD - LAHOUSSOIE.
        Tail of column to be clear of ALBERT before 10.0 a.m. each day.

5. Details to be arranged between Brigade Commanders.

6. Completion of each stage of relief to be reported to this office by wire.

7. 50th Divisional Trench Mortar Batteries will move to their forward camp at S.19.d.50 on the 29th Dec. and will relieve 1st Divisional Trench Mortars in the line on Jan. 1st.
   Details to be arranged between Divisional Trench Mortar Officers concerned.

8. 50 D.A.H.Q. will relieve 1st D.A.H.Q. at 12 noon on Jan. 2nd at which hour command of Right Group D.A. (3rd Corps) will pass to C.R.A. 50 D.A.

9. H.Q. 50 D.A. will close at 8.30 a.m. at BAVELINCOURT on Jan. 2nd and open at FRICOURT FARM at 10.0 a.m. the same day.

10. Acknowledge.

Major, R.A.
B.M. 50 D.A.

Issued at 12 noon.

Copies to - 1 - R.A. IIIrd Corps.
2 - 250 Bde. R.F.A.
3 - 251 Bde. R.F.A.
4 - 252 Bde. R.F.A.
5 - 50th D.A.C.
6 - D.T.M.O.50 Div.
7 - Right Group D.A.(3rd Corps)
8 - 1st Division.
9 and 10 - 50th Div.
11- R.A. IIIrd Corps.

12 - 50th Div.Train A.S.C.
13 - A.D.M.S. 50th Div.
14 - A.D.V.S. 50th Div.
15 and 16 - War Diary.
17 and 18 - Spare.

Relief of batteries of 50th D.A. and of 113th battery R.F.A. by batteries of 50th D....

| Relieving Unit. | | Unit to be relieved. | | | |
|---|---|---|---|---|---|
| Unit. | Rest Area Position. | Unit. | Position | Wagon Lines | Time of Relief. | Remarks. |
| B/250 | PARKINCOURT | *113 Bty. R.F.A. | S.3.c.85 | X.30.a. | Night of 30/31 Dec. and 31 Dec./1 Jan. | 1. Commands of batteries will pass on completion or relief. 2. Guns and ammunition will be taken over in situ. 3. All wagons and limbers will move out empty. |
| A/252 | PAVILINCOURT | †A/251 | S.5.c.42 | X.29.a.41 | 1/2 Jan and 2/3 Jan. | |
| B/252 | PARKINCOURT | †B/251 | S.4.d.65 | X.29.a.35 | 3/4 Jan and 4/5 Jan. | |
| D/252 | PAVILINCOURT | †D/250 | S.11.b.15 | X.29.a.45 | 5/6 Jan. and 6/7 Jan. | |

* Centre Bde. Group R.F....

† Right Bde. Group R.F.A.

www.ingramcontent.com/pod-product-compliance
Lightning Source LLC
Chambersburg PA
CBHW080824010526
44111CB00015B/2603